# Issues in Prayer Book Revision

# Issues in Prayer Book Revision
## • VOLUME 1 •

*edited by*
## Robert W. Prichard

Contributors:

James W. Farwell
Nathan G. Jennings
Patrick Malloy
Andrew McGowan
Robert W. Prichard

William Bradley Roberts
Amy C. Schifrin
Bryan D. Spinks
Shawn O. Strout
James F. Turrell

Copyright © 2018 by Robert W. Prichard

All rights reserved. No part of this book may be reproduced, stored in a retrieval system, or transmitted in any form or by any means, electronic or mechanical, including photocopying, recording, or otherwise, without the written permission of the publisher.

Unless otherwise noted, the Scripture quotations contained herein are from the New Revised Standard Version Bible, copyright © 1989 by the Division of Christian Education of the National Council of Churches of Christ in the U.S.A. Used by permission. All rights reserved.

Church Publishing
19 East 34th Street
New York, NY 10016
www.churchpublishing.org

Cover design by Jennifer Kopec, 2Pug Design
Typeset by PerfecType, Nashville, Tennessee

A record of this book is available from the Library of Congress.

ISBN-13: 978-1-64065-125-8 (pbk.)
ISBN-13: 978-1-64065-126-5 (ebook)

In thanksgiving for the work of the
Standing Commission on Liturgy and Music

# CONTENTS

| | |
|---|---|
| Tables | ix |
| Preface | xi |

1. Criteria for Prayer Book Revision and the Preface to the 1549 Prayer Book  
   Nathan G. Jennings — 1

2. The Language of Worship  
   Robert W. Prichard — 19

3. Moving Offices: Daily Prayer in the 1979 Book of Common Prayer and Beyond  
   Andrew McGowan — 49

4. The Baptismal Revolution of 1979  
   James F. Turrell — 71

5. The 1979 Prayer Book's Baptismal Office and the Potential of Revision  
   James F. Turrell — 87

6. A Reflection on the Eucharistic Prayer in Light of the Possible Revision of the 1979 Book of Common Prayer  
   James W. Farwell — 105

7. Calling Down the Holy Spirit: A Consideration of the Implications of the Texts of the Epiclesis in the Episcopal Eucharistic Liturgies  
   Amy C. Schifrin — 121

8. "The Word of the Lord": An Examination of the Use of
   Lectionaries in the Episcopal Church  143
   Shawn O. Strout

9. Burial Rites  169
   Patrick Malloy

10. The Apostolic Tradition and Liturgical Revision  203
    Bryan D. Spinks

11. Has the Time Come for Hymnal Revision?  213
    William Bradley Roberts

12. The Style and Format of the Book of Common Prayer  221
    Robert W. Prichard

Index  241

# TABLES

Number of Days of Commemoration and Saints     161

Number of OT References in *Lesser Feasts and Fasts 2006*
and *Holy Women, Holy Men*     162

Number of Epistle References in *Lesser Feasts and Fasts 2006*
and *Holy Women, Holy Men*     162

Number of Gospel References in *Lesser Feasts and Fasts 2006*
and *Holy Women, Holy Men*     163

# PREFACE

By the time this volume appears in print, the 2018 General Convention will have responded to a report on which the Standing Commission on Liturgy and Music has been working since 2015. The convention in that year asked the commission to prepare "a plan for the comprehensive revision of the current Book of Common Prayer" for presentation in 2018.[1] The commission responded with a "Blue Book Report" that laid out two different options.[2]

Option one, presented as Resolution 2018-A068, is to begin a full revision of the Book of Common Prayer, a multistep process that would take twelve years or longer to complete and would, the commission estimated, ultimately cost $7 to $8 million. The first three-year period (2018–21) would be devoted to data collection (interviews, consultations, surveys) and planning (formation of subcommittees, identification of consultants). It would be followed in subsequent triennia by drafting of texts (2021–24), trial use of those texts (2024–27), and adoption of a Book of Common Prayer (2030)

---

1. Resolution 2015-A169, General Convention, *Journal of the General Convention of . . . the Episcopal Church, Salt Lake City, 2015* (New York: General Convention, 2015), 886–87.
2. The Blue Book is a collection of the reports of commissions, committees, agencies, and boards of the Episcopal Church. Known by the blue covers that it initially—but not always—had, it also contains the resolutions that those bodies have prepared for consideration at convention.

by action of the 2027 and 2030 conventions.[3] The process, however, could take considerably longer.[4]

The second option, suggested by Resolution 2018-A069, would be a process of review and engagement with the current liturgy over the period from 2018 to 2021, with the anticipated outcome being a deeper understanding of the current liturgy and the introduction of resolutions allowing a wider use of non–prayer book materials.[5] While no specifics are identified, such changes might include compilation, editing, and publication of the various authorized materials in the Enriching Our Worship series and other approved supplemental liturgies into a single authoritative volume, whose status would be clarified by the adoption of new canonical legislation.[6] It might also include new canonical legislation supportive of the 1979 prayer book's declaration that "Holy Baptism is full initiation by water and the Holy Spirit into Christ's Body the Church."[7]

---

3. Standing Commission on Liturgy and Music, "Blue Book Report," 56–61, https://extranet.generalconvention.org/staff/files/download/21031 (accessed March 16, 2018). The page numbers refer to pages in the online document; when all Blue Book reports are combined in a single volume, pages will be renumbered.

4. The time period might be substantially longer. The time allotted for trial use, projected for three years in the current proposal, took nine years (1967–76) in the process leading up to the current Book of Common Prayer (1979). In the case of the Book of Common Prayer (1892), the process of approval, envisioned in the commission's proposal as the work of two conventions meeting at a three-year interval, required the action of four conventions (1883, 1886, 1889, 1892).

5. Standing Commission on Liturgy and Music, "Blue Book Report," 62–66.

6. Other materials that have been received, approved for study or use, or issued by General Convention include *I Will Bless You and You Will Be a Blessing* (a set of marriage rites appropriate for same sex couples), *Changes* (a set of liturgies marking rites of passage), and *Daily Prayer for All Seasons*.

7. Book of Common Prayer (1979), 298. For a discussion of the implications of this affirmation about full initiation, see chapters 4 and 5 of this collection.

This approach or a hybrid arrangement of options one and two might allow for what the Standing Commission on Liturgy and Music has called "technical fixes" to the Book of Common Prayer (1979). Standing Commission chair Devon Anderson explained the difference between such fixes and a full-blown revision in a December 20, 2016, posting on the commission's website: "Technical fixes are adjustments in grammar, punctuation, and word choice that do not change the theology, poetry, or intended meaning of the text," which presumably would change in a full-blown revision. She provided examples of "technical fixes" from Eucharistic Prayer C—"changing 'you made us the *rulers* of creation' to 'you made us the *stewards* of creation' or adding the matriarchs along with the patriarchs."[8]

This volume was prepared at a point in which it was not yet clear which of these two options—or what other alternative—would be adopted by the General Convention in 2018. It is extremely likely, however, that the Episcopal Church will be devoting additional time in the immediate future to deep engagement and study of the forms of worship that shape common life, and to consideration of ways in which the Book of Common Prayer (1979) might be supplemented or revised.

The authors of this volume offer their essays to the church to assist in the engagement, reflection, and study that will be needed to support the ongoing discussion about the church's liturgy. The authors, most of whom are current faculty members at Episcopal seminaries, explain the background to current texts, summarize parallel resources in other church bodies, and raise questions about how the Episcopal Church might best support or revise the Book of

---

8. Devon Anderson, "Four Possible Paths for the Book of Common Prayer," December 20, 2016, https://standingcommissiononliturgyandmusic.org/page/3/ (accessed March 16, 2018).

Common Prayer (1979).[9] The authors are not of one mind, but they do share a common conviction about the importance of worship in the life of the church and the care that must be taken in contemplating change.

Two initial chapters focus on important preliminary issues—the principles that underlie revision and the language used in liturgical rites. In the first chapter Nathan G. Jennings suggests the principles that have been followed in previous revisions of the prayer book. The second chapter looks at the use of Elizabethan and balanced language in the Episcopal Church, and makes suggestions about the language of future revisions or "technical fixes."

Chapters 3 to 10 then focus on particular portions of the prayer book. Andrew McGowan notes that the expansion of options in the 1979 Book of Common Prayer's Daily Offices (Morning and Evening Prayer, and the briefer services for Noonday and Compline) creates a level of potential confusion. He commends the examples of other churches of the Anglican Communion that have matched the expansion of allowable canticles and prayers with clear directions about which are to be used on which specific days, thereby preserving a level of uniformity and simplicity. In chapters 4 and 5, James F. Turrell reminds us of the radical reworking of the rites of initiation (baptism and confirmation) in 1979, and challenges the church to live into the implications of that change. In chapters 6 and 7, James W. Farwell and Amy C. Schifrin consider the contents of the Eucharistic Prayers of the Episcopal Church. Farwell

---

9. There are two exceptions to this pattern. Patrick Malloy was previously the Professor of Liturgy at the General Theological Seminary but is currently serving as the Cathedral Canon for Liturgy and the Arts at St. John the Divine Cathedral in New York. Shawn O. Strout is a former teaching assistant in liturgy at the Virginia Theological Seminary and is currently completing a PhD in liturgical studies/sacramental theology at the Catholic University of America.

notes that Anglican Eucharistic prayers have frequently focused on Christ's death and resurrection to the exclusion of other themes in his life. He looks to the early church and to the liturgies of other Christian bodies for models of prayers with references to Jesus Christ's teaching and ministry, and suggests that future editions of the prayer book should add such themes. Schifrin makes a lyric appeal for a wider recognition of the role of transforming power of the Holy Spirit in Eucharistic prayers. In chapter 8, Shawn O. Strout surveys the multiple lectionaries of the Episcopal Church and calls for greater simplicity. In chapter 9, Patrick Malloy traces the introduction in the 1928 edition of the Book of Common Prayer of optional prayer *for* the dead—something that was not part of the Episcopal burial office before that time.[10] He notes the expansion of such prayers in 1979 and points to shifts in popular culture related to death that might call for further changes. In chapter 10, Bryan D. Spinks looks at the influence of the document known as *Apostolic Tradition* on the 1979 revision, cites the current reappraisal of that work, and ends with a pointed question about the ordination service.

Chapters 11 and 12 deal with general concerns rather than specific rites. In chapter 11, William Bradley Roberts asks whether it is time to begin work on a new hymnal and concludes that the logical sequence would be for hymnal revision to follow prayer book revision. Chapter 12 cautions that the decisions about graphic design have considerable influence on the reception of new editions of the prayer book in the church.

The authors of these articles wrote prior to the 2018 General Convention; the various ideas advanced should nonetheless prove

---

10. Previous prayer books included prayers that gave thanks for the example provided by the departed and anticipated reunion with them on the Last Day. They did not, however, petition God to treat the dead in any particular way, assuming that God needed no instruction in that regard.

useful for whatever the course of action the General Convention has selected.

Robert W. Prichard
Alexandria, Virginia
March 24, 2018

*Postscript:*

The General Convention, which concluded on this day, adopted a revision of 2018-A068 that sought something of a middle path between the options that the Standing Commission on Liturgy and Music had presented to it. On one hand, it "authorized the ongoing work of liturgical and Prayer Book revision" based on "a dynamic process for discerning common worship, engaging all the baptized, while practicing accountability to the Episcopal Church" that would involve "worshipping communities in experimentation and the creation of alternative texts to offer to the wider church." On the other hand, the resolution "memorialized the 1979 Book of Common Prayer as a Prayer Book of the church preserving the psalter, liturgies, The Lambeth Quadrilateral, Historical Documents, and Trinitarian Formularies ensuring its continued use" and called for continued engagement with its "deep Baptismal and Eucharistic theology and practice." Rather than entrusting this complicated work to the Standing Commission on Liturgy and Music alone, the resolution created a new "Task Force on Liturgical and Prayer Book Revision." Clearly, the General Convention of 2018 has expanded rather than ended the discussion of liturgical revision, for which this volume is intended as a resource.

Robert W. Prichard
July 13, 2018

# 1

# Criteria for Prayer Book Revision and the Preface to the 1549 Prayer Book

## Nathan G. Jennings[1]

The Standing Commission on Liturgy and Music (SCLM) has responded to the General Convention's resolution 2015-A169 directing it "to prepare a plan for the comprehensive revision of the current Book of Common Prayer and present that plan to the 79th General Convention."[2] It is difficult to predict in advance how the General Convention will respond, but whatever the decision it reaches, it will certainly be appropriate to reflect on the criteria underlying any plan of revision or correction, or any judgment that alteration is not appropriate at this time. I suggest we

---

1. The Rev. Dr. Nathan G. Jennings is the J. Milton Richardson Associate Professor of Liturgics and Anglican Studies and Director of Community Worship at the Seminary of the Southwest.
2. General Convention, *Journal of the General Convention of . . . the Episcopal Church, Salt Lake City, 2015* (New York: General Convention, 2015), 886–87.

return to the criteria of the preface to the 1549 prayer book,[3] the first prayer book in our tradition, as guideposts to look at and to reflect on before we begin to take up the task of any future revision. These criteria are: (1) that the worship of the church should be grounded upon Holy Scriptures, (2) that it should be agreeable to the order of the primitive church, (3) that worship should be unifying to the church, and (4) that it should be edifying to the people. My reasoning is not due to a belief that we ought to be antiquarian or because of a belief that the Episcopal Church is simply defined by our tradition in a strict or a legalistic way. Rather, the suggestion stems from the fact that these criteria have, in a haphazard, organic way, become a part of our "DNA," our "genetic" inheritance as Anglicans and as Episcopalians.

In addition to these four well-established criteria, I suggest another. But before I do, allow me a brief literary digression. Science fiction author Isaac Asimov devised "Three Laws of Robotics" for his fictional world. These laws were intended to protect humanity from the rising power of the robots. Yet in his short story collection, *I, Robot*,[4] machines nearly take over the human race. As a result, Asimov imagined the development of a "Zeroth Law." Because the previous three had been hardwired into the robots in logical order, the scientists and engineers in Asimoz's story could not simply add a fourth law and achieve the result of human protection. Asimov

---

3. I am emphasizing the 1549 preface over Cranmer's authorship, as his sole authorship has recently come into doubt: "[I]t remains difficult to know how much of 'Cranmer's Prayer Book' is actually Cranmer's personal composition." Diarmaid MacCulloch, *Thomas Cranmer: A Life* (New Haven, CT: Yale University Press, 1996), 414.
4. The Zeroth Law isn't named as such until *Robots and Empire*, and R. Daneel Olivaw, one of Asimov's continuing characters, hardwires it into his own brain over thousands of years. See Isaac Asimov, *I, Robot* (1950; Bantam hardcover ed., New York: Bantam, 2004) and *Robots and Empire* (New York: Doubleday, 1985).

described this Zeroth Law as more binding, even, than the first of the Three Laws of Robotics.

Similarly, even though these four explicit criteria of Cranmer are present in the 1549 Book of Common Prayer, I propose a "Zeroth" criterion be added, in the spirit of Asimov. This Zeroth criterion is implicit in the manner in which Thomas Cranmer went about his work of liturgical reformation. I would sum up this Zeroth principle of the prayer book tradition as "continuity with immediate inheritance." When Cranmer began compiling the English liturgy for the Church of England in the 1540s, he did not do what Anabaptists, Reformed Christians, and some Lutherans did elsewhere in Europe. These other traditions, to varying degrees, simply discarded much of the previous liturgical inheritance of the Western church.[5]

Of all the Protestant traditions, the Church of England, and therefore, our own Anglican tradition thereafter, was the most liturgical. When Cranmer applied these four explicit criteria to the reform of worship in the Church of England, the Zeroth criterion was always in play. For the most significant action Cranmer took to reform the liturgy was simply to translate much of the current Sarum use of the Roman rite—that is, the text, lectionary, calendar, and rubrics of the form of the Roman rite in use at Salisbury Cathedral—from Latin into sixteenth-century English vernacular. Simply translating into English was itself an act of reform, a radical one that was subject to much dispute. Thus the founding act of our prayer book tradition is the maintenance of continuity with previous inheritance. In this

---

5. Martin Luther's Latin Mass (*Formula Missae*) of 1523 retained much of the received liturgical tradition. It was, however, intended for use only in Wittenberg; Luther encouraged other churches in sympathy with his reform to make their own revisions. The *Formulae Missae* was, moreover, followed by other revisions that were less tied to the received Roman rite. In general, however, the Lutherans did keep more of the liturgical inheritance than the continental churches of the Reformed tradition.

case, it was done through translation of previous liturgy. This Zeroth criterion of continuity with our immediate inheritance, like Asimov's Zeroth Law of Robotics, manifests a more fundamental commitment of our prayer book tradition than even that of the explicit four.

In the following essay, I discuss each of these criteria one by one, starting with the first and ending on the Zeroth. Each section of commentary includes what the criterion meant in its context, and how it appeared and was used during the Liturgical Movement of the twentieth century that would develop our 1979 prayer book. Then I reflect on how the criterion suggests we might best go forward with liturgical revision today.

## I. Grounded upon Holy Scripture

The prayer book is the result of the Reformation in the Church of England, and that reformation was, in large part, a desire to reform church practice and teaching based on a return to Holy Scripture. At least, that is how the reformers saw their own efforts. In many ways, they lacked historically accurate knowledge of both scripture and the early liturgy that might have aided their fulfilling this goal more clearly and succinctly than they were able, however much that this was their goal.

As Cranmer went about making his changes in order to develop the Book of Common Prayer, at times he found himself unable simply to translate the Sarum rite into English due to his commitment to the Reformation's theological trends. He would then paraphrase the prayer grounded upon his discernment of its function in the liturgy into a form more acceptable to a Reformed theologian's ear and heart. His chosen method was to draw upon scripture, either by directly quoting it, or by making an allusion or reference to it, resulting in prayers more theologically satisfactory to a Reformer.

I would like briefly to note that the way in which this criterion works in Anglicanism is different than, say, the way in which the regulative criterion works in the Reformed tradition of our neighbors. The criterion of *sola scriptura* was applied to worship as the regulative principle by our Reformed neighbors thusly: if it is not in scripture, it ought not be in worship. To this day, certain branches of Presbyterian churches will not sing hymns during the divine service on Sunday mornings. Only psalms are sung at worship because they are found in scripture.

What is interesting here is that although the English Reformation falls under the greater umbrella of the Reformed tradition (more so than, say, the Lutheran-Evangelical tradition), we did not, in our Thirty-Nine Articles, for example, simply take up *sola scriptura* as a principle and thereby take on the Reformed regulative principle for worship. Instead, the phrase "grounded upon holy scripture" corresponds in the Articles to the notion that we cannot teach anything in the church that is "repugnant to scripture." There is a great deal of difference between these two guiding criteria.

When applied to worship, it means that we no longer need to have a regulative criterion that says that we cannot, in worship, have anything not explicitly found in scripture. Instead, we hold up the act of worship to the light of scripture, and if we discern that it is not repugnant to scripture, we simply keep it.[6] Take for example, the *Sursum corda*, the Latin name for the dialogue between celebrant and congregation that precedes the Eucharistic Prayer. When examined through the regulative principle, we have to deny it; it must be deleted from Reformed worship. But if we hold it up rather to the criterion of avoiding anything repugnant to scripture, as there is nothing in the *Sursum corda* repugnant to scripture, we find that we are inclined to keep it. Thus, even though not found in scripture,

---

6. This tendency to keep whatever we can points forward to the Zeroth principle of continuity with immediate inheritance.

because it is not repugnant to scripture, we have the *Sursum corda* in our worship to this day.

At the time of the Liturgical Movement, the twentieth-century Roman Catholic and Anglican reform that led to the revision of the Roman Catholic missal after Vatican II (1962–65) and to our current 1979 Book of Common Prayer, this criterion of scripture was not forgotten, of course. The framers of the 1979 prayer book used this criterion in a way quite similar to Thomas Cranmer's own. That is to say, when the time came for new prayers to be composed, the framers of the 1979 prayer book deliberately looked to scripture and did their best to compose new prayers that either directly quoted scripture, paraphrased, or alluded to it. I would hope that any future prayer book revision will uphold this criterion genetic to our inheritance as Anglicans.

Much of the liturgical supplementary material that has come out of the SCLM since the publishing of the 1979 prayer book has continued to uphold the Anglican criterion of direct scriptural quotation, or paraphrase, or allusion. However, some of the material seems to bear the stamp of more heady academic theology currently in vogue, or other secular ideologies that we have "baptized" as the direction in which the church ought to go, or that the church as "chaplain" to current society ought to baptize. My hope, going forward, is that prayer book revision, whenever new prayers are incorporated, would continue to uphold the tradition of grounding any newly composed liturgical material strictly upon scripture in this same manner. Whatever liturgical supplementary material we consider for addition to a future revision of the prayer book, our decision would benefit from a stricter interpretation of what it means to have our liturgy grounded upon Holy Scripture.

## II. Worship Agreeable to the Order of the Primitive Church

Thomas Cranmer had available to him the various attempts at performing worship that scholars of the continental Reformed tradition and the Lutheran-Evangelical tradition had made before him or were making concurrently. He also had before him various forms of the Roman rite, especially the Sarum use, and it seems evident that he also had before him Eastern liturgical material such as the liturgy of St. Chrysostom.[7] In addition, he had the Church Fathers to which to refer, especially St. Augustine, St. Chrysostom, St. Gregory of Nazianzus, and others, who wrote about, and alluded to, the liturgies they used. In the main, however, we do not have much of an historical record of early liturgies, for these were part of the oral tradition of the church and prior to the fourth century were in many ways deliberately kept oral and not written down. Cranmer and other reformers did the best they could to reconstruct what early Christian worship might have been, triangulating from all this disparate material what might have been the practice of the early church.

At the time of the Liturgical Movement, an explosion in new historical scholarship concerning Christian liturgies burst into the Western world and Western church; for example, many translations of ancient liturgies became available in the vernacular, including English. People who were passionate about liturgy were thrilled by

---

7. Ashley Null, a contemporary Thomas Cranmer scholar, has been working for the past decade on Cranmer's commonplace books, his collections of source quotations. The books offer concrete evidence of the sources that Cranmer used. Null's "Cranmer and the Sacraments," in *Christian Theologies of the Sacraments: A Comparative Introduction*, ed. Justin S. Holcomb and David A. Johnson (New York: NYU Press, 2017), traces the deep influence of Cyril of Alexandria on Cranmer's Eucharistic doctrine. Volume three of Null's projected multivolume Oxford Cranmer project will deal more broadly with Cranmer's Eucharistic sources under Edward VI, but that work is still a few years off.

these discoveries. For us as Anglicans, the result was a large amount of liturgical renewal across the Anglican Communion; the result for us as Episcopalians was the 1979 Book of Common Prayer. We already had as our inheritance, in a way not present for other liturgical traditions such as Roman Catholics or even Lutherans, a desire to have worship agreeable to the order of the primitive church. Whenever we as Anglicans or Episcopalians discover more about early Christian liturgies, we get excited about it and want to give it a try.[8] That's exactly what occurred leading up to, and finally resulting in, the 1979 prayer book.

Since the time of the 1979 prayer book, however, further historical studies have called into question many of the basic assumptions upon which the framers of that prayer book relied. We need to continue to revise prayers books with this second criterion of agreeability to ancient forms of worship. When new historical knowledge comes to light, it is always something we ought to consider. However, just looking at what happened in the 1979 prayer book should perhaps slow us down a bit. We need to be careful in thinking that current historians have reconstructed the most final and most accurate knowledge of a historical reality.[9] If we were suddenly to so modify our 1979 prayer book inheritance according to current historical liturgical trends, we might find ourselves disappointed in yet another generation to discover that we were yet again wrong to assume we had found the ultimate reconstruction of ancient liturgies. Scholarship often reopens issues that members of one

---

8. Another example of this from our history is the way in which Thomas Rattray's commentary on the liturgy of St. James of Jerusalem led to the formation of the eighteenth-century revision of the communion service in the Wee Bookies of the Protestant Episcopal Church of Scotland.
9. See, for example, the chapter ten in this volume in which Bryan Spinks discusses the changing scholarship on a document once assumed to be *Apostolic Tradition* by Hippolytus of Rome.

generation were convinced they had settled once and for all. So we need to be wary of buying too wholesale into any currently popular academic reconstruction of ancient historical liturgies.

## III. Worship Should Be Unifying to the Church

Of course, it is important to recall that the Book of Common Prayer was to be common. In the way that common law is common, in the way that common parliamentary procedure is common, Cranmer wanted a prayer book that allowed commonality across the English people, so that they could be unified in their worship. This represents a trend in liturgical change; throughout history, liturgy follows pendulum swings. This pendulum swings throughout history in general, in the West in particular, and especially for us as a Reformation church and tradition. The two movements of this pendulum swing consist of a movement toward greater liturgical proliferation on the one hand, and then a swing back to greater liturgical unification on the other. The first move of the pendulum pushes boundaries and expands options. The second moves toward unity and the filtering out of the unnecessary.

Both of these movements have positive and negative aspects. The movement to push boundaries is positive because, again, it expands options, it allows for localization and for greater diversity and catholicity of observance. However, what is negative about that direction is that it can tend toward festooning the liturgy unnecessarily, toward proliferation of unneeded prayers and rites, and toward dividing Christians from one another as they become increasingly unable to recognize that their worship unites them.

The other direction also has its positive and negative. On the positive side, the pendulum-swing in the direction of unity sorts and shifts, selecting liturgical material of lasting value to the community and to greater unity. On the negative side, the move toward unity can suppress local diversity and create a hierarchical control. These two movements bring balance to the Christian observance of liturgy in general, and balance to our Anglican and Episcopalian observance in particular.[10]

At the time of the Reformation, Cranmer was trying to move toward greater unity, suppressing many different uses of the Roman rite throughout the English realm, not to mention throughout Christendom in general at the time, and to bring about a conformity of practice so that all English-speaking Christians could know that they were members of the same church, being formed and transformed by the same liturgical activity.

At the time of the development of the 1979 prayer book, the pendulum was swinging the other way. The 1979 prayer book was an attempt to push boundaries, to expand options, to try out new and different things, and to bring forward more ancient practices. The theory in play in 1979 was roughly that we would be committed to a shared order of worship but provide for interchangeable parts—a range of Eucharistic prayers, prayers of the people, optional lesser feasts, alternate forms, etc. The approach is likely drawn from Gregory Dix's idea in *The Shape of the Liturgy* that the liturgy has an unchangeable shape that itself conveys meaning. Now is a good time to reflect on how well the fixed-structure-with-flexible-parts approach has functioned to unite the people. So, for example, it may be time to drop the second postcommunion prayer from Rite II, or to specify that the option to drop the confession in the Eucharist is not to be exercised during Lent, or to give seasonal direction to

---

10. I am indebted to a conversation with Bob Prichard, the Professor of Church History and Instructor in Liturgies at Virginia Theological Seminary, for this particular insight. Prichard himself was drawing upon the insights of Anton Baumstark (1872–1948), who posited a set of "laws" descriptive of the ways in which liturgies develop over time.

the use of the various forms of the Prayers of the People and the Eucharistic Prayers.

Since then, the liturgical materials produced and given as supplementary options by the SCLM have continued this trend toward the pushing of boundaries, the expanding of options, and allowing for more localization, but also bringing further division. One can go to the East Coast, the West Coast, the Midwest, and feel that one is worshiping in different Episcopal churches in each of these places. In many ways, this is a sign of catholic diversity; however, equally yet oppositely, in many ways it can be a sign of division and a lack of common prayer.

We may be tempted in a further prayer book revision to continue moving in the direction of pushing boundaries, expanding options, continuing unnecessary proliferation, and festooning of the liturgy. We've done this enough, and it is time to return to the ancient Anglican criterion of worship being unifying to the church. We would be wise to allow the pendulum to swing now in that direction.

## IV. Worship of the Church Should Be Edifying to the People

Included within the criterion of "edifying to the people" is the now-famous phrase from the Thirty-Nine Articles that the liturgy ought to be a language "understood of the people."[11] So the first and most basic meaning of the liturgy being edifying to the people is that the liturgy be in a language that the people understand. The liturgy is indeed a mystery, but it ought not be a mystery because we cannot understand the words being said. Translation of the liturgy is a basic criterion of the various Eastern churches and is a criterion

---

11. Article XXIV, "Historical Documents," Book of Common Prayer (1979), 872.

of all Protestant churches. We are a people of the Word, the Word made flesh, and so understanding is core.

Furthermore, what was meant by "edifying to the people" at the time of the Reformation was a Reformation focus on being didactic, and frankly, just "teach-y" and "preachy" in the liturgy. One can see in the liturgy various points at which Cranmer and the other framers of the prayer book tradition inserted teaching moments—doctrinal point moments—to ensure that our good Protestant laity were properly educated as to what is occurring in worship so that they do not err and stray from good Protestant ways into Romish thinking or perhaps thinking that it is too nonconformist.

For example, we have an exhortation, which may be said prior to Rite I communion being celebrated.[12] This exhortation is an introduction to the communion service so that we know what we are really celebrating and how we ought to prepare ourselves. We have a kind of introduction to the Daily Office in the bidding to confession in the Rite I Morning Prayer, letting people know what the office is supposed to be for and how it is supposed to be used and approached.[13] We have the introduction to the marriage service that is now so famous that Hollywood and television make use of it: "Dearly beloved, we are gathered here today. . . ."[14] Again, it is built-in homily to the service itself in order to ensure that everyone, including priests, who at the time of the Reformation might not know what they were doing, understood what was actually occurring in a good, Protestant, Reformed, theological fashion.

This very didactic approach to liturgy is not the meaning of the criterion of edifying to the people taken at the time of the

---

12. Book of Common Prayer (1979), 316–17. The 1979 exhortation draws on elements from the three separate exhortations that were found in the 1928 and early editions of the prayer book. See Book of Common Prayer (1928), 85–89.
13. Book of Common Prayer (1979), 41.
14. Ibid., 423–24.

framing of the 1979 prayer book. At that time an important, and potentially misleading, phrase was popular: *lex orandi, lex credendi*, sometimes parsed into English as "praying shapes believing." Therefore, the liturgy was understood to be edifying to the people by those framers as something that shaped the very beliefs of the church, forming the foundation of the beliefs and doctrines of the Christian people.

Some of the new edifying material wound up in the *Book of Occasional Services*. We tried to adopt something like Rites of Christian Initiation for Adults, as the Roman Catholics had developed in Vatican II, but modified for use in our context. *The Book of Occasional Services* contains a series of catechetical and mystagogical meetings and worship services designed to prepare people for and understand initiation as Christians in the Episcopal Church.[15] This has not been used as much as might have been hoped. But that worship should be edifying to the people is fundamental to our inheritance as Episcopalians.

In recent liturgical scholarship, there has been a slight reinterpretation of the role of worship in edifying the people. For some, the shape of the liturgy is no longer understood to have any historical or theological content of its own, but is rather understood as an empty mold into which one can pour any language and any theological presumptions that inculcate the current theological or ideological vogue. The nineteenth-century Roman Catholic scholars who revived the tag *lex orandi, lex credendi* understood the liturgy to be a fixed category that offered a counterbalance to changing theological ideas in their church; many Episcopalians today regard the liturgy from the opposite perspective, as a vehicle for shaping laity into believing more what we think the church ought to believe in

---

15. Catechetical instruction generally precedes participation in the sacraments, while mystagogical instruction follows.

our day. We thus turn the liturgy into a tool for community formation and frankly, a tool for propaganda.[16]

We need to be very careful in approaching liturgical revision from this perspective. For the liturgy to be edifying of the people, the main point is that it be in the language understood by the people, thus ensuring that we continue to have contemporary language available without skewing our traditional language inheritance, due to its importance in our worship and in our English language. Having truly sound liturgical materials available so that people understand what they are engaging is the second part of this. However, when we compose liturgical verbiage for current theological and ideological trends, I believe we violate the first of Cranmer's criteria, which is that liturgy needs to be grounded upon Holy Scripture. If the prayers and rites that we compose and compile in our prayer book revisions do not sound like Holy Scripture to us, do not sound like the scripture is speaking to God and God is speaking to us through scripture—either through direct quotation or by paraphrase and allusion—then we have strayed from our first criterion of grounded upon scripture, in an exaggerated attempt to be true to our fourth criterion of being edifying to the people.

### The Zeroth Criterion

To conclude, I return to my proposed Zeroth criterion, that of continuity with immediate inheritance. This criterion is not explicit in any of Cranmer's writings, but I would argue that it is implicit in the way in which he applied the four explicit criteria. For example, when Cranmer went about revising the liturgy he inherited into the

---

16. For a thoughtful examination of the concept of *lex orandi, lex credendi*, see chapters 7 and 8 of Geoffrey Wainwright, *Doxology: The Praise of God in Worship, Doctrine, and Life: A Systematic Theology* (New York: Oxford University Press, 1980).

first and second prayer books, what he did was not simply to eliminate all liturgy received in the Western Catholic church of his day. Rather, he looked at the worship available, looked at other reformers' efforts, looked to the East, and then compiled a liturgy that had continuity, for English people, with their previous inheritance, while conforming to the theology and teachings of the Reformation of the Western church.

The first way in which Cranmer wanted to reform worship was to use the printing press to get all of the worship books used by a Western Catholic priest of the time into one book. There were several books that needed to be used by any particular parish priest in order to get through one liturgical year. He wanted it all compressed into one book; first and foremost, that meant reformation of the liturgy through editing, redacting, cutting—things just dropped onto the cutting room floor, so to speak. As soon as a Reformed theologian like himself looked through the liturgy of the day and found something that seemed repugnant to scripture or a bit too "Romish," the first and easiest action to take was simply to excise it.

It is important to remember that the next action he took was simply to translate. Cranmer did not write new liturgies, he inherited the Roman rite focusing on its Sarum use, and translated much of it. As examples we have the *Sursum corda*, the Preface, the *Sanctus*, and in the 1549 prayer book, still the *Benedictus qui venit*.[17] He simply translated from Latin into Elizabethan vernacular.

When Cranmer came across something he thought he could not simply cut, but that he was also uncomfortable merely translating, he would paraphrase it into something more fitting to his Reformed

---

17. The *Benedictus qui venit* (the initial Latin words of the phrase "Blessed is he who comes in the name of the Lord") was included at the end of the *Sanctus* ("Holy, Holy, Holy") in the 1549 edition of the Book of Common Prayer. It was dropped in the 1552 and subsequent editions of the prayer book and not restored until the American 1979 and other late twentieth-century prayer book editions. See Book of Common Prayer (1979), 334, 362.

theology, using scriptural quotations or allusions. Failing that, only then would he compose a new prayer whole cloth, nevertheless still following the inherited structures and forms of his immediate inheritance. For example, we still have in our current prayer book many collects Cranmer composed that very strictly follow the form of a collect inherited in the Western Catholic tradition.

So this is our inheritance as Anglicans and as Episcopalians: not simply to follow Cranmer's four criteria in some sort of liturgical vacuum, but to apply these four criteria to the current liturgical inheritance. In many ways, this is still the case in our 1979 prayer book; people might especially point to Rite I. However, many of those who put together the current prayer book and many of those who continued on the Standing Commission on Liturgy and Music assumed that we would eventually phase out Rite I and simply move to contemporary language.[18] If that were the case, we would then lose the anaphora (the Eucharistic Prayer) that has characterized Anglican worship, especially our Scottish/American Episcopal tradition of the Holy Communion that has shaped us for hundreds of years.[19] That would be a sad loss, one that I would not recommend.

However, in many places of the 1979 prayer book, we simply lost any liturgical continuity whatsoever.[20] Many scholars have written about the way in which the current Rites of Initiation, especially the Rite of Holy Baptism, have much work that needs to be done,

---

18. See the second chapter in the volume for a further discussion of the rationale for retention of Rite I texts in a future edition of the prayer book.
19. The American and Scottish prayer books retain a Eucharistic Prayer based on that in the English 1549 Book of Common Prayer. Most other churches of the Anglican Communion used a form of the Eucharistic Prayer from the English 1552 Book of Common Prayer. See Book of Common Prayer (1979), 333–36.
20. It should be noted that the 1979 prayer book is a new prayer book. All other prayer books in the United States of America are revisions of the 1789 prayer book.

such as reordering the shape. However, no one has made the simple point that the current rite of baptism in the 1979 prayer book has no verbal continuity with any other rite that we have inherited as Anglicans. There is absolutely no continuity between our previous 1789 prayer book tradition and our current prayer book. Much of this is for good and inevitable reasons because our baptismal theology has undergone deep transformation. However, in the baptismal rites and in many other rites, I suggest that, going forward, the best way is not only to maintain continuity with our immediate inheritance—in this case, the 1979 prayer book—but also to retrieve better, and greater, continuity with our previous inheritance of our 1789 prayer book tradition.

Trying to create a better amalgamation between the 1928 and the 1979 prayer books before we have lost the generation that remembers worshiping under the 1928 would be wise. For example, in the baptismal rite, we could keep much of the fundamental actions of the rite that we have in the 1979 prayer book, reshaping it according to more recent historical and theological scholarship, but also retrieving and renewing some of the traditional verbiage that has been formative for Anglicans for over 400 years. Doing this, and other similar revisions throughout our current prayer book, would place ourselves not only in touch with the four explicit principles of the 1549 prayer book, but would also reground us within their shared, more fundamental assumption: a criterion of continuity with previous inheritance.

# 2

# The Language of Worship

## Robert W. Prichard[1]

During the last half of the twentieth century, Episcopalians wrestled with two different but related questions about the language of worship. One concerned comprehensibility, and the other concerned justice. The first two sections of this essay will consider these two issues in the order in which they were raised in the Episcopal Church, looking first at the concern for comprehensibility, and second with the concern for justice. A third section will consider the future of Rite I texts, and a concluding section will make recommendations about future revision.

### Elizabethan Language and the Question of Comprehensibility

By the middle of the twentieth century, it became evident to many people that there was a problem with the language commonly used

---

[1]. The Rev. Robert W. Prichard, PhD, is the Arthur Lee Kinsolving Professor of Christianity in America and Instructor in Liturgics at Virginia Theological Seminary.

in English-language worship. To put matters simply, they recognized that it took effort to understand the sixteenth-century and early seventeenth-century English of the King James Version (KJV) of the Bible and the Book of Common Prayer. Not all saw this effort as negative. The Elizabethan language of those works were a part of the literary heritage of the English-speaking people that is also to be found in the plays of Shakespeare and in much poetry and hymnody.[2] Some would argue that the effort to understand such language was well spent. Others argued that the difficulty involved was an obstacle to comprehension.

Six elements distinguished Elizabethan English from contemporary use. (1) Spelling was not yet standardized in the sixteenth and seventeenth centuries, with decisions made by individual authors and printers. Subsequent editions and printings of the Book of Common Prayer and the King James Bible gradually adjusted spelling, however, to conform to the increasing standardization of the English language. In the case of the 1928 edition of the Book of Common Prayer, archaic spellings survived in such words as *throughly* for *thoroughly* and *ensample* for *example*.[3]

(2) Some words had acquired new meaning or passed out of common speech in the intervening centuries. Such words as *prevent* (meaning to go before rather than to hinder) or *meet* (meaning fitting) in the 1928 prayer book fell into this category.[4]

(3) The most noticeable element of the English of the King James Bible and the Book of Common Prayer was the treatment of second- and third-person pronouns and verbs. In the place of

---

2. The King James Version of the Bible was produced during the reign of James I. The language of that revision might, therefore, be designated *Jacobean*, rather than Elizabethan. For the sake of simplicity, however, this essay will use the designation *Elizabethan*.
3. See the Collect for the Second Sunday after Easter and Psalm 51:2 in Book of Common Prayer (1928), 171, 403.
4. Book of Common Prayer (1928), 76, 213.

the all-purpose *you* that we now employ for all second-person pronouns, Elizabethan English used the pronoun *thou* with its related forms *thee* (objective case), *thy* and *thine* (possessive forms with *thine* reserved for use before vowels), and a nominative plural form (*ye*) distinguished from the objective plural form (*you*). Thus, the celebrant would say to the congregation in the Book of Common Prayer, "the Lord be with *you* (second person plural)," while the congregation would reply, "And with *thy* (second person singular) spirit."[5] The *thou* forms required separate verb endings with *t* or *st*: thou *art*, thou *shalt*, thou *didst*. . . . The singular forms would be used even where the second-person singular address (*thou*) was implied but not actually written or spoken: "Our Father, who *art* in heaven." Third-person pronouns were not distinctive—except in the treatment of gender that will be discussed in feature six below—but Elizabethan English did employ distinctive verb endings for third-person singular subjects: *-th* present tense verb forms that were in the process of being replaced in England in the sixteenth and seventeenth centuries by the *-s* more typical of Northern European Germanic languages: he *saith*, she *hath*, who *liveth*, here *endeth*, he *doth* or *doeth*.[6]

(4) A fourth feature of Elizabethan English was what the Standing Liturgical Commission (the body created by General Convention to provide leadership in liturgical review and revision) would identify as "the 'Latin' Style of sentence-structure." The Commission used the collects "with their involved subordinated

---

5. It is the lack of this precision in contemporary English that leads modern speakers to adopt nonstandard plural forms: you all, you guys, you-uns, youse, etc.

6. *Determinants of Grammatical Variations in English*, ed. Günter Rhodenburg and Britta Mondorf, vol. 43 of Topics in English Linguistics (Berlin: Mouton de Gruyter, 2003), 19.

clauses, or the Consecration Prayer, with its parentheses and participial constructions" as examples of this style.[7]

(5) The King James Bible and the Book of Common Prayer followed a fifth feature of Elizabethan English only sparingly—the practice of addressing individual persons of high status with plural pronoun forms. Some English speakers had begun in the thirteenth century to adopt this practice, which was more common in some other European languages. Editions of the Book of Common Prayer followed this convention only with bishops in the services of confirmation ("upon whom . . . *we* have now laid *our* hands") and ordination ("Reverend Father in God, I present unto *you*, these persons present, to be admitted Deacons").[8] Surprisingly, however, the parish priest and God were not referred to in this way. In the major public services of the church and in the King James Bible, the *thou–ye* distinction was used consistently to indicate number and not status.

---

7. The Standing Liturgical Commission of the Protestant Episcopal Church in the United States of America, *Prayer Book Studies XVII: The Liturgy of the Lord's Supper, a Revision of Prayer Book Studies IV* (New York: Church Pension Fund, 1966), 53. The collects are short variable prayers composed for particular days or themes such as The Collect for the First Sunday in Advent or A Collect for Grace.

8. Book of Common Prayer (1928), 298 and 530. The Book of Common Prayer did not contain any first- or second-person references to the monarch. For a description of the origin of this plural use of pronouns and verbs with individuals in authority and its adoption in English later than in other European languages, see Roger Brown and Albert Gilman, "The Pronouns of Power and Solidarity," in *Style in Language*, ed. Thomas A. Sebeok (London: MIT Press, 1960), 253–76. See especially page 266, in which the authors note the earliest use of the plural approach in English in the thirteenth century and their judgment that "the English seem always to have moved more freely from one form to another than did the Continental Europeans." Certainly, the prayer book use (outside of that addressed to bishops) was an important example of resisting the plural use for individuals.

(6) There was a clear rule for gender: masculine pronouns and the word *man* were used for mixed groups or where gender was indeterminate.

Mid-twentieth-century Americans who had a general knowledge of English literature—and a number who did not—were able to navigate the traditional prayer book services and to read the King James Bible with comprehension. A knowledge of European languages that continued to distinguish between multiple forms of second-person pronouns also proved helpful. Biblical scholars and church leaders were worried by the middle of the twentieth century, however, about the number of people who found the traditional language off-putting and confusing.

One of the first serious responses to this problem was the preparation and publication of the Revised Standard Version (RSV) of the Bible in 1952 by the Division of Education of the National Council of Churches. It corrected spelling, updated vocabulary, and simplified some Latin sentence structure. It offered a compromise solution for the use of second-person pronouns—it retained the *thou* form of address but only in references to the deity. It also dropped the *-th* forms of the third person singular and *ye* as the nominative case for the second person plural. Thus, the Lord's Prayer (which was addressed to God the Father) survived unchanged, but "Ask, and it shall be given you; seek, and *ye* shall find" (Matthew 7:7 KJV) became "Ask, and it will be given you; seek, and *you* will find" (RSV). The Revised Standard Version retained male generic pronouns.

The Standing Liturgical Commission was slow in following the lead of the revisers of the Revised Standard Version of the Bible in seeking a replacement of Elizabethan language.[9] The process that would eventually lead to the adoption of the 1979 edition of

---

9. The Standing Liturgical Commission acknowledged this reticence in the introduction to *Prayer Book Studies XVII*. See *Prayer Book Studies XVII*, 54–55.

the Book of Common Prayer began in earnest with the publication in 1950 of the initial two volumes of what would eventually be a thirty-volume *Prayer Book Studies* series (1950–89). The series considered and provided sample texts for revision of the Book of Common Prayer, and after the adoption of the 1979 edition provided resources for its introduction and use. Volumes I to XVI (1950–63) continued, however, to use Elizabethan language and to print lessons from the King James Version of the Bible. It would not be until the publication of *Prayer Book Studies XVII* in 1966 that the Standing Liturgical Commission published its first discussion of Elizabethan language. The explanatory essay in that volume titled "Rationale of Proposed Revision" listed ten issues related to revision, most of which had to do with the structure of the service. The tenth was a catch-all "Other Consideration," which addressed language and length. In this portion of the essay, the Commission devoted its attention primarily to features 3 (second- and third-person pronouns and verbs) and 4 (Latin sentence structure), noting that such issues were "much deeper than its scattered archaisms" (features 1 and 2). The Commission did not address feature 5 (use of plural pronouns by bishops).[10] It would, however, eliminate plural use with individual bishops in the *Services for Trial Use* (1971). The Commission's 1966 statement was silent on feature 6 (use of male pronouns); the Commission would not begin to address the issue until 1976, very late in the revision process. In the liturgical text that was included in *Prayer Book Studies XVII*, which with General Convention's approval in the following year was published separately as *The Liturgy of the Lord's Supper*, the Standing Liturgical Commission took an approach similar, though not identical, to that of the Revised Standard Version of the Bible. *Prayer Book Studies XVII* explained:

---

10. *Prayer Book Studies XVII*, 55–56.

In this proposal, we have endeavored to take several steps toward a more contemporary language (if not style), and a wider outlook toward the world about us today:

We have retained the archaic use of the second person singular (Thou, thee, thy) in all formularies addressed directly to God. But we have consistently substituted the modern "you" and "yours" in all other exchanges with or biddings to the congregation. This follows the usage of the Revised Standard Version. . . .

Biblical citations have been generally made from the Revised Standard Version. Where we have departed from it, the reason has been one of rhythm of phrase.[11]

The departures from the Revised Standard Version generally involved use of the *-th* forms of the third person singular. The Revised Standard Version had converted all third person singulars to the modern *-s* form. *Prayer Book Studies XVII* did so in most cases, with the exception of references to persons of the Trinity. Thus, Jesus Christ continued to be the one who "*takest* away the sin of the world" and "*sitteth* at the right hand of God the Father" in the *Gloria in excelsis,* and God the Father "*didst* make us" in his own image in the Eucharistic Prayer.[12]

---

11. Ibid., 55.
12. *Prayer Book Studies XVII* also followed one other Elizabethan convention that had been dropped in the Revised Standard Version. Elizabethan English, like modern German, sometimes used the verb *to be* rather than the verb *to have* to create perfect tenses. This use survived in the fraction anthem "Christ our passover *is* sacrificed for us" (1 Corinthians 5:7, KJV), which the Revised Standard Version had rendered as "Christ, our paschal lamb, *has* been sacrificed." Curiously, this Elizabethan perfect tense would later be used in the 1979 Rite II Eucharist, while a modern form of perfect tense would be used in Rite II Morning Prayer. See Book of Common Prayer (1979), 83, 337, 364.

The Standing Liturgical Commission made a further change of direction in the following four years. *Prayer Book Studies 18: Holy Baptism with the Laying-on-of-Hands* (1970) and *Prayer Book Studies 20: The Ordination of Bishops, Priests, and Deacons* (1970) abandoned the Revised Standard Version approach by dropping the use of *thou* as a form of address for God. The Standing Liturgical Commission also dropped the *-th* forms of second-person singular verbs in references to the persons of the Trinity.[13] The introductions to the two volumes did not offer any explanation for this shift, but it undoubtedly reflected the ecumenical effort to agree upon liturgical texts that followed the Second Vatican Council (1962–65) and the Roman Catholic Church's decision to replace Latin with vernacular languages. The Roman Catholic Church created the International Commission on English in the Liturgy (ICEL) in 1963; it then cooperated with other churches to create the ecumenical International Consultation on English Texts (ICET) in 1969. The first chairs of the latter body were Roman Catholic Canon Harold Winstone and Anglican Canon Ronald Jasper. In 1969 the International Consultation on English Texts agreed upon its first set of liturgical texts, which were circulated for comment and published the following year under the title *Prayers We Have in Common*.[14] All the texts were in contemporary English; none preserved the Elizabethan pronouns or verb endings.

In 1970 the Standing Liturgical Commission responded to complaints about the disappearance of Elizabethan language by offering two versions of selected liturgical texts—a contemporary language version following the approach of *Prayer Book Studies 18* to *20* that

---

13. In contrast to the first seventeen volumes in the *Prayer Book Studies* series, volume 18 and beyond used Arabic rather than Roman numerals in their titles.
14. International Consultation on English Texts, *Prayers We Have in Common: Agreed Liturgical Texts Proposed by the International Consultation on English Texts* (Philadelphia: Fortress Press, 1970).

made use of the new International Consultation on English Texts translations and a modified Elizabethan version. This new approach was followed in a series of *Prayer Book Studies* published in 1970: *Prayer Book Studies 19: The Church Year*, *Prayer Book Studies 21: The Holy Eucharist*, *Prayer Book Studies 22: The Daily Office*, and *Prayer Book Studies 24: The Pastoral Offices*. *Prayer Book Studies 19* listed two forms of each collect: a contemporary version followed by an Elizabethan version. The order was reversed in *Prayer Book Studies 21, 22,* and *24*, which placed an Elizabethan language First Service before the contemporary Second Service. *Prayer Book Studies 23: The Psalter, Part I* offered only a single contemporary version, but the First Service of the Daily Office and the Burial Office *(Prayer Book Studies 22* and *24)* preserved some psalms from the *Great Bible* Psalter that had been in prayer books since the sixteenth century.[15]

These modified Elizabethan texts in *Prayer Book Studies 18–24* took a partial step back from the Revised Standard Version approach of *Prayer Book Studies XVII* in the direction of the 1928 and earlier editions of the prayer books. The use of *thou* for singular references to individuals was no longer restricted to references to God. So, for example, "And with *thy* spirit" returned as the congregation's response to a (single) celebrant. *Ye* returned as a nominative plural

---

15. In 1611 James I approved what would become known as the King James Version of the Bible as a means to end divisions in the Church of England over two competing vernacular translations: the Great Bible, which was a version of the Coverdale Bible that had been approved by the English government for use in the 1530s, and the Geneva Bible, published in 1560 by English exiles in Switzerland who had fled the Roman Catholic policies of Mary I. While the new King James Version became the standard for the reading of lessons in the Church of England (and other English-speaking Protestant churches), the Great Bible translation in the Book of Common Prayer and its Psalter would remain unchanged until the revisions of the late twentieth century.

form in the invitation to confession: "*Ye* who do truly and earnestly repent you of your sins."[16] As in *Prayer Book Studies XVII*, however, the *-th* forms of third-person singular verbs were retained for persons of the Trinity but not for human beings. "St. Paul *exhorteth*" of the Exhortation of the Eucharist became "St. Paul *exhorts*."[17]

The General Convention of 1970 accepted the *Prayer Book Studies 18* through *24* as presented for trial use, though it did make some modifications concerning the role of the bishop in the rites of initiation in *Prayer Book Studies 18*. The texts were collected and published as *Services for Trial Use* (1971), widely called the "Green Book" because of its olive cover. The Preface to the Book explained the linguistic choices made:

> Certain of the services and prayers contained in the present edition appear in two forms: a contemporary and a traditional form. This is true of the Holy Eucharist, where two complete services are given (and also an Order for Celebrating the Holy Eucharist on occasions other than the principal service on Sundays and other Feasts of our Lord); the Daily Office, where two forms are given for Morning and Evening Prayer;

---

16. The first service of the burial order in *Prayer Book Studies 24* wavered between the Revised Standard Version approach of *Prayer Book Studies XVII*, which had retained Elizabethan second-person singular (but not third-person singular) forms for references to God and the approach of the Daily Office and the Eucharist of *Prayer Books Studies 21* and *22*, which had retained more Elizabethan elements. The prayers in the burial order were in Elizabethan language, but biblical anthems were from the Revised Standard Version of the Bible. The psalms printed in the office were from the Great Bible, and some versicles and responses were in contemporary English. The congregational response to "the Lord we with *you*" was, for example, "And with *your* spirit."

17. Book of Common Prayer (1928), 85; *Services for Trial Use* (New York: Church Hymnal Corp., 1971), 59.

the Order for Burial of the Dead; and the Collects for Sundays, Holy Days and special occasions.

This duality of form is a direct result of the comments on and reactions to, the trial use of *The Liturgy of the Lord's Supper* received by the Standing Liturgical Commission during the triennium 1967–1970. A substantial minority of those who responded to the Commission's Questionnaires showed a deep-seated attachment to the traditional language of The Book of Common Prayer.[18]

The preface went on to say that the creation of two forms of service "was not done . . . with a view to encourage the formation of partisan groups within the Church, some wedded to one style, some to another. Rather, as the Introduction to the Holy Eucharist points out, the Commission 'offers these services for the whole Church, and not for separate parts of it.'"[19] Such hopes would soon be frustrated, however. In the same year in which *Services for Trial Use* appeared (1971), a group of Episcopalians gathered in Sewanee, Tennessee, to create an organization to lobby against replacement of the 1928 prayer book. Initially named the Society for the Preservation of the Book of Common Prayer, the organization later shortened its name to the Prayer Book Society.

The existence of an organized opposition may have contributed to the incremental increase in the use of Elizabethan texts in the second trial liturgy volume (*Authorized Services 1973*, often called the "Zebra Book" because of its cover design) and in the final product of the revision (the Book of Common Prayer edition of 1979).

---

18. Preface, *Services for Trial Use*, viii–ix. The parenthetical reference to an Order for Celebrating the Holy Eucharist is potentially confusing. The order did not contain any traditional language texts; its rubrics did, however, allow use of the traditional language Eucharistic Prayers in the First Service.

19. Preface, *Services for Trial Use*, ix.

An expanded edition of *Authorized Services* eliminated the confusion of having the contemporary collects listed first, while contemporary services followed the Elizabethan versions and were labeled as "second"; it reversed the order of the collects and separated them into two sections rather than one integrated list, a decision that would have connotations for calendar materials as a whole.[20]

The Book of Common Prayer (1979) would go further. The entire 1928 Eucharistic Prayer was added as an option to the Rite I (as the First Service had been retitled) Eucharist. The book contained an order for marriage that could be used either for an innovative marriage service or as a justification to follow the service as it appeared in the Book of Common Prayer (1928). It conformed the linguistic style of the Rite I Burial of the Dead to that of the Rite I Daily Office and Eucharist.

A section of Prayers and Thanksgivings included certain prayers in Elizabethan language in which verbs and pronouns were italicized to assist those who wanted to render them into contemporary language. An instruction at the beginning of the book allowed the reverse procedure—conforming "the contemporary idiom . . . to traditional language" where Elizabethan forms were lacking, but it offered no clear instructions of how that might be done.[21]

When Charles P. Price (acting on behalf of the Standing Liturgical Commission) penned a general introduction to the texts

---

20. *Services for Trial Use* had united most lectionary material in one section, titled "the Proper." It included both forms of the collect, the eucharistic lessons for all three years of the lectionary, and the indication of the preface to be used all on a single page. In addition, liturgies for special days, such as Ash Wednesday and Holy Week, were integrated within this listing. The initial edition of *Authorized Services* did not include the collects or lectionary. An expanded edition followed that added collects and both the eucharistic and Daily Office lectionaries. Once the two sets of collects were divided, it became impossible to put all lectionary material in one sequence.
21. Book of Common Prayer (1979), 14.

that would become the 1979 edition, he offered a theological justification for the use of contemporary language, one that pointed to the deficiencies of Rite I language.

> We continue to believe that it is important to be able to use contemporary language for worship.
>
> The reason for this conviction can be stated briefly. It is shared by those engaged in liturgical revisions in every Western Church, namely, that in a religion centered on the Word made flesh, liturgy should be rooted in the language of the people. Such language will necessarily be different from that of the Book of Common Prayer in a number of significant respects.[22]

Price and his colleagues on the Standing Liturgical Commission believed that the Rite II contemporary texts offered a language of worship that was comprehensible to Americans of the late twentieth century. Rite II language, he argued, was able to "convey reverence and dignity in the presence of God by means of twentieth-century words and style" just as well as "sixteenth-century words and style."[23] Price offered no rationale for the retention of modified Elizabethan Rite I texts.

Many of the clergy and lay leaders who began to have significant adult involvement in the Episcopal Church in the 1960s, 70s, and 80s assumed at the time that Rite I texts were only being preserved to mollify older parishioners who were attached to older forms. They disregarded the appeal the Standing Liturgical Commission made in 1971 that all revised texts were offered "for the whole Church" and used Rite I texts as a targeted pastoral strategy for

---

22. Charles P. Price for the Standing Liturgical Commission, *Introducing the Draft Proposed Book of Common Prayer*, Prayer Book Studies 29 (New York: Church Hymnal Corp., 1976), 24.
23. Ibid., 27.

older parishioners.[24] A common parish practice was to offer the Rite I Eucharist at an early Sunday celebration of Eucharist, scheduled at a time inconvenient to families with young children, and exclusively to offer Rite II services later in the day.

This attitude survives in many clergy and lay leaders of the baby boom—my own—generation today. A 2010 posting on Episcopal Café by a retired priest from the Diocese of Newark identified Rite I, for example, as "something best consigned to the Historical Documents section of the BCP" and contrasted it with Rite II services that reflect the "common language that ordinary people understand."[25] Yet Rite I continues to persist in the life of the church, often in ways that few would have predicted in the 1970s.

## Language and Justice

Members of the Standing Liturgical Commission belatedly began to consider the final aspect of the received Elizabethan language—the grammatical convention of using male gender to refer to groups or individuals of mixed or indeterminant sex—in 1976. Texts produced by the Commission prior to that time showed little concern about that matter and in some cases introduced new male language not found in the Book of Common Prayer (1928). *Prayer Book Studies XVII* (1966) was typical. In its introduction Commission members explained that they had "introduced into the Prayers of intercession new themes, particularly with reference to *men's* vocations in the world of today, and to the proper use of God's created order." A corresponding new petition asked for God's help that those in commerce,

---

24. "Preface," *Services for Trial Use*, ix.
25. Paul Woodrum, Episcopal Café, comments on the Book of Common Prayer in 4 Minutes, June 25, 2010, http://www.episcopalcafe.com/the_book_of_common_prayer_in_four_minutes/ (accessed September 30, 2016; link no longer active). Used with permission from the author.

industry, education, and child care might "be worthy of their calling to serve thee and their fellow *men*." The Commission also retained the reference in the Nicene Creed to "us *men* and for our salvation," and added a new opening acclamation in which his God the Father was identified with a male pronoun, "And blessed be *his* kingdom, now and forever."[26] The use of ecumenical International Consultation on English Texts' translations in *Service for Trial Use* (1971) and *Authorized Services 1973* introduced additional use of male gender. The consultation's Nicene Creed in those books broke up some of the long sentences of 1928 and earlier prayer books, and in the process replaced "the Holy Ghost . . . who spake by the Prophets" in the third paragraph with "the Holy Spirit. . . . *He* has spoken through the Prophets." The *Sursum corda* (the dialogue at the beginning of the Eucharistic Prayer) changed "It is meet and right so to do" to "It is right to give *him* thanks and praise."[27] Similarly, the version of the Psalter that was begun in *Services for Trial Use* ("The Psalter Part I: A Selection of the Most Frequently Appointed Psalms") and completed in *Authorized Services 1973* made no attempt to reduce male language, and it may have slightly increased that use because of the attempt to simplify sentence structure. Psalm 15:6 appeared in the Book of Common Prayer (1928) as "*He* that hath not given his money upon usury, nor taken reward against the innocent," but in the new Psalter as "*He* does not give his money in hope of gain, nor does *he* take a bribe against the innocent."[28]

When the Standing Liturgical Commission presented the *Draft Proposed Book of Common Prayer* to the General Convention of 1976, commission member Charles P. Price acknowledged that some

---

26. *Prayer Book Studies XVII*, 55 (introduction), and 3, 8, 10 (text of service). (Emphasis added.)
27. *Services for Trial Use* (1971), 68 and 71; *Authorized Services 1973*, 60 and 63. (Emphasis added.)
28. Book of Common Prayer (1928), 357; *Services for Trial Use* (1971), 140; and *Authorized Services 1973*, 229 (emphasis added).

in the church had begun to complain about the use of the terms *man* and *men* to refer to human beings. Writing on behalf of the Standing Liturgical Commission in *Introducing the Draft Proposed Book*, he explained this issue in terms of removing ambiguity.

> In response to a widespread, though admittedly not universal, sense that the word "man" in many such instances is ambiguous, and can be taken to designate males only instead of including females as well, [the Standing Liturgical Commission] has taken a careful review of all generic references, and has sought to eliminate ambiguity where possible. . . . Not every generic "man" or "brother" has been eliminated . . . and no single rule for making the change has been employed. But it is hoped that many ambiguities have been clarified.[29]

Later in the volume Price acknowledge that a "number of critics" were arguing that this ambiguity had serious theological implications:

> In the Nicene Creed, [the *Draft Proposed Book*] has elected to drop the word *men* from the line, "who for us men and for our salvation." As a generic term, it adds nothing to sense of the line and a number of critics have felt that the word excludes women from Christ's saving work. [*The Draft Proposed Book*] reads "For us and for *our* salvation."[30]

The Standing Liturgical Commission removed most generic uses of the word *man* and *brother*, but it left male pronouns and personal adjectives unchanged in most of the *Draft Proposed Book of Common Prayer*. The third collect in the Rite II burial office, for example, explained that "we remember before you this day our brother (sister) N. We thank you for giving *him* to us, *his* family and

---

29. Price, *Introducing the Draft Proposed Book of Common Prayer*, 26–27.
30. Ibid., 36.

friends. . . ."[31] The italics appeared in the original text in order to signal a change might be made for a female.

The Psalter was a notable exception. Price explained that "a careful study has been made of the generic words" in that portion of the book. He mentioned that revisions had been made to the new translation that had appeared in the 1971 and 1973 trial liturgies with the intent "to eliminate masculine nouns where a generic meaning is intended." Many pronouns and personal adjectives referring to human beings were also changed. The revised form of 1976 retained male pronouns, however, in cases "where the reference is unmistakably messianic, and where a familiar New Testament allusion and liturgical implication would be destroyed by an alteration."[32]

These changes only concerned references to human beings, however. No changes were made in the *Draft Proposed Book of Common Prayer* in relationship to the language about the persons of the Trinity. The *Draft Proposed Book of Common Prayer* would, for example, retain the reference in the Nicene Creed to the Holy Spirit as *he*, which had been introduced with the International Consultation on English Texts' translation in *Service for Trial Use* in 1971.[33]

After approval by the General Conventions of 1976 and 1979, the *Draft Proposed Book* became the Book of Common Prayer (1979). Its adoption did not bring an end, however, to the criticism that Price had noted in 1976. The timing of this criticism was significant in one aspect. It came at a point after the separation of Rite I and Rite II texts. This meant the generic language debate was introduced as a critique of Rite II contemporary language rites, rather than an indictment of Elizabethan language.

---

31. *The Draft Proposed Book of Common Prayer* (New York: Church Hymnal Corp., 1976), 493.
32. Price, *Introducing the Draft Proposed Book of Common Prayer*, 110.
33. Book of Common Prayer (1979), 359.

By 1979, use of male generic language was increasingly seen as a matter of justice and human rights, rather than of style and comprehensibility. This new perspective on language had reached the United States from Europe in the 1960s and 1970s by way of university departments of language, philosophy, and anthropology. Anglo-German linguistic philosophers were, for example, questioning the long-standing assumption that language offered labels for preexisting things in some neutral way. In his *Philosophical Investigations* (1945), the linguistic philosopher Ludwig Wittgenstein examined the internal logic of language and rejected this traditional idea that "every word has a meaning [that] is the object for which the word stands," in favor of a "language game" by which society assigned meaning to words.[34] French anthropologist Claude Lévi-Strauss, a leading figure in the field of structural anthropology, suggested that "language not only implies life in a society but is indeed the very foundation of that life . . . the most perfect and most complex of those communications systems in which all social life consists."[35] In *The Second Sex* (1949), social theorist Simone de Beauvoir argued that the inferior position which women held in society was a social creation, rather than some natural order. While she focused her attention in the work on portrayals of women in fiction, she laid the groundwork for those who would point out that what she noted about the society's treatment of women in fiction could be applied to language itself: "Society, being codified by man, decrees that woman is inferior. . . . It was neither a changeless essence nor a mistaken choice that doomed her to imminence, to inferiority. They were imposed on her."[36]

---

34. Ludwig Wittgenstein, *Philosophical Investigations*, trans. G. E. M. Anscombe, 3rd ed. (New York: Macmillan, 1958), 1.1, 1.7.
35. Claude Lévi-Strauss, *Structural Anthropology*, 2 vols. (New York: Basic Books, 2008), 2:9–10.
36. Simone de Beauvoir, *The Second Sex*, trans. H. M. Parshley (New York: Alfred A. Knopf, 1953), 717.

By the 1970s American academics were putting these pieces together. Editors Casey Miller and Kate Swift's *Words and Women* explained how this happened in their case. Assigned the task of editing a junior high school sex education text in 1970, they

> discovered that whatever the author's intention, the message coming through was that girls are not as important, responsible, or self-sufficient as boys or as healthy in their outlook on life. This impression was conveyed in part by the materials, both secular and religious, around which the course was structured, but *it was also communicated by the standard English the author used.*[37]

The two women went on to produce the influential *Handbook of Nonsexist Writing* in 1980.[38] Miller and Swift were not theologians, but they became convinced that Western religions had a particularly serious problem with language:

> Nowhere are the semantic roadblocks to sexual equality more apparent—or significant—than in the language of dominant organized religions.... Since the major Western religions all originated in patriarchal societies and continue to defend a patriarchal world view, the metaphors used to express their insights are by tradition and habit overwhelmingly male-oriented. As apologists of these religions have insisted for tens of centuries, the symbolization of a male God must not be taken to mean that God really *is* male. In fact, it must be understood that God has no sex at all. But inevitably, when words like father and king are used to evoke the image of

---

37. Casey Miller and Kate Swift, *Words and Women* (Garden City, NY: Anchor Press/Doubleday, 1976), ix. (Emphasis added.)
38. Casey Miller and Kate Swift, *The Handbook of Nonsexist Writing: For Writers, Editors and Speakers* (New York: Harper & Row, 1980).

a personal God, at some level of consciousness it is a male image that takes hold.[39]

Within two years of the adoption of the Book of Common Prayer (1979), the Standing Liturgical Commission began to wrestle with this perspective, one that made male generic language not only a matter of intelligibility but of justice as well. In November of 1981, the Standing Liturgical Commission scheduled a meeting with a group of people, most of whom had connections to the Episcopal Divinity School (EDS), to assist with this discussion.

In October 1984 Professor Robert Bennett of EDS presented a paper to the Standing Liturgical Commission titled "The Power and Promise of Language in Worship," in which he argued that "the cultural context of the Judeo-Christian heritage has been male-oriented, and this patriarchal way of viewing reality has affected the way we perceive God and one another." He argued that "Jesus calls us to move beyond cultural patterns of dominance and powerlessness."[40] A September 1993 consultation at Seabury-Western Theological Seminary, then located in Evanston, Illinois, led to the publication of *Liturgical Studies 2*, which continued the discussion on language.

This new concern for language provided the rationale for the publication of a series of experimental liturgies. The first of the texts, *Liturgical Texts for Evaluation* (1987), was approved for use on specific dates at a limited number of selected sites, many of which were theological seminaries. This first text was followed by *Supplemental Liturgical Texts* (1989), for which more general use was allowed,

---

39. Miller and Swift, *Words and Women*, 71.
40. Bennett's paper was published three years later. See Robert Bennett, "The Power and Promise of Language in Worship: Inclusive Language Guidelines for the Church," *The Occasional Papers of the Standing Liturgical Commission*, Collection Number One (New York: Church Hymnal Corp., 1987), 39, 43. This was the only volume of *Occasional Papers* published.

provided the bishop consented. These two volumes attempted to create a nonsexist liturgy from which all male language in references to the Trinity or to the people was removed. These efforts were both a call for reform and an attempt to bring order to process of revision that was beginning to be made in some parishes.

The effort to find alternatives to use for masculine pronouns proved to be difficult. By the 1990s some members of the House of Bishops began, for example, to have misgivings about the major strategy used to avoid male language in these first two alternative liturgies—identifying persons of the Trinity by function (Creator, Redeemer, Sanctifier, etc.). Some complained that the approach obscured the personhood of God and bordered on the early heresy of Modalism.[41] In the 1990s, therefore, the Standing Liturgical Commission changed its approach, moving from *nonsexist* to *balanced* language. Rather than removing all male Trinitarian language, the effort was made to diminish the frequency of masculine references to God and to balance them with female images drawn from scripture and the history of the church. This was the approach followed in *Supplemental Liturgical Materials* (1991) and *Enriching Our Worship 1* (1998). Both of these rites were incomplete; they did not contain complete services, but rather elements that could be used to supplement Rite II texts in the Book of Common Prayer (1979).[42] Both volumes incorporated ecumenical texts from the English Language Liturgical Consultation (ELLC). That body, created in 1985, sought to continue and expand the earlier work of

---

41. The Modalists was the name given to early third-century Christians who spoke in ways that suggested that the Son had no independent existence but was simply a mode in which God the Father chose to appear. This was one of the theological opinions that was rejected by the Ecumenical Councils of Nicaea (325) and Constantinople (381).
42. See note 20 in chapter 3 for a discussion of the confusing instructions about use found in *Enriching Our Worship 1*.

the International Consultation on English Texts but with an added "sensitivity . . . to the need for inclusive language."[43] By the end of the 1990s, discussion in the church moved on to other language issues, seeking to develop *expansive* language that not only recognized male-female bias as a problem, but also addressed such issues as bias based on ethnicity, age, or disability. This turn to a broader discussion in the late 1990s was aided by a decision of the 1997 General Convention to merge the Standing Liturgical Commission with the Standing Commission on Church Music into one Standing Commission on Liturgy and Music. Those involved with church music already had a long track record of incorporating multiple cultures and perspectives. That effort by musicians—but not always those on the Standing Commission on Church Music—resulted in the publication of such works as *Lift Every Voice and Sing* (1981), *Lift Every Voice and Sing II* (1993), and *El Himnario* (1998). This expansive language perspective has informed the later volumes in the Enriching Our Worship series.

## A Revival of Interest in Elizabethan Language

Back in 1897 American humorist Mark Twain responded to inquiries from the *New York Journal* about rumors of his death. He famously replied, "The report of my death was an exaggeration."[44] One could well say something similar about the use of Rite I language in the Episcopal Church. Ever since the introduction of

---

43. English Language Liturgical Consultation, *Praying Together* (1988), 5–6. Electronic version available at http://englishtexts.org/ELLC-Documents/ELLC-Texts (accessed March 15, 2018).

44. Later writers have often paraphrased his response as, "The reports of my death are greatly exaggerated." See Famous Quotations and Phrases Linked to Each Day of the Year, May 31, 2015, http://www.thisdayinquotes.com/2010/06/reports-of-my-death-are-greatly.html (accessed September 28, 2016), for an image of the letter in which Twain made his quip.

separate contemporary and traditional language rite in *Services for Trial Use* (1971), members of the baby boom generation have been predicting or announcing the death of traditional language forms of worship.[45]

Not all agreed, however. The members of the Standing Commission on Church Music showed, for example, continued interest in the use of Elizabethan language. The amended form of their *Proposed Text for the Hymnal 1982 as submitted . . . by the Standing Commission on Church Music* was adopted by the General Convention as the *Hymnal 1982*. The majority of the texts in the book—56.1 percent—contained Rite I language.[46] In addition, the General Convention of 1982 chose not to withdraw permission for the continued use of the *Hymnal 1940*.[47] Musicians continued to see hymns with Elizabethan language as viable options.

---

45. The Preface to *Service for Trial Use* explained that "certain of the services contained in the present edition appear in two forms: a contemporary and a traditional form." These services were labeled as "First Service" and "Second Service." This designation continued in *Authorized Services 1973* but was changed in the Book of Common Prayer 1979 to "Rite One" and "Rite Two." See "Preface," *Services for Trial Use* (New York: Church Hymnal Corp., 1971), viii.

46. This percentage is based on an examination of the use of second-person pronouns and third-person singular verb forms in the 720 hymns in the volume. This numeration counts each of the 720 entries. This involves some duplication since the hymnal uses sequential numbers for texts that appear with more than one musical setting. There is also a separate numbering system for the service music, which is not included in this count. It is possible, therefore, to come up with alternative percentages of Rite I texts. The difference would, however, be slight.

47. General Convention Resolution 1982-A093 authorized and approved the 1982 Hymnal for use in the church, without removing the previous permission for use of the *Hymnal 1940*. See General Convention, *Journal of the General Convention of . . . the Episcopal Church, New Orleans, 1982* (New York: General Convention, 1983), C-13.

By the 1990s it was evident that younger members of the Episcopal Church were among those finding Rite I language attractive. The balanced approach to language could be understood as supportive of a variety of differing approaches, which could include a reappropriation of Elizabethan language. Emily Wachner, who is a Lecturer in Practical Theology and Director of Integrative Programs at the General Theological Seminary, has explained the dynamics of reappropriation in terms of a congregation she served.[48] Most of the young people in that congregation grew up hearing what she characterizes as the "top 40 Protestant hymns." Such hymns often contain traditional language, yet they resonated with her parishioners in a way that "a diet of praise music and Taizé hymns" would not. The parishioners, Wachner suggested, "did not in general have trouble with hymnody that focused on God the Father" and "get that the liturgy was created in time and place, and that male language was intended to include both men and women." She had no doubt, however, that the reaction to traditional language would have been different if the celebrants were uniformly male, and women were excluded from leadership. "It matters," she explained "who uses a word and whether it has been used in oppressive ways." The presence of female celebrants, assisting clergy, Eucharistic ministers, and lectors provides a context in which the younger members of the congregation that she served could worship without offense, using music that employed Elizabethan language.[49]

In 1991, a parish in Pennsylvania prepared the first of what might be called a "Rite I prayer book," a volume that took advantage

---

48. "Reappropriation" is the intentional self-application of language that has been previously perceived as demeaning. For a psychological description of the effects of reappropriation, see Adam D. Galinski, Cynthia S. Wang. Jennifer A. Whitson, et. al., "The Reappropriation of Stigmatizing Labels: The Reciprocal Relationship Between Power and Self-Labeling," *Psychological Science* 24 (October 2013): 2010–19.

49. Emily Wachner, phone conversation with the author (October 6, 2016).

of the rubric allowing the transformation of Rite II texts to Rite I language.[50] The General Convention of 2000 authorized the occasional use of "the texts of the Daily Offices and Holy Communion contained in the 1928 edition of the Book of Common Prayer," provided the use received ecclesiastical approval parallel to that specified in the "guidelines for supplemental liturgical materials."[51] In 2002 a new group was formed in New York—Episcopalians for Traditional Faith—that advocated taking advantage of this provision and using 1928 Book of Common Prayer texts. In 2014 the group would change its name to "The 1928 Prayer Book Alliance."[52]

Episcopalians were not the only ones to suggest that traditional language still had a place in Christian worship. Songwriters Amy Grant and Michael W. Smith's "Thy Word," which mixes Elizabethan and contemporary language, has been a popular favorite among Evangelical Christians since its introduction in 1984 on Grant's album *Straight Ahead.* In 2003 the Roman Catholic Church issued an edited version of the Episcopal prayer book with multiple use of Rite I texts—*The Book of Divine Worship*—for parishes of former Episcopalians in the United States who had aligned with the Roman Catholic Church.[53] Clearly, interest in the use of Elizabethan language in worship had not disappeared.

---

50. The book contained Elizabethan forms of most prayers used for public worship with the notable exception of Eucharistic Prayer C. See *The Anglican Service Book: A Traditional Language Adaptation of the 1979 Book of Common Prayer Together with the Psalter or Psalms of David and Additional Devotions* (Rosemont, PA: Church of the Good Shepherd, 1991). For the enabling prayer book rubric, see Book of Common Prayer (1979), 14.
51. General Convention, *Journal of the General Convention of . . . the Episcopal Church, Denver, 2000* (New York: General Convention, 2001), 681.
52. The 1928 Prayer Book Alliance, "Our Story," http://www.1928prayerbookalliance.org/our-story (accessed September 30, 2016).
53. *The Book of Divine Worship: Being Elements of the Book of Common Prayer Revised and Adapted According to the Roman Rite for Use by Roman*

Rite I is no longer an infallible sign of an aging congregation. St. Paul's K Street in Washington, DC, which is located near George Washington University, has a lively ministry to people in their 20s and 30s and uses only Rite I services. A growing percentage of the younger students that I teach at Virginia Theological Seminary, who are drawn from across the country, have an interest in traditional forms of worship that at times surprises older faculty members.

Not all young adult Episcopalians find inspiration from Elizabethan texts, of course. Stephen R. Shaver, who is a 2017 PhD graduate from the Graduate Theological Union and an adjunct faculty member at the Church Divinity School of the Pacific, sees young adults who have an interest in traditional language of worship as constituting one of two "particularly but not exclusively among younger" adult populations that are often found where there is "numeric and spiritual" growth in the Episcopal Church today:

> The first kind sees itself as living at the center of the prayer book tradition in ways that self-consciously claim continuity with, and even a kind of counter-cultural obedience to, practices inherited from the Christian past (even if that past is always to some extent a constructed one). The second kind sees itself as creatively riffing on the prayer book tradition, treating it as a precious and beloved resource but also as a foundation for creative reinvention.[54]

He identified the "tribal markers" of the first group as "things like *a preference for Rite I* and for eastward eucharistic celebration; an interest in correctness of performance and a willingness to

---

*Catholics Coming from the Anglican Tradition* (Mt. Pocono, PA: Newman House Press, 2003). In 2015 the Roman Catholic Church issued a replacement volume, titled *Divine Worship: The Missal*.

54. Stephen R. Shaver, "On Pronouns, Politics, and Process," (paper delivered at the Once and Future Prayer Book Conference, Part II, the University of the South, Sewanee, Tennessee, October 10, 2017).

engage in long discussions of rubrical principles (would that we all took the rubrics so seriously!); and, often, a level of suspicion toward *Enriching Our Worship*, other recent supplementary materials. . . ." He suggests that the tribal markers of the second strand "include the open invitation to receive communion regardless of baptism; an interest in incorporating non-prayer book material, and emending prayer book material to fix perceived problems of inclusion; a love of the questions included in the baptismal covenant of 1979. . . ."[55]

While such observations do not constitute a systematic study of national trends, they should at least suggest the need for caution about the total elimination of Rite I services; they do not simply meet the spiritual needs of the oldest among us. Some younger people find beauty and meaning in traditional language worship.

## What Then Should We Do?

Episcopalians—young and old—continue to show both an interest in modified Elizabethan worship and a concern about balanced and expansive language. What strategies might be followed if the 2018 General Convention adopts one of the Standing Commission on Liturgy and Music's 2018 proposals about liturgical revision or subsequent proposals directed to the same end? Clearly, the revisers of the next prayer book have two language issues to address, which might be identified as Enriching Our Worship and Rite I issues.

### Enriching Our Worship Issues

The General Convention should build on the work of the 1990s and follow the balanced language approach of supplementing Rite II Trinitarian language with feminine images drawn from scripture, rather than rejecting all uses of male imagery and language for

---

55. Ibid. (Emphasis added.)

persons of the Trinity. Nonetheless, it would be wise for General Convention to replace the controversial texts in the Book of Common Prayer (1979) that followed the International Consultation on English Texts in introducing a new use of masculine pronouns in reference to persons of the Trinity: "Blessed be *his* kingdom," "*He* has spoken through the Prophets," and "It is right to give *him* thanks and Praise."[56] These texts are already being widely amended in individual Episcopal congregations, and the Roman Catholic Church's 2011 revised liturgy no longer contains them.[57] It might also make sense for General Convention to address one other text introduced in 1979—Eucharistic Prayer C. It might approve a new rubric allowing the addition of other names after the listing of the patriarchs.[58]

General Convention should consider whether it would be appropriate to take a further step and replace all the International Consultation on English Texts ecumenical texts for common portions of the liturgy (Lord's Prayer, Gloria, Nicene Creed, etc.). These appear with slight modifications in the Book of Common Prayer (1979). They could be replaced with the newer ecumenical texts suggested by the English Language Liturgical Consultation in *Praying Together* (1988).[59]

The General Convention could include selected texts from the Enriching Our Worship series in a future edition of the Book of Common Prayer. This could include Eucharistic Prayers, Canticles, and pastoral prayers and offices. As an addition or alternative to

---

56. Book of Common Prayer (1979), 355, 359, 361.
57. CatholicBridge.com, "Text of the New English Roman Catholic Mass," http://www.catholicbridge.com/catholic/catholic_mass_full_text.php#greeting (accessed March 1, 2018).
58. Book of Common Prayer (1979), 372.
59. English Language Liturgical Consultation, *Praying Together* (1988), electronic version available at http://englishtexts.org/ELLC-Documents/ELLC-Texts (accessed March 15, 2018).

this approach, the General Convention could move some Enriching Our Worship texts to the *Book of Occasional Services*, the use of which is less restricted than that directed in the Enriching Our Worship series.

## *Rite I Issues*

The General Convention might decide to add an introduction about Elizabethan language to a future prayer book to aid those who participate in such services. It might also approve a revision of the rubric on page 14 of the 1979 Book of Common Prayer (1979) to say directly what it is now generally interpreted to mean—that any Rite II text can be converted to Rite I language—and add to it some explanation of how that might be done.

General Convention might also decide to expand Rite I forms in the Book of Common Prayer to include Noonday, An Order for Worship for the Evening, Compline, Baptism, and An Order for Celebration of the Holy Eucharist so that all the regular public services of the Church would be available in both contemporary and traditional language.

The General Convention could decide to list only one form of the collect—either a contemporary collect that could be converted to a traditional form (a practice allowed by the rubric on page 14 of the 1979 Book of Common Prayer) or a traditional form that could be converted to a contemporary language (a pattern allowed by a rubric on page 814 of the 1979 Book of Common Prayer for certain "classic prayers"). This would allow a return to the *Services for Trial Use*'s practice of uniting lectionary materials in one place, saving space and providing a more accessible way to use lectionary materials.

If the bishops and deputies at General Convention fear that such strategies might create a prayer book that would be so large as to be unwieldy, it might be possible to pursue a two-book approach.[60] The convention could follow the English example by according permanent status to the Book of Common Prayer (1979), while creating a comprehensive Alternative Book that would bring together materials from the Enriching Our Worship series, the *Book of Occasional Services, Lesser Feasts and Fasts,* and other supplemental volumes. Alternatively, the General Convention could follow the example of the General Convention's decisions about the hymnal in 1982 and authorize a new prayer book without removing permission for previous editions.

This is not an exhaustive list of language proposals, but it does suggest some directions that conversation about language might take.

---

60. See pages 179-80 of this volume for a further explanation of the English use of alternative books.

# 3

# Moving Offices: Daily Prayer in the 1979 Book of Common Prayer and Beyond

### Andrew McGowan[1]

> *Moreover the nombre and hardnes of the rules... and the manifolde chaunginges of the service, was the cause, y$^t$ to turne the boke onlye, was so hard and intricate a matter, that many times, there was more busines to fynd out what should be read, then to read it when it was faunde out.*[2]

## The Daily Office in the 1979 Book of Common Prayer

Few people pondering the Book of Common Prayer adopted by the Episcopal Church in 1979 are likely to mention the Daily Office as

---

1. The Very Rev. Dr. Andrew McGowan is the Dean and President of Berkeley Divinity School and McFaddin Professor of Anglican Studies and Pastoral Theology at Yale University.

2. Cranmer's preface from 1549; published in *The First Prayer Book of King Edward VI*, ed. Vernon Staley (London: Alexander Moring, 1903), 3.

a highlight of that book's originality, or as a window onto its distinctive concerns.[3] The main offices of Morning and Evening Prayer are in fact among the most conservative elements of the book, and reflect little either of fresh contemporary insight, or of that wisdom, older even than Cranmer's and derived from ancient Christian patterns of worship, on which those who formed the 1979 book drew in many other ways.

This is hardly to say those services have no merit; they continue to reflect the heart of Archbishop of Canterbury Thomas Cranmer's sixteenth-century reshaping of the Daily Office and its emphasis on Psalter and scripture. There are also new services that expand the range of offices for individuals and groups to use at different times of day. Yet in many ways the 1979 Book of Common Prayer—unlike many others adopted around the Anglican Communion—seems to have passed over the question of significant reform of Christian daily prayer. In addition, the subsequent resources made available for use in the Episcopal Church do not show the expected engagement either with ecumenical or other Anglican scholarship or practice in the interim. As conversation about prayer book revisions gains momentum, this seems to be an area where the status quo is not where it is for other rites.

In what follows I place the Daily Office of the 1979 Book of Common Prayer in context and consider how the reform of communal prayer took shape in other parts of Anglicanism across the same period. Considering also the newer resources of *Enriching Our Worship 1* and *Daily Prayer for All Seasons*, I offer some suggestions for next steps that would take the Daily Office forward to

---

3. I use the term "the Episcopal Church" as that preferred by the organization and as self-evident in this context, granted that other churches of the Anglican Communion that refer to themselves as "Episcopal" in their title must indicate, unsurprisingly, their specific national or geographical identities.

a place that reflects both the distinctive American tradition of the Book of Common Prayer, and a deeper connection with daily prayer in the wider Church.

## Cranmer's Book and Ours

Three things about the Daily Office as found in the early Books of Common Prayer have remained influential in the way members of the Anglican Communion undertake their versions of the Christian tradition of daily prayer. First is the consolidation of the monastic hours into two, the daily Morning and Evening Prayer services whose structures have shaped many communities and individuals since. Second is the relative simplicity of a mostly invariable structure, without the inherited complexity about which Cranmer's preface to the first Book of Common Prayer (see above) wryly complained.

Third, and hardly least, is the priority these offices give to the Psalter and to the Bible as a whole, whose praying and reading *in toto* are prescribed in ways that reflect earlier monastic tradition, and whose centrality in the exercise are ensured by the simplicity of the rest.

This two-fold, simple, and scripture-centered pattern constitutes the heart of Cranmer's achievement in the Daily Office, and through the global influence of the 1662 book in particular has become the hallmark of Anglican daily prayer, even while its specific language has become a less universal feature. Like other elements of liturgy, however, the Daily Office has sustained considerable scrutiny in the last century and continues to be the object of reflection and reform.

Prior to the 1979 book, Morning Prayer had been the principal Sunday service in numerous parishes in the Episcopal Church, especially those of a classically low-church tradition. The new book however was, and is, distinguished by an emphasis on Eucharist and on baptism, which reflects changes in thinking not just in the United States of America or Anglicanism but in the wider Church of the mid-twentieth century. The new—or rather the ancient—centrality given to the Eucharist implied that the era of Morning and Evening Prayer as events shared by the typical congregation on Sunday was all but over. Although the new Book of Common Prayer (1979) allowed that both the Holy Eucharist and "Daily Morning and Evening Prayer, as set forth in this book, are the regular services appointed for public worship in this Church," the Eucharist was now called "the principal act of Christian worship on the Lord's Day."[4]

While the 1979 baptismal and eucharistic liturgies themselves thus reflect radical liturgical ideas, ancient and modern alike, the effect on the Daily Office of this shift of interest was close to stagnation. In the case of the Eucharist, there was clearly a new liturgy, whether in traditional (Rite I) or modern (Rite II) language; the two classic Daily Offices, however, are remarkably similar to those in the 1928 book. The most significant innovation in daily prayer lay outside them, in the addition of a group of shorter services, which together implied a recognition that the future of the offices lay in private and smaller group use. The Daily Office had been left not just to the weekdays in Church, but on the sidelines in liturgical revision.

## From 1928 to 1979: Tweaks

The conservatism of the rites themselves is the clearest evidence that the framers of the 1979 book were not, relatively speaking, very interested in the revision of the Daily Office. Two editions of *Prayer Book Studies*—the small books presenting the thinking of the Standing Liturgical Commission to the wider Church during the

---

4. Book of Common Prayer (1979), 13.

revision process—were devoted to daily prayer, published in 1957 and 1970. Most of the concern in these is for increased flexibility, and for changes to outmoded language. These were perhaps large enough issues for most to contend with or celebrate in the 1960s and 70s, with the energy focused elsewhere in the revision process.

The result is that the Daily Office in the 1979 book, or at least the two-fold office of Morning and Evening Prayer, is simply that of the Book of Common Prayer 1928, modestly adapted. Rite I is of course closer to the older book in language; Rite II is basically a translation of Rite I, with some additional materials. The modest changes of content that do occur reflect issues already discussed in the 1950s, while language issues had become more pressing in the 1970s.[5]

Rite I Morning Prayer, which can serve as representative of the two main offices in both rites, differs from that of 1928 in four more or less significant ways. First, there is a new framework of section headings, which makes no explicit difference to the celebration of the office, but reflects a new interest in order or shape that had been prominent in liturgical thinking particularly since Gregory Dix's 1945 study, *The Shape of the Liturgy*.[6] Where the 1928 service had presented its elements simply as a sequence of texts or prayers, the 1979 Book of Common Prayer follows its opening sentences and confession with a portentous "Invitatory and Psalter" heading (of the same size as the division of Holy Eucharist into "The Word of God" and "Holy Communion"). Next comes "The Lessons" (which

---

5. See Standing Liturgical Commission of the Protestant Episcopal Church in the United States of America, *Prayer Book Studies VI: Morning and Evening Prayer; Prayer Book Studies VII: The Penitential Office* (New York: Church Pension Fund, 1957); and Standing Liturgical Commission of the Episcopal Church, ed., *Prayer Book Studies 22: The Daily Office* (New York: Church Hymnal Corp., 1970).
6. Gregory Dix, *The Shape of the Liturgy*, new ed. (New York: Continuum, 2005).

actually includes canticles and the Apostles' Creed), then "The Prayers." These three headings do not accompany any actual change of substance or structure but seem rather to be an attempt to reveal one in the existing rite. The result, more or less a three-fold form of psalms, scripture, and prayers, remains a faithful rendition of the Cranmerian tradition.

Second, there is an expansion of options in the canticles, especially for the morning office. The 1928 book offered *Venite* as invitatory, then a choice of *Te Deum, Benedictus es,* or *Benedicite* to follow the first lesson, and *Benedictus* or *Jubilate Deo* (Psalm 100) to follow the second. The 1979 book gives a choice between *Venite* or *Jubilate* to begin,[7] then offers seven more canticles among which to choose *ad lib* as the two to follow the readings (including *Gloria in excelsis* and *Magnificat,* both more traditional in other contexts).[8] This emphasis on variety mirrors the approach taken in other rites in the book, such as for Eucharistic Prayers. For whatever reason, Rite II has more options than Rite I, although the Rite I rubrics also offer those additional canticles, or at least their page numbers, to intrepid officiants. Evening Prayer in both rites is, perhaps by accident, more conservative about canticles; the hymn *Phos hilaron* is added as a parallel to the use of *Venite* in the morning as an invitatory, which may be the single most significant change of rite across the offices, but only the traditional *Magnificat* and *Nunc dimittis* are provided as canticles, unless a rubrical invitation to wade into the reservoirs already offered for Morning Prayer is followed.

This change toward variety, and the first regarding structure, are closely related. In this regard at least, the spirit of the new Book

---

7. Also envisaged in the 1950s; see Standing Liturgical Commission of the Protestant Episcopal Church in the United States of America, *Prayer Book Studies VI: Morning and Evening Prayer; Prayer Book Studies VII: The Penitential Office.*

8. Although *Gloria in excelsis* had been an odd inclusion in earlier American books, as an alternative to *Gloria Patri.*

of Common Prayer (1979) was present in the revision of the offices: a shift was evident in the "commonality" of Common Prayer, from being understood as uniformity of text to a unity of structure. The dilemmas created by this new range of options were acknowledged by provision of a table of suggested canticles for Morning and Evening Prayer each day of the week, with some provision for seasonal variation but maintaining the oddity already noted about the Evening Prayer canticles.[9]

Third, some editing of language is notable, particularly in the confession. This has a less penitential introduction (as well as a much shorter alternative form), text, and absolution, achieved mostly by redaction rather than new composition. These will be evident to most readers at a glance and do reflect the shift toward a more optimistic and affirming theology of the human person redeemed in Christ that is characteristic of the book as a whole, as well as some desire to constrain wordiness. Yet the continued provision of confession and Apostles' Creed as normal parts of the office on a daily basis suggests little interest in simplification per se.

Fourth, the section now titled "The Prayers" has been expanded, relative to the 1928 book. Two changes link the offices more closely with the English book of 1662, curiously enough. The Lord's Prayer has been moved from its early placement after the confession to the beginning of the Prayers, corresponding to the second of two places it appears in 1662; earlier American books had kept the first, but not the second.[10] This change seems to fit with the book's consolidation or clarification of "prayers" as a section, and also to present the Lord's Prayer more clearly as a model of Christian prayer

---

9. Book of Common Prayer (1979), 144–45.
10. Already envisaged in 1957; see Standing Liturgical Commission of the Protestant Episcopal Church in the United States of America, *Prayer Book Studies VI: Morning and Evening Prayer; Prayer Book Studies VII: The Penitential Office*, 7–8.

generally. The suffrages, truncated to two versicles and responses in the three earlier Episcopal Church books, were now expanded into an updated version of 1662 (form A), with the latter verses of the *Te Deum* as an alternative (B). Given the general emphasis on ancient Christian patterns and ecumenical alignment in the new Book, this apparent glance back at the English liturgy is surprising, but the changes can be understood as reflecting the mind of the revisers in other respects. The collects are also revised; collects for Sundays, Fridays, and Saturdays are now provided, reflecting the emphasis on time, and on Sunday in particular, throughout the book.

The overall effect of these changes is to lessen the penitential feel of the older forms, but especially to add to the variable elements. In practice, the extent to which the variable elements can result in actual flexibility depends on the level of preparation by the officiant, and on a liturgical skill previously unknown or unnecessary—the constant announcement of page numbers. There is therefore some degree of unwitting return here of the "hard and intricate matter" Cranmer bemoaned, of "manifolde chaunginges."

## The Additional Offices

More significant, at least in theory, than these changes to the Episcopal Church's versions of Cranmer's two-fold scheme was the addition of three new forms for different times of day provided in 1979: An Order of Service for Noonday, An Order of Worship for the Evening, and An Order for Compline (a service for the end of the day). These are placed in the book so as to suggest a sequence across the day along with the Rite II services, but the new forms share more with each other than with the two major offices.

The Noonday Order is closest to the traditional offices and has the same structure (without the prominent headings to assert it, perhaps because it is less encumbered by additional features). Beginning with the same response as Evening Prayer ("O God, make speed . . ."), it proceeds to a small and invariable selection of psalms and a choice of three very short readings (both features apparently modelled on the Compline order, on which see below). Last come prayers consisting of the responsive *Kyrie*, Lord's Prayer, collects, and "free intercessions" (a term only used here and at the new Compline in the whole Book of Common Prayer). This is more like what has been termed a "Cathedral" form of office, emphasizing a small amount of material in scripture and Psalter repeated daily, rather than the more "monastic" pattern of the major offices adopted by Cranmer that reads (almost) the whole Bible and recites all the Psalms.[11] This is a common feature with the other two new services, the Order for Evening and Compline.

The Order for Evening is the most distinctive of the three, taking the form of a short *Lucernarium* or service of light, an ancient tradition which makes this the most obvious place where the eastward-leaning eclecticism of the 1979 book appears in the forms of daily prayer. The investment of the Book of Common Prayer (1979) framers in this liturgical curiosity is reflected in overexplanation: there are two sets of instructions (108 and then 142–43) before and after, and then unusually full rubrics within the service as printed (112). The office itself, however, consists simply of opening sentences, a "Prayer for the Light" before candle and lamp lighting, and the hymn *Phos hilaron*. Its explicit use of symbol and ritual—a unique feature—also reflects a shift to the "Cathedral" model with its simpler, more repetitious, and more communal focus. Rubrics indicate this service can be used before one or other of Evening Prayer or Eucharist, before "a meal or other activity," or "as a complete evening Office" with (unspecified) psalmody, Bible reading, canticle, prayers, and dismissal. This list, by the way, seems to be the clearest

---

11. See Paul F. Bradshaw, *Two Ways of Praying* (Nashville: Abingdon Press, 1995).

statement by the framers of the 1979 Book of Common Prayer about what any office should entail, and reflects the structure of them all.

Compline follows closely a form in the Proposed Book of 1928 for the Church of England,[12] and similar versions of this later evening service had been reclaimed around the Anglican Communion after the Anglo-Catholic revival of the nineteenth century. After opening sentences, it has confession and absolution, then a choice of four psalms and the same number of very short readings, as in Noonday Prayer. A responsory ("In your hands . . .") comes before the familiar quartet of *Kyrie*, Lord's Prayer, collects, and "free intercessions." *Nunc dimittis*, with antiphons from the old monastic office, functions as a closing canticle, one of a few features here that do not really belong with the general shape of these newer offices but seem to have found favor with the editors because of use elsewhere and earlier.

Taken as a set, these new offices give more insight into the ethos of the 1979 book, or the interests of its editors, than the conservative revisions of Morning and Evening Prayer. As noted already, these new services sit closer to the pole that liturgists often describe as "Cathedral" prayer, emphasizing repeated simple elements of psalmody and scripture, rather than the arguably more "Monastic" pattern of the Cranmerian two-fold office, where the whole of the Bible and the Psalter are used. Each of these three new services has psalmody, scripture, and prayer also, but the place of psalms and readings is heavily constrained, not just in brevity but fixity. This makes for a curious contrast with the revised Morning and Evening

---

12. The Church of England prepared a revision of the Book of Common Prayer around the same time as the effort that led to the 1928 American edition. The British Parliament, however, which formally has authority over public worship for the established Church of England, did not approve the proposed book, although its services came into partial use under different mechanisms. The more recent English services discussed below have been authorized as supplements to, rather than replacements for, the 1662 book.

Prayer, which not only retain the full use of Psalter and scripture, but now offer a significant and very different complexity and variety in the otherwise "fixed" elements of canticles and collects.

Any sense these new forms could actually constitute a series of hours of prayer with the two traditional offices of Rite II, as the page order of the Book of Common Prayer (1979) attempts to suggest, is thus unconvincing. Experience and observation further suggest that the other two, the more classical Anglican forms, have continued to be more widely and consistently used in those places where the offices are actually said.[13] If the three new offices have found regular users, they seem likely to have been small groups such as participants in conferences or other residential experiences, vowed religious, or individuals engaged in private prayer.

## Meanwhile, Elsewhere in the Anglican Communion . . .[14]

The conservatism of the 1979 Book of Common Prayer is more striking when compared to developments in other parts of Anglicanism through the same period. While the Episcopal Church book stayed close to the form of its early modern predecessors, at least some other national Churches were imagining quite different uses for daily prayer and providing for them accordingly.

Just as shifts in the dynamics of the Communion as a whole were taking place, so too developments in daily prayer far away from the traditional center in England were initially more important, and in this case those in the antipodes and in religious communities were most interesting.

---

13. Commentary leading up to the revision suggests the use of the two other offices is assumed; see Standing Liturgical Commission of the Episcopal Church, *Prayer Book Studies 22: The Daily Office*, 29.

14. See John Gibaut, "The Daily Office," in *The Oxford Guide to the Book of Common Prayer: A Worldwide Survey*, ed. Charles Hefling and Cynthia Shattuck (Oxford: Oxford University Press, 2006).

While the Church of England's *Alternative Service Book* (1980) had reflected only the same issues, and a very similar result, as the 1979 Book of Common Prayer,[15] the Daily Office as revised for the Society of St Francis, the Anglican Communion's main group of Franciscan orders, had wide influence. *Daily Office SSF*, which was published in different forms from the 1970s on, provided a different version of daily prayer for each morning and evening, including different canticles and prayers in a common structure. It also introduced new canticles, particularly some based on biblical texts. These were provided as daily and seasonal variations rather than merely in a reservoir of material for use *ad lib*. While reflecting the same desire for varied material as the Episcopal Church book, the SSF model placed this diversity in a shared pattern rather than in the hands of officiants—a telling contrast.

This model, of variety reflected in community and calendar rather than individual leaders' choices, was followed elsewhere quickly. The first major revision in Australia, *An Australian Prayer Book* of 1978—published prior to the Episcopal Church book—was one of the first of a national church to offer not just a revised or translated form of the 1662 or similar offices, but also both a simpler structure (opening versicle, canticle, psalmody, readings, canticle, prayers) and specific forms for each morning and evening of the week. This model is repeated, with some influences in content from later English books, in the current *A Prayer Book for Australia* (1992).

The *New Zealand Prayer Book*, better known (if perhaps not better understood) in the United States of America, has a similar pattern, with a "Morning and Evening Worship" related to the 1662 form and intended for larger groups, but also daily services

---

15. Interestingly a pattern like that discussed in what follows was provided by the Joint Liturgical Group in *The Daily Office Revised: With Other Prayers and Services*, ed. Ronald Jasper (London: SPCK, 1978).

reflecting the Franciscan pattern discussed above.[16] The New Zealand book was to have some influence in later Episcopal Church conversations, but not by way of a different model or structure. When published in a new form as *Celebrating Common Prayer* in 1992, the Franciscan office book already reflected collaboration with the Church of England's Liturgical Commission. *Celebrating Common Prayer* exemplified a number of the new trends in the Daily Office that would become widespread in Anglican and other settings, and made them more widely available in the Church of England and elsewhere. When the *Common Worship* resources for the Church of England were published more recently to succeed the *Alternative Service Book*, a further revised version of that Franciscan office had effectively become the daily prayer of the Church of England.

*Common Worship* itself is not a book but a collection of materials, supplemental in theory at least to the 1662 Book of Common Prayer, which remains nominally in force in the Church of England. *Common Worship*, however, finds form in different physical books, for Sunday use, pastoral offices, and others, including a massive Daily Office book. This expands the options—the canticles and the other variable elements—of *Celebrating Common Prayer* onto both the days of the week and the liturgical year, so that a different version of Morning and Evening Prayer is provided for each day of the week in each season. While it thus involves a new kind of complexity, the *Common Worship* model exemplifies a way of dealing with options quite different from the Episcopal Church 1979 book (or *Enriching Our Worship*). Where the Episcopal Church resources place a large amount of discretionary power in the officiants' hands and require participants to move back and forth in the book via announcements that emphasize the role of the leader in a

---

16. Stephen Burns, "'Learning Again and Again to Pray': Anglican Forms of Daily Prayer," *Journal of Anglican Studies* 15, no. 1 (May 2017): 13–15.

direct way, *Common Worship* makes collective decisions based on seasons and on theological themes connected with the cycle of the week, and allows a continuous flow through a few pages at each office, with the officiant simply beginning to recite each element, the Psalter excepted.

One thing each of these models share is a relative simplicity and brevity. Creeds and confessions are typically optional, and while some have opening canticles, the idea of an "invitatory" is rare. The canticles and other elements provide more clearly a frame for the central elements of the office, which remain the recitation of the Psalms and the reading of the Bible.

## *Enriching Our Worship*

There were of course further developments in the Episcopal Church after 1979. The use of inclusive and expansive language and image in the Supplemental Liturgical Texts that became *Enriching Our Worship 1* (to many, just *Enriching Our Worship*) has been celebrated by some, and criticized by others.[17] In the context of the Daily Office, however, *Enriching Our Worship*'s failings or success lie not in radicalism, but in a conservatism that is still essentially that of the 1979 Book of Common Prayer's approach to the offices. That is to say, *Enriching Our Worship*, like the Book of Common Prayer (1979), offers no new idea or rite, but simply an expanded range of texts for use with the essentially conservative Rite II.

While debate has continued about its language and about some of the unintended consequences of that commitment on issues such as Trinitarian doctrine, liturgically speaking *Enriching Our Worship* suffers from a problem just as fundamental, but quite different: a basic tension that goes back to its predecessors, the Supplemental

---

17. Standing Liturgical Commission, *Enriching Our Worship: Supplemental Liturgical Materials* (New York: Church Publishing, 1997).

Liturgical Texts that constituted *Prayer Book Studies 30* and the subsequent *Supplemental Liturgical Materials*,[18] and to the General Convention resolutions that set the process of developing them in motion.[19] In these, and in commentary on them, there is a tug of war between two different projects or agendas: on the one hand, a push to change further the actual rites of the 1979 book in the direction of inclusion, with a possible new liturgy as the result; on the other the more modest but important possibility of offering additional materials to complement what was already a set of variable options for the key texts of most Book of Common Prayer (1979) rites.

The "final" result in *Enriching Our Worship* is not a set of rites at all. Texts are presented in the order they appear in the Rite II, but without the elements for which no alternative has been offered. Thus, there is no attempt at any complete liturgy in *Enriching Our Worship*—but just enough visual similarity to them to be confusing. The prefatory material, which was supplied at the time of publication rather than adopted by General Convention, is contradictory.[20] The

---

18. Standing Liturgical Commission of the Episcopal Church, *Supplemental Liturgical Texts* (New York: Church Hymnal Corp., 1989); Sarah Motley, ed., *Supplemental Liturgical Materials* (New York: Church Hymnal Corp., 1991); Standing Liturgical Commission, *Enriching Our Worship*.

19. The Standing Liturgical Commission was to "prepare inclusive language liturgies" in 1985, but to "study, develop, and evaluate supplemental . . . texts" in 1989. Standing Liturgical Commission of the Episcopal Church, *Commentary on Prayer Book Studies 30 Containing Supplemental Liturgical Texts* (New York: Church Hymnal Corp., 1989), C-15.

20. Then Presiding Bishop Frank Griswold's preface clearly states that *Enriching Our Worship* seeks "to provide additional resources to assist worshiping communities wishing to expand the language, images and metaphors used in worship" (5); in the introduction, Phoebe Pettingell writes clearly that *Enriching Our Worship* "avoids supplying complete rites, providing instead a collection of texts" (9); yet the unsigned instructions for use state, "The texts may be used in two very different ways. First, any of the texts may be used in conjunction with the Rite II liturgies of the 1979 BCP. . . . A second option is to develop an entire liturgy using the supplemental texts"

confusion has encouraged some enthusiastic but unreflective readers both for and against the Enriching Our Worship project to imagine that it does present whole rites, and hence to imagine *Enriching Our Worship* as, for good or ill, an alternative rather than a supplement.

In any case, for Morning and Evening Prayer even more than for Eucharist, *Enriching Our Worship* cannot be considered a rite, but a set of resources that expands options for Rite II. It offers inclusive-language alternatives for the confession, opening versicles, doxology after the Psalms, ending for lessons, salutation, and closing sentence, among the fixed elements, arguably making these variable by doing so. Of the already variable parts, the new canticles are undoubtedly the highlight. *Enriching Our Worship* borrows and/or adapts sixteen canticles from Anglican sources (especially *Celebrating Common Prayer* and the *New Zealand Prayer Book*) and Roman Catholic ones, mostly biblical in origin.[21] A new table of suggested canticles for morning and evening each day is provided (44–45), with much greater complexity than the Book of Common Prayer (1979) version. It also offers a pair of "Morning Psalms" distinguished in some undefined way from "Invitatory Psalms" but offered for the same purpose, and similarly three "Evening Psalms" including a metrical setting of *Phos hilaron* (not a psalm).[22] Other new options include a further set of suffrages.

---

(14). The instructions for use were an edited form of a set of instructions added in the editorial process for an "expanded edition" of *Supplemental Liturgical Materials* that was published in 1996. See Standing Liturgical Commission, *Enriching Our Worship*, 5, 9, 14; and Standing Liturgical Commission, *Supplemental Liturgical Materials*, expanded ed. (New York: Church Hymnal Corp., 1996), 11–15.
21. Standing Liturgical Commission, *Enriching Our Worship*, 9.
22. Perhaps its least successful feature as a book useable alongside the Book of Common Prayer (1979) for actual communities is the placement of new antiphons for these "psalms" after their actual texts, when they are expected

Of the three new or lesser offices added in the 1979 book, only the Order of Worship for the Evening receives any attention in *Enriching Our Worship*, and then only in the form of an alternative opening versicle, some references to the "Evening Psalms" provided for the two major offices, and mention of forms of blessing provided for the Holy Eucharist.

Despite the confusion about its purpose, which continues in its ongoing reception in the Episcopal Church for the Daily Office as well as for the better-known eucharistic texts, *Enriching Our Worship* simply adds to the options for existing variable elements of Rite II and offers a number of alternative forms for some "invariable" elements. There is, however, still no different structure or rite for the Daily Office, any more than for the Eucharist. Ritually speaking, *Enriching Our Worship* is thus as conservative as the Book of Common Prayer (1979) itself, or more so. While this may seem surprising, given the wider evolution of daily prayer in other parts of the Anglican Communion that had long been going on before it was published, this reality is merely the outworking of the assumptions that were brought to the genesis of *Enriching Our Worship*.

## *Daily Prayer for All Seasons*

In 2014 the Standing Commission issued a further publication called *Daily Prayer for All Seasons*, which consists of short forms of prayer connected consciously if loosely to the older monastic hours combined or removed by Cranmer. These are divided into something like greater and lesser hours (to use traditional terms), with forms for private use at the beginning and end of the day, and then so-called "Shorter" hours (which seem at a glance often to be longer

---

to be used before. Standing Liturgical Commission, *Enriching Our Worship*, 24–25.

than the others), intended for communal use. These are mapped onto the eight Benedictine hours, but concepts such as "wisdom" or "trust" are substituted for the traditional names.[23]

While it describes itself as a "variation on [the] theme" of the Daily Office, *Daily Prayer for All Seasons* is not in any obvious way linked either to the prayer book tradition, or—despite its claim to evoke Benedictine patterns—to wider patterns of daily prayer discernable across Christian tradition which emphasize the Psalter in particular and scripture in general. The Psalms have no particular place in this scheme, except as part of a larger corpus of material that yields words amenable to the framers' intention.

There are two ways in which *Daily Prayer for All Seasons* does reflect wider conversations or movements in the Anglican Communion and beyond. One is that familiar emphasis on structure or form itself, which is raised to a new level of prominence, whether or not convincingly: the preface explains the common form for the opening and closing hours as "Entering and Going Out (or Closing)," "Scripture," "Meditation," "Prayer." The "shorter" hours are said to add "Prayer," "Praise," "Meditation," "Prayer." This redundancy hints that the elements of the *Daily Prayer for All Seasons* form an assemblage of resources for private prayer; granted that there is a shape all the forms share, the forms do not quite succeed in connecting with a sense of communal or liturgical activity.

Second and more interesting is an attempt to combine seasonal themes with those of the hours of prayer. Each of the hours is provided in sets that reflect the basic seasons of the liturgical year, although there is no sign of a sanctoral calendar. This hints at some influence from how recent resources already discussed have given greater emphasis to seasonality, in their provision of varied material, while holding at bay the logistical difficulties of "manifolde

---

23. Standing Commission on Liturgy and Music of the Episcopal Church, *Daily Prayer for All Seasons* (New York: Church Publishing, 2014).

chaunginges." To its credit, *Daily Prayer for All Seasons* does not require much in the way of page-flicking. While the resource itself makes much of its connection to "monastic" tradition, its use of short and repeated texts (at least across the whole pattern of the week) is much closer to what liturgists call the "Cathedral" model of daily prayer.

Assessment of *Daily Prayer for All Seasons* depends very much on how its purpose is understood. It is a collection of interesting material for prayer, and has much in common with other devotional aids for personal or small group use that have sprung up in recent decades, and which reflect the hunger of many for prayer that is variously contemporary, inclusive, global, etc. It shows a renewed interest in the Benedictine tradition (or at least in the idea of it), in versions of Celtic spirituality, and in other voices often left unheard in the existing composed prayers of Anglican tradition. Its strength lies in these elements, and in the possibility that it will thus prove a useful devotional aid for individuals especially, and perhaps for some groups too.

If, on the other hand, *Daily Prayer for All Seasons* is taken at its word, as a form of the liturgy of the hours or the Daily Office, judgment will be less favorable. Apart from the hint of influence around emphasizing seasonality, *Daily Prayer for All Seasons* seems to have appeared in a bubble of sorts. It borrows freely in content but does not reflect a strong connection either with its own tradition as manifested in the Book of Common Prayer (1979) or *Enriching Our Worship*, or knowledge of the wider Anglican and ecumenical conversation about the hours of prayer as reflected in resources like *Common Worship*.

"Prayer" for *Daily Prayer for All Seasons* does not really seem to mean the services or hours of prayer as events or distinctive practices, nor do the hours mean more than times. "Daily prayer" is not so much that distinctive Christian practice formed in the historic community of faith, centered especially on the Psalter, but a means for expression of what comes from within the praying individual. This distance from other traditional and contemporary assumptions or definitions gives even the eclecticism of *Daily Prayer for All Seasons* an exceptionalist feel, if taken at its word as an attempt at contributing to the tradition of the Daily Office.

If read as a step toward what might appear in a future prayer book or supplementary resource, *Daily Prayer for All Seasons* is then a missed opportunity—but this might be to misread its intent. In either case, it underlines further the extent to which the Episcopal Church has left itself outside a global conversation about the renewal of daily prayer that otherwise reflects some consensus, as well as some ongoing contests.

## Conclusions and Prospects

If the Daily Office is to be considered either as part of a formal revision of the Book of Common Prayer for the Episcopal Church, or in consideration of further alternative and supplemental materials to stand alongside it, there are some issues that need significant attention.

The Episcopal Church was lagging behind the wave of liturgical reform in this area even when the otherwise rich and influential 1979 book was published. Subsequent supplemental and alternative materials have provided additional texts but have left the issue of substantial renewal of the Daily Office itself hanging, for a number of reasons. Developments in the wider Anglican Communion suggest some of the contours that a renewed landscape of communal prayer could and should have.

In the 1979 Book of Common Prayer and *Enriching Our Worship*, the addition of large amounts of variable material, in the canticles in particular, has unwittingly created a variety of expressions subservient to personal preferences rather than to a deeper sense of community or seasonality. Elsewhere in the Communion, the same kind of variety has been provided for in set patterns based on weeks and seasons, as part of a common mind expressed by national churches and their liturgical commissions. It is not hard to imagine how the content of the 1979 Book of Common Prayer, including the important new canticles in *Enriching Our Worship*, could be set into a framework that provided more clearly for daily and/or seasonal variation. Berkeley Divinity School at Yale has recently experimented with such an office solidly grounded in the Episcopal Church texts, including *Enriching Our Worship*, but with a simplified structure, and providing for the varied use of canticles, suffrages, and other materials according to a pattern mapped onto the calendar.

One issue that deserves more discussion is the tension between the more "Monastic" and specifically Cranmerian pattern of the two major offices in the Episcopal Church book, and the "Cathedral" style prayer embodied in the three lesser offices introduced in 1979. English liturgist Paul Bradshaw has suggested that the "Cathedral" style deserves more positive attention, and points out that daily prayer in *Common Worship* can already be used with a simpler and less exhaustive set of readings and psalms.[24] While it seems unlikely that the modest if not trivial number of individuals and communities who already use the Daily Office regularly in the Episcopal Church will be attracted to a model without the rigor or depth of the patterns set by Cranmer, a simpler set of psalms and readings could indeed be provided for Morning and Evening Prayer too, not least with a view to wider use. This may be part of what *Daily Prayer for All Seasons* intended, but its retreat from the centrality of the Psalter in particular makes it problematic as a model.

Last but not least, the differences between private or small group uses, and the potential for different forms of public worship,

---

24. Paul F. Bradshaw, "The Daily Offices in the Prayer Book Tradition," *Anglican Theological Review* 95, no. 3 (June 1, 2013): 447–60.

deserve more attention. The older Anglican forms were framed as public, but were used as such just on Sundays, other than in cathedrals and collegiate churches. The Sunday public use of Morning and Evening Prayer is now mostly gone in the Episcopal Church, yet recent experience suggests the public character of Christian prayer is not irrelevant. There is a growing appreciation in many places of the value of Compline, which has become popular on many college campuses, or of the forms from the Taizé community, not just as spiritually helpful for insiders but as an evocative presentation of Christian prayer for those who may not yet fully understand either prayer or Christianity itself, and hence for whom eucharistic worship is not fully accessible.

So there is room for different expressions of the Daily Office, both as private devotion and as public worship, which map diversity onto the lives of communities, rather than merely giving clergy more choices or offering individuals more varied resources for private prayer. The doctrine of the 1979 book concerning the centrality of eucharistic celebration can be taken as a given for the Episcopal Church; yet the future of the Daily Office lies not just in its capacity to deepen the prayer lives of the baptized, individually and communally, but also as a form of divine service based in the words of Psalter and Scripture, overlain on the structure of day and night, and hence offered to the wider reality of human life, including to a wider public, as well as to its creator.[25]

---

25. My thanks to those who have discussed these issues in a variety of settings, especially my colleague Bryan Spinks who offered helpful comment, and to the editor of this volume for suggestions that have certainly improved the result. Shortcomings that remain are my own.

# 4

# The Baptismal Revolution of 1979

## James F. Turrell[1]

The 1979 Book of Common Prayer represented a revolution in the theology of baptism, with profound implications for the life of the church. It was a departure from the prayer books that had preceded it, both in its overall pattern of initiation and in its theology of baptism. This departure in turn sparked substantial developments in sacramental practice, ecclesiology, and Christian formation. Perhaps because of its radical nature, the book has only partially been appropriated by the Episcopal Church in its daily life. Those drafting the next revision of the prayer book—whenever it comes—will need to decide if they wish to continue in the path set by the 1979 BCP or reject its baptismal pattern and theology. Indeed, because of the partial reception of the initiatory

---

1. The Reverend Canon James F. Turrell, PhD, is the Norma and Olan Mills Professor of Divinity, the Associate Dean for Academic Affairs, and the Sub-Dean of the Chapel of the Apostles at the School of Theology of the University of the South in Sewanee, Tennessee.

theology of the prayer book, revisers may decide it is too soon to undertake revision, until we have fully lived into the baptismal pattern of the 1979 prayer book.

## Initiation Before the 1979 Prayer Book

The initiatory sequence in the 1979 prayer book was both an innovation and a recovery of an earlier tradition. It represented a sharp break with the English prayer book tradition dating from the sixteenth century, but it was at the same time a recovery of a patristic pattern of Christian initiation. It was, in its way, both a conservative work, mining the tradition, and a radical departure, rejecting the pattern set by Archbishop of Canterbury Thomas Cranmer in the first two editions of the prayer book (1549, 1552) and maintained by all of the subsequent editions of the Book of Common Prayer.

The first century or two after the apostles showed a remarkable diversity of initiatory process, with separate patterns followed by different geographic and linguistic groups. In time, particularly after the Emperor Constantine designated Christianity as an allowable religion in the Roman Empire (313), these multiple patterns were replaced by a single pattern.

In Syria in the first centuries, it appears that there was a preliminary anointing before a water bath, but no ceremonies following. This preliminary anointing was seen as pneumatic, conveying the Holy Spirit to the candidate. In the West, the water bath was followed by handlaying and (pneumatic) anointing. The diversity of baptismal practice continued until the fourth and fifth centuries, when we see a general homogenization of practice, with West Syrian rites adding post-bath anointings (not added in Eastern Syria), mirroring the Western pattern, and reframing their pre-bath anointings as exorcistic (a casting out of evil), rather than pneumatic (an infusion of the Holy Spirit).

The sequence through most of the church, from the fourth century onward, could be characterized as "bath-anointing-first communion," with allowance for some local variations: the Gallican rite—the form of the liturgy used in the Roman province of Gaul, which is roughly equivalent to today's France—had a single postbath anointing, for example, while the early Roman rite had two, one by a presbyter and one by the bishop. Nevertheless, the core of the sequence was shared.[2]

Many candidates for baptism in the early church were adults (though some persons were baptized as infants), and the norm of adult baptism shaped both baptismal preparation and baptismal procedures. In an era of evangelization, as the church grew and expanded its reach, more people likely came into the church through conversion than by birth. The church in several places devised programs of formation for those converts, in the ancient catechumenate.[3] The adult converts, termed *catechumens* (those who receiving catechesis—i.e., instruction in the Christian faith), were typically dismissed from the worshiping assembly before the Eucharistic Prayer and given instruction. As the date of their baptisms approached, they were exorcised repeatedly as a sort of spiritual preparation. The baptism of adults allowed the church to undertake significant education and formation of baptismal candidates, something that would have been absurd for infants. More important, though, was the expectation (voiced in some early rites themselves) that baptism meant a reordering of one's life around the imperatives of the gospel. Catechesis was not simply learning a Christian message or absorbing doctrine, but taking on a new way of living in the world. Baptismal candidates typically went into the waters naked, in baptisteries separate from the main worship space

---

2. Maxwell Johnson, *The Rites of Christian Initiation: Their Evolution and Interpretation*, rev. ed. (Collegeville, MN: Liturgical Press, 2007), 42–200.
3. Ibid., 36, 119, 198.

of a church building. Once baptized and clothed, the neophytes (new Christians) were brought into the main worship space of the church, where they joined in the prayer of the faithful, exchanged the peace, and shared in the Eucharist for the first time. Baptism thus entailed considerable preparation, before taking place in a eucharistic context.[4]

Over time, however, the practice of adult baptism declined and the baptism of infants became predominant. By the sixth and seventh centuries, most candidates were infants.[5] Christianity was no longer primarily a religion of converts, so there was a higher proportion of children of believers in the community; infant mortality and fear of the consequences of original sin gave an incentive for baptism; and the development, in time, of means of dealing with postbaptismal sin (through penance) meant that there were not strong disincentives to early baptism.[6] This change in the age of customary candidates meant that the process of catechesis, intended to help adult candidates in the reordering of their life around a new,

---

4. Aidan Kavanagh, *Shape of Baptism: The Rite of Christian Initiation* (Collegeville, MN: Liturgical Press, 1978), 56–67; Johnson, *Rites of Christian Initiation*, 98–106, 122–24; see also Justin Martyr, "First Apology," *Documents of the Baptismal Liturgy*, ed. E. C. Whitaker and Maxwell E. Johnson (Collegeville, MN: Liturgical Press, 2003), 3; "Apostolic Constitutions" III.16 in Whitaker and Johnson, *Documents*, 36.
5. Paul Turner, *Ages of Initiation: The First Two Christian Millennia* (Collegeville, MN: Liturgical Press, 2000), 9–16.
6. Cyprian and other church leaders in North Africa in the mid-third century defended baptism soon after birth (Cyprian, "To Fidus, on the Baptism of Infants," Epistle LVIII in *The Ante-Nicene Fathers: The Writings of the Fathers Down to A.D. 325*, ed. Alexander Roberts, James Donaldson, and A. Cleveland Coxe, vol. 5 [Grand Rapids, MI: Eerdmans, 1957], 353–54). They did so during a period of persecution, and it may be that Christian parents feared that they might not live to raise their children to maturity. After legalization of Christianity, Christians reenvisioned the practice as a response to the high rate of infant mortality.

Christian identity, was now irrelevant.[7] Infant candidates within weeks of birth were not really engaged in a process of conversion from one way of life to another, nor were they able to absorb doctrinal teaching (though older children would be a different matter).

In roughly the same period, the unified initiatory rite of bath-anointing-first communion broke apart in the West. The initiatory rite fragmented because the Roman rite became the predominant liturgical rite in the West. It had maintained two post-bath anointings, reserving the second one to the bishop. In the geographically compact dioceses of the Italian peninsula, it was not unreasonable to expect baptisms to take place in the presence of the bishop, so that the final anointing could be supplied. In those rare cases in which the bishop was absent, the final anointing was deferred until the candidate could be brought to the bishop. When the Roman rite spread throughout the West, displacing local liturgical patterns, it brought with it the requirement of the second, episcopal anointing (i.e., one given by the bishop). This made less practical sense, however, in the geographically large dioceses of Northern Europe, in which it was rare for a layperson to encounter a bishop. Tied with this was the emergence, then, of the *quam primum* baptism of infants—baptism as soon as possible after birth. The result was that the post-bath anointing at the hands of a bishop was often significantly delayed after baptism, if it happened at all. This separated handlaying came to be known as confirmation.[8] It was expected to be done as soon as possible after baptism (which by now was often done without the congregation present), and medieval art portrays infants being confirmed by bishops (some of whom even confirmed

---

7. Johnson, *Rites of Christian Initiation*, 260–61.
8. Ibid., 246–60; Marion Hatchett, *Commentary on the American Prayer Book* (New York: Seabury Press, 1980), 257–58; Mark Searle, "Infant Baptism Reconsidered," in *Living Water, Sealing Spirit: Readings on Christian Initiation*, ed. Maxwell Johnson (Collegeville, MN: Liturgical Press, 1995), 370–71.

from horseback),⁹ but many adults were never confirmed at all. Nevertheless, once they reached the "age of discretion," as young as seven or as old as fourteen, individuals were to make their first confession and receive absolution. The Fourth Lateran Council (1215) expected individuals to receive communion annually, and first communion seems to have happened as young as seven or as old as eighteen. In any case, they were not to receive unless they had had confession and absolution.[10] Beginning in the thirteenth century, confirmation itself came to be delayed until the age of discretion.[11] This is the pattern that Thomas Cranmer inherited: what once had been a unified rite of initiation was fragmented into three—baptism, confirmation, and first communion.[12]

Cranmer altered the theology behind the rites he inherited, but he kept their basic pattern. Cranmer's first baptismal rite (in the 1549 Book of Common Prayer) largely preserved medieval ceremonies, but it borrowed some texts and some theology from the continental reformers. For example, it retained exorcism of the candidate, a pre-bath signing with the cross, and a post-bath anointing, while adding the Flood Prayer found in Luther's baptismal rite, which compared the dying to sin in baptism to Noah's flood. The

---

9. Ann Eljenholm Nichols, *Seeable Signs: The Iconography of the Seven Sacraments, 1350–1544* (Woodbridge, Suffolk: Boydell Press, 1994), 209–13, 216–17; Joseph Lynch, *The Medieval Church: A Brief History* (London: Longman, 1992), 279.
10. Turner, *Ages of Initiation*, 30–31.
11. Searle, "Infant Baptism Reconsidered," 370–71.
12. Baptism developed in different ways in the Eastern churches, however, with bishops authorizing presbyters to anoint (Johnson, *Rites of Christian Initiation*, 269–307). In some places there may have been an extended catechumenate beginning in infancy and concluding with childhood baptism (Byron D. Stuhlman, *The Initiatory Process in the Byzantine Tradition: Texts in Translation from Early Manuscripts of the Euchology and Typikon of the Hagia Sophia in Constantinople with a Brief Commentary* [Piscataway, NJ: Gorgias Press, 2009]).

addition of the Flood Prayer did create an odd redundancy: it stated that Jesus' baptism "diddest sanctifye the flud Jordane & all other waters, to the misticall washing awaye of sinne," while Cranmer nevertheless retained a form calling for God to sanctify the water in the font immediately before the administration of the water. This form was only used when the water was changed, at least monthly.[13] Cranmer's concept of consecration was distinctive: to consecrate was to set aside for a holy use, and so the prayer asking for God to sanctify the water frames this in terms of the spiritual benefits it is to convey to the baptismal candidate.[14]

The 1552 prayer book eliminated the remaining traditional ceremonies (such as exorcism and anointing), with the exception of the signing of the candidate with the cross, which was moved from its old position prior to the bath to a new location as a post-bath ceremony. It also altered the two texts used in the 1549 book to consecrate the water when the font was changed. The first text, a lengthy set of petitions, asked God to "Sanctifie this fountain of baptisme . . . ," in the midst of requests that God might give spiritual benefits to the candidates. The second text, a collect, asked that all baptized in this water might "receive the fulnesse of thy grace, and ever remain in the noumbre of thy faithfull and elect children." In the 1552 revision, Cranmer omitted the petition to sanctify the water while retaining the other petitions and the concluding collect, and he directed that these texts be used at each baptism, not

---

13. F. E. Brightman, *The English Rite: Being a Synopsis of the Sources and Revisions of the Book of Common Prayer* (London: Rivingtons, 1915), 726–29, 738–41. For Luther's version of the Flood Prayer, see Martin Luther, "The Order of Baptism 1523," trans. Paul Zeller Strodach in *Luther's Works*, vol. 53, ed. Ulrich S. Leupold (Philadelphia: Fortress Press, 1965), 97.

14. Gordon Jeanes, *Signs of God's Promise: Thomas Cranmer's Sacramental Theology and the Book of Common Prayer* (London: T&T Clark, 2008), 197–206.

merely when the water was changed.[15] The only remaining nod toward a sanctification of water, as opposed to the newly baptized, lay in the Flood Prayer. The 1552 baptismal rite became the pattern for all subsequent Anglican baptismal rites until the revisions of the twentieth century.

The 1662 prayer book retained the 1552 structure, though it made a few modifications to the rite. It retained the Flood Prayer's description of Jesus' entrance into the water at baptism as consecrating water, but then specifically identified only "the river Jordan" rather than "the fludde Jordan, and al other waters" of earlier prayers. The 1662 service also modified the 1552 collect before the administration of water, adding a petition to "sanctify this water to the mysticall washing away of sin," in effect restoring what Cranmer had eliminated in 1552.[16] The inclusion of this petition, paired with the elimination of the vague reference to "all water" in the Flood Prayer, clarified that the font's water was being sanctified in the midst of the liturgy itself, directly before use. Otherwise, the 1552 structure was intact. Similarly, the 1662 book added a form for "Ministration of Baptism to such as are of riper years," but this mirrored the structure for infant baptism, with alterations to allow candidates to speak for themselves and the substitution of a passage from John 3 in place of the customary Gospel reading from Mark 10, telling the story of people bringing their children to Jesus.

Cranmer had also preserved the separate rite of confirmation. His 1549 rite contained a signing with the cross that was dropped in 1552, but otherwise there was not much that changed in his second edition. The 1662 prayer book added an explanatory preface at the start of the rite itself, a query renewing the candidate's baptismal promises, the recitation of the Lord's Prayer, and a prayer for the

---

15. Brightman, *English Rite*, 738–41.
16. Ibid., 726–29, 740–41.

candidate's obedience to God's laws, but the rite is still recognizably the offspring of Cranmer's 1552 version.[17]

While the English prayer books had maintained the medieval pattern of assuming the baptism of infants as normative, their treatment of confirmation was different. In 1549, Cranmer followed Luther's example, requiring instruction in the catechism before one could be presented for confirmation. Thus, confirmation became an adolescent rite of passage. Complicating matters still further, Cranmer also retained a thirteenth-century English regulation, promulgated by Archbishop Robert Peckham, that asserted that one must be confirmed before one could receive communion. This had been instituted in an effort to encourage more confirmations, but it had the effect now of posing a barrier to communion. All subsequent English Books of Common Prayer continued to tie confirmation to instruction, and communion to confirmation. This resulted in a two-stage initiation: individuals were made members of the church in baptism, but they were not full, participatory members. Instead, the prayer book required a second initiatory rite, confirmation, which was to follow several years later. In reality, most individuals never received confirmation, at least until the end of the seventeenth century and beginning of the eighteenth. Instead, the enforcement mechanisms of the church insisted on knowledge of the catechism as the necessary prerequisite for full, participatory membership. The 1662 prayer book finally introduced the loophole into the prayer book itself: now persons must be confirmed or "ready and desirous of confirmation" in order to receive communion. Loopholes notwithstanding, it was clear that baptism was simply the first stage of multipart initiation.[18]

---

17. Ibid., 724–99.
18. For a more thorough discussion, see James F. Turrell, "Confirmation, Conversion, and Catechizing: Patterns of Incorporation in the Early Modern Church of England" (PhD diss., Vanderbilt University, 2002).

The American prayer books retained the Cranmerian pattern. The 1789 prayer book simplified the liturgy, permitted several changes in practice (making the signing with the cross optional and allowing parents to make promises for their children, in place of godparents) and made several bits of text optional, but the structure still resembled that of 1552. The 1789 prayer book retained separate rites for the baptism of adults and private baptism, but these, too, resembled their English forebears. The prayer book revision in 1892 did not change these fundamental elements.[19]

The 1928 prayer book consolidated the separate rites for adults and children and for public and private baptisms, and reworked the liturgical structure, but it left Cranmer's basic pattern unchanged. The prayer book continued to assume infant candidates as the norm. It did add two new questions for adult candidates, asking "Dost thou believe in Jesus Christ, the Son of the Living God?" and "Dost thou accept him, and desire to follow him as thy Saviour and Lord?"[20] Most significantly, the blessing of the font was altered: the text asking God to "sanctify this Water to the mystical washing away of sin" and that the candidate might receive grace was changed from the "collect" form in the earlier prayer books to a structure resembling the communion service's prayer of consecration. It began with a dialogue, then gave thanks to God in language reminiscent of the prayer of consecration in the communion office ("It is very meet, right, and our bounden duty, that we should give thanks unto thee . . .").[21] By opening with a dialogue and recasting it in the context of thanksgiving, the framers of the 1928 prayer book put the two sacraments of baptism and the Eucharist into parallel liturgical forms, and it emphasized the blessing of the water, placing

---

19. Paul V. Marshall, ed., *Prayer Book Parallels*, vol. 1 (New York: Church Hymnal Corp., 1989), 234, 240–56.
20. Ibid., 245–47, 266–79.
21. Ibid., 254–55.

it on the same footing as the consecration of bread and wine in the Eucharist. Yet despite these structural adjustments, the basic lines of Cranmer's 1552 baptismal rite remained, as well as the underlying initiatory pattern of infant baptism–adolescent confirmation–subsequent communion.

All of the prayer book baptismal rites from 1549 to 1928 shared a theology of baptism that centered on the cleansing of the candidate from sin. The 1549 baptismal rite featured a prayer prior to the bath, asking that the infant candidates "may receyue remission of theyr sinnes, by spirituall regeneracion."[22] The prayer accompanying the post-bath anointing referred to God, "who hath regenerate thee by water and the holy gost."[23] Subsequent prayer books underscored this emphasis on regeneration and cleansing from sin. The 1552 book, for example, added a prayer of thanksgiving that God had been pleased to "regenerate this infant" and to "receive him for thy own child by adoption."[24] The 1662 book added the petition noted above to "sanctify this water to the mysticall washing away of sin" to the prayer just prior to the baptismal washing.[25] The emphasis on new birth was carried over in the American prayer books, with prayers that asked God to grant the infant candidate "spiritual regeneration" and a prayer over the water asking God to sanctify it "to the mystical washing away of sin."[26]

Discipleship was not a primary emphasis of the baptismal rites before 1979. Cranmer's baptismal rite had included an admonition to the godparents to see that their charges were "vertuously brought up to leade a godly and Christian life."[27] To the original, Cranmerian

---

22. *The First and Second Prayer Books of Edward VI* (London: Prayer Book Society, 1999), 237.
23. Ibid., 241.
24. Brightman, *English Rite*, 724–47.
25. Ibid., 724–47.
26. Marshall, *Prayer Book Parallels*, 240–41, 254–55.
27. *The First and Second Prayer Books of Edward VI*, 241.

structure, the 1662 BCP had added a vow to "obediently keep God's holy will and commandments, and walk in the same" at the end of the affirmation of the Creed.[28] The vow survived in all of the American books through 1928. The American prayer books of 1789 and 1892 retained the admonition to the godparents, though it was dropped in 1928.[29] Following Jesus had a moral dimension, but it was not a primary emphasis of the prayer books, nor was it articulated in ways that went beyond virtuous living.

The initiatory pattern of the pre-1979 Books of Common Prayer then assumed infant baptism and adolescent confirmation; the separation of baptism, anointing/handlaying ("confirmation"), and first communion; and an emphasis on cleansing from sin and regeneration. This reflected elements of both the church's medieval heritage (the separation of the components of Christian initiation) and its Reformation heritage (Luther's reinvention of confirmation as a ceremony after catechizing). Baptism was, as my liturgy professor stated, "celestial fire insurance," while confirmation was an educational opportunity required for full participation in the church.

## Initiation in the 1979 Book of Common Prayer

The process of revision leading to the 1979 prayer book's initiatory rites has been masterfully addressed by Ruth Meyers of the Church Divinity School of the Pacific, and so the narrative of that process and its successive draft liturgies need not divert us here.[30] It is enough to note that the original plan of the framers of the prayer book, embodied in *Prayer Book Studies 18*, was for a restoration of the early church's unified rite of initiation. The separate rite of

---

28. Brightman, *English Rite*, 724–47.
29. Marshall, *Prayer Book Parallels*, 250–63.
30. See Ruth A. Meyers, *Continuing the Reformation: Re-Visioning Baptism in the Episcopal Church* (New York: Church Publishing, 1997).

confirmation came back through a series of revisions (in *Prayer Books Studies 26*, the *Draft Proposed Book of Common Prayer*, and finally in revisions at the General Convention to the draft proposed book). Now joined with optional formulae for the reception of persons into the communion of this church and for the reaffirmation of baptismal vows by those already confirmed, the new confirmation rite was printed among the "Pastoral Services" in the book. The resuscitation of confirmation left substantially unchanged, however, the shape of the revised baptismal rite that had first been proposed in *Prayer Book Studies 18*.

The 1979 BCP's baptismal liturgy introduced significant structural changes. It included a water bath, a post-bath handlaying with optional anointing, and the expectation that the baptism took place in the context of the Eucharist. This amounted to a revival of the unified rite of initiation from the early church. Similarly, adult baptism was now the "liturgical norm" for the rite, giving it shape and meaning.[31] The new prayer book also adjusted the theology of the baptismal rite. The new prayer book added a "baptismal covenant," tacking onto the recitation of the Apostles' Creed a series of behavioral promises. The post-bath handlaying was accompanied by a prayer for the gifts of the Holy Spirit, formerly associated with confirmation. Finally, a note in the prayer book stated, "Holy Baptism is full initiation by water and the Holy Spirit into Christ's Body the Church."[32]

The shift toward adult baptism as the "liturgical norm" (though not the statistical norm) for the Episcopal Church brought with it the revival of the ancient church's catechumenate, published in the parallel *Book of Occasional Services* in 1979 (and revised periodically thereafter). The presence of the catechumenate suggests to all,

---

31. For a discussion of the concept of a "liturgical norm," see Kavanagh, *Shape of Baptism*, 106–10.
32. Book of Common Prayer (1979), 298.

even those who have been baptized as infants, that baptism is a serious undertaking requiring serious preparation, not merely a milestone rite for babies. Catechumens themselves, with the personal narratives that drew them to the font, underscore that Christian life is a choice, not a genetic inheritance. The catechumenate is, in Aidan Kavanagh's words, "conversion therapy," as the catechumens reassemble their identity and their life around Jesus Christ.[33] The shift to adult baptism as the liturgical norm makes clear that baptism is not child's play, though it may be done to children as well as adults.

Similarly, the inclusion of an explicit baptismal covenant, with detailed promises governing behavior, reflects an emphasis on discipleship. The baptismal rite in the 1979 prayer book makes it clear that Christian identity entails certain behavioral expectations that go beyond mere moral virtue, in contrast to the terse and therefore ambiguous commitments required in earlier prayer books since 1662. The covenant requires a commitment to repentance and to social justice, which can be seen as an application of the moral law, but the candidate also commits to proclaim the gospel and to participate in eucharistic worship. These latter commitments are less self-evident in the single vow in the older prayer books—at the very least, the new vows render explicit what was formerly indistinct. This was the goal of the drafters: "to spell out—as it were, to flesh out— the implications of keeping God's holy will and commandments."[34] Baptism was still about new life and cleansing from sin, but it also became a matter of discipleship, of following Jesus in action.

---

33. Aidan Kavanagh, "Catechesis: Formation in Stages," in *The Baptismal Ministry and the Catechumenate*, ed. Michael W. Merriman (New York: Church Hymnal Corp., 1990), 37.
34. Louis Weil, "When Signs Signify: The Baptismal Covenant in Its Sacramental Context," *Open: Journal of Associated Parishes for Liturgy and Mission* (Spring 2008): 8; see also Meyers, *Continuing the Reformation*, 205–6.

Above all, the 1979 prayer book made it clear that baptism was full initiation. In part, this was the result of structural changes to the rite: by restoring handlaying (and optional anointing) after the water bath, together with a prayer for the gifts of the Holy Spirit, in a liturgy that assumes a eucharistic context, the 1979 prayer book had reassembled the unified baptismal rite of antiquity. There was nothing left to be supplied later. In case that was too subtle, the prayer book printed an explicit statement in the preliminary notes "Concerning the Service": "Holy Baptism is full initiation."[35] While this would appear difficult to argue around, some have tried: in one article, New Testament scholar Reginald Fuller, of the Seabury-Western Theological Seminary (1955–66), Union Theological Seminary, New York (1966–72), and Virginia Theological Seminary (1972–85) faculties, argued that "full initiation" meant "full sacramental initiation," allowing for the exclusion of the baptized-but-unconfirmed from some aspects of church life.[36] Such a reading flies in the face of the plain meaning of the prayer book text.

Finally, the 1979 prayer book reflects, in large and small ways, an ecclesiology grounded in baptism. The prayer book catechism is the most direct in its treatment: the Church is "the Body of which Jesus Christ is the Head and of which all baptized persons are members . . . the ministers of the Church are lay persons, bishops, priests, and deacons . . . [and] the ministry of lay persons is to represent Christ and his Church; to bear witness to him wherever they may be; and, according to the gifts given them, to carry on Christ's work of reconciliation in the world; and to take their place in the life, worship, and governance of the Church."[37] This is reflected in new roles

---

35. Book of Common Prayer (1979), 298.
36. Reginald H. Fuller, "Confirmation in the Episcopal Church and in the Church of England," in *Confirmation Re-Examined*, ed. Kendig Brubaker Cully (Wilton, CN: Morehouse-Barlow, 1982), 18.
37. Book of Common Prayer (1979), 854–55.

within the liturgical rites of the book: for example, laypersons may officiate at the Daily Office, are to read the lessons, and may lead the prayers of the people at the Eucharist.[38] Even at ordinations, which in the past could be clerical affairs, laypersons are to serve as presenters, read the lessons, and take other roles in the liturgy.[39]

In the next essay, I will consider the advisability of revision of the current baptismal office.

---

38. Ibid., 74, 354.
39. E.g., ibid., 511, 513, 515.

# 5

# The 1979 Prayer Book's Baptismal Office and the Potential of Revision[1]

## JAMES F. TURRELL[2]

The church has generally accepted the baptismal ecclesiology taught by the 1979 prayer book and explained in the previous chapter of this book. One sees this both in the larger life of the church and in its ritual practice. In the church's liturgical life, the role for laypersons has expanded significantly beyond what would have been imaginable at the start of the twentieth century.

---

1. An oral presentation based on portions of this material was delivered at the School of Theology of the University of the South on October 9, 2017, as part of the Once and Future Prayer Book Conference. A version of that presentation was published in the Christmas 2017 issue of the *Sewanee Theological Review* (volume 61:1).

2. The Reverend Canon James F. Turrell, PhD, is the Norma and Olan Mills Professor of Divinity, the Associate Dean for Academic Affairs, and the Sub-Dean of the Chapel of the Apostles at the School of Theology of the University of the South in Sewanee, Tennessee.

The canons have expanded opportunities for laypersons to share in formally recognized, liturgical ministries. Most parishes have licensed lay chalice bearers, laypersons who read the lessons, and those who take other roles in the service. In some respects, present usage has gone further than the prayer book text itself: while the prayer book permits licensed laypersons to administer the chalice only "in the absence of sufficient deacons and priests," in some parishes it is now customary for vested clergy to sit out while a layperson administers the chalice, and in some places one even finds laypersons administering bread.[3]

The portion of the service designated as "the Baptismal Covenant" itself has come to loom large in the consciousness of Episcopalians, in part because of the widespread practice of its renewal on the four baptismal feasts of the church calendar, even if there are no actual baptisms on those dates. The covenant is also a convenient authority to which preachers appeal, a way of summing up what Christian life requires, and it has been a benchmark in catechumenal preparation of candidates for baptism.[4] Theological commentaries on the baptismal rite, ranging from specialist treatises on the liturgy to popular introductions, have placed the covenant in interpretive context for a variety of audiences.[5] The covenant has

---

3. The General Convention of 1988 replaced references in the canons to lay distribution of the *chalice* with references to distribution of the *elements*, a change understood to authorize lay distribution of the bread. While this provision has survived subsequent revisions of the canons, no corresponding change has been made to the additional directions in the prayer book about distribution that mention only the chalice. See Resolution A123 in General Convention, *Journal of the General Convention of . . . the Episcopal Church, Detroit, 1988* (New York: General Convention, 1989), 239; Canon III.4, Episcopal Church, *Constitution and Canons 2015* (New York: General Convention Office, 2016), 68–70; and Book of Common Prayer (1979), 408.
4. Weil, "When Signs Signify," 9.
5. E.g., Marianne Micks, *Deep Waters: An Introduction to Baptism* (Cambridge, MA: Cowley Publications, 1996), 66–76; Daniel Stevick, *Baptismal Moments,*

been borrowed by other churches as well, sometimes with subtle alterations.[6]

## The Failure to Implement Other Elements of the Prayer Book's Ethos

By contrast with its enthusiasm for the covenant, the church has been slow to embrace the new liturgical norm of the adult baptism, at least in practice. In numerous aspects, large and small, parishes demonstrate their assumptions that baptism is a rite of passage for infants: the frequently observed practice of calling children up to the font to see the baptism (while it is rare to see a parish priest call the children closer to the altar to see the eucharistic action, in the other dominical sacrament); the practice of parading newly baptized infants but not adults; the practice of ignoring the baptismal feasts in the church's calendar in favor of baptism on seemingly random Sundays to accommodate the convenience of traveling relatives, or worse, to ensure that the ancestral baptismal gown still fits; the omission of the baptismal covenant.[7] All of these surviving practices indicate that the church imagines baptism as something

---

*Baptismal Meanings* (New York: Church Hymnal Corp., 1987), 156–58; Anne E. Kitch, *Taking the Plunge: Baptism and Parenting* (New York: Morehouse Publishing, 2006), 43–48; Hatchett, *Commentary on the American Prayer Book*, 273–74; Leonel L. Mitchell, *Praying Shapes Believing: A Theological Commentary on the Book of Common Prayer* (Harrisburg, PA: Morehouse Publishing, 1985), 101–2.

6. Stephen Burns and Bryan Cones, "A Prayer Book for the Twenty-First Century?" *Anglican Theological Review* 96 (2014): 645–46.

7. Paul V. Marshall, "Trite Rite: Field Notes on the Trivialization of Christian Initiation," in *Leaps and Boundaries: The Prayer Book in the 21st Century*, ed. Paul V. Marshall and Lesley A. Northup (Harrisburg, PA: Morehouse Publishing, 1997), 73; James F. Turrell, *Celebrating the Rites of Initiation: A Practical Ceremonial Guide for Clergy and Other Liturgical Ministers* (New York: Church Publishing, 2013), x.

done to infants, a sort of hangover from the 1928 prayer book and its predecessors, memorably described by bishop and liturgical scholar Paul Marshall: "Salvation without discipleship (Christendom)—the transformation of 'mysteries' to be enacted into things to be received, gazed upon, or carried about (sacraments)—created a situation where costly and life-changing initiation was neither necessary nor desirable."[8] This amounts to the trivialization of the baptismal liturgy.

Perhaps the slow appropriation of adult baptism as normative and the continued infantilization of the rite of baptism reflects the failure of the church to evangelize. The framers of the prayer book determined that they were in a post-Constantinian context, in which the culture no longer bore the Christian message and in which the church would need to reach out deliberately and vigorously to bring persons to the knowledge of the gospel and the love of the Lord. While they were correct in their assessment of the culture, the Episcopal Church has not engaged in the widespread, evangelistic effort to the unchurched that the framers expected. As a consequence, most baptismal candidates in Episcopal parishes are infants, and the church's numbers have declined.[9]

---

8. Marshall, "Trite Rite," 72.
9. The decline in religious affiliation in the United States has been well documented (e.g., Pew Research Center, "America's Changing Religious Landscape" http://www.pewforum.org/2015/05/12/americas-changing-religious-landscape/ [accessed April 20, 2017]). There has been a 19.2 percent decline in baptized membership in the domestic dioceses of the Episcopal Church from 2005 to 2015 (http://www.episcopalchurch.org/files/baptized_members_by_province_and_diocese_2005-2015.pdf [accessed April 20, 2017]). While much of the decline since 1966 can be attributed to the declining birthrate, there has been no discernible increase in adult converts to offset the lower numbers of infants born within the church (C. Kirk Hadaway, "Is the Episcopal Church Growing (or Declining)?", http://www.episcopalchurch.org/files/2004GrowthReport(1).pdf [accessed April 20, 2017]).

The church has failed to implement other elements of the prayer book's ethos as well. One still hears of private baptisms, even though the book is clear that baptism should be reserved for the chief liturgy on a Sunday or major feast. Not all parishes have taken to heart the book's clear preference that baptisms be reserved for four baptismal feasts or the visit of the bishop, and so one hears of baptisms taking place on other Sundays (though at least a congregation is present).[10] One hears of baptisms even in Lent, the traditional season for the preparation of candidates, suggesting a lack of understanding of both baptism and the church year.

The church has developed selective amnesia concerning aspects of baptismal ministry. Baptism is, as noted, "full initiation," and it entails certain behavioral promises. After baptism is conferred, there is no higher dignity that the church can bestow: even ordination is merely the setting aside of an individual for certain functions for the good of the *ekklesia*, the assembly. One struggles, then, to grasp the call for new commissioning rites for laypersons' ministries in the world.[11] For that matter, the profusion of commissioning rites in the 2003 edition of the *Book of Occasional Services* for every possible functionary in the life of the local congregation obscures the reality that we are commissioned for service in the world by virtue of our baptisms, not some additional rite.[12]

Most serious is the practice of communion without baptism, which reflects a profound misunderstanding of the sacramental

---

10. Book of Common Prayer (1979), 298, 312; for discussion, see Hatchett, *Commentary on the American Prayer Book*, 267–68, 284–85. (Most of those private baptisms do not occur in a eucharistic context, another point of departure from the structure and ethos of the prayer book.)
11. Lisa Fishbeck, "Called to Ministry in the World: What If We Ordained the Laity?" July 13, 2013, https://www.episcopalcafe.com/called_to_ministry _in_the_world_what_if_we_ordained_the_laity/ (accessed April 17, 2017).
12. *The Book of Occasional Services 2003* (New York: Church Publishing, 2004), 179–95.

"grammar" of the 1979 prayer book. The 1979 book restored the three-part, unified rite of initiation from the church of the fourth century or so: baptism, handlaying (with optional chrism), and first communion. Each time one subsequently receives communion, one reiterates that third, repeatable part of the initiation rite.[13] Communion becomes, in part, a renewal of baptism. The understanding that communion is for the baptized is embedded in various parts of the prayer book: the promise in the baptismal covenant to continue in "the breaking of bread"; the postcommunion prayers in which we note that God has "graciously accepted us as living members of [God's] Son our Savior Jesus Christ," and that through the Eucharist we are assured "that we are living members of the Body of your Son," an incorporation into the Body of Christ that happens only through baptism; and the invitation to communion, "The Gifts of God for the People of God," a status that Gentiles achieve through baptism. Eucharistic Prayer C and the proper preface of the Holy Spirit (available for prayers A and B) both make explicit the norm that only the baptized participate in the Eucharist: the celebrant in prayer C prays, "And so, Father, we who have been redeemed by him, and made a new people by water and the Spirit, now bring before you these gifts," while in the preface she prays, "For by water and the Holy Spirit you have made us a new people in Jesus Christ our Lord, to show forth your glory in all the world."[14] As Virginia Theological Seminary liturgical theologian James Farwell has noted, the church has accepted parts of the prayer book at different speeds: enthusiastic embrace of weekly Eucharist, moderate embrace of the emphasis on baptism, and slow embrace of the Holy Week liturgies. As a result, the Eucharist has been cut loose from

---

13. Mitchell, *Praying Shapes Believing*, 116.
14. Book of Common Prayer (1979), 304, 364–366, 371, 378; Robert MacSwain, "'The Gifts of God for the People of God': Some Thoughts on Baptism and Eucharist," *Sewanee Theological Review* 56 (2012): 71–84.

the meaning it finds in the context of baptism and the paschal mystery.[15] The 1979 prayer book assumes that baptism precedes participation in the Eucharist, and proponents of communion without baptism reject this foundational tenet of the book.

The desire to remove baptism as the ordinary precondition for sharing in the Eucharist (perhaps through canonical change, as was attempted at the 2012 General Convention) reflects several related desires, among them the desire to be hospitable and the desire to reflect what some believe to be the example of Jesus. A debate in the pages of the *Anglican Theological Review* between Kathryn Tanner of Yale and the University of Chicago and James Farwell develops the issues in greater depth than one can here.[16] We do well, though, to note that frequently lost in the debate is the difference between rules and norms, the latter being those standards that give shape and meaning to our liturgical life. No responsible proponent of the prayer book's approach of baptism-before-communion imagines checking baptismal certificates or communion tokens at the communion rail. Mainstream pastoral practice has (with rare exceptions) dictated that one gives communion to anyone who presents herself at the altar expecting to receive it: only later does one follow up with those one knows to be unbaptized, to explain the church's traditional pattern and to invite the person to consider baptism. At the parish level, the question of baptism-before-communion or communion-without-baptism is generally played out in the

---

15. James Farwell, "Baptism, Eucharist, and the Hospitality of Jesus: On the Practice of 'Open Communion,'" *Anglican Theological Review* 86 (2004): 229–31.
16. Ibid., 215–38; Kathryn Tanner, "In Praise of Open Communion: A Rejoinder to James Farwell," *Anglican Theological Review* 86 (2004): 473–85; James Farwell, "A Brief Reflection on Kathryn Tanner's Response to 'Baptism, Eucharist, and the Hospitality of Jesus,'" *Anglican Theological Review* 87 (2005): 303–10. For another helpful analysis, see Thomas E. Breidenthal, "Following Jesus Outside: Reflections on the Open Table," *Anglican Theological Review* 94 (2012): 257–62.

announcements, spoken or printed, inviting persons to communion: does one invite "all baptized Christians," or simply, "all"? It is not clear how many parishes no longer expect baptism to precede communion. In part, this is likely because of the canonical prohibition on communion without baptism—not all parishes publicize their canonical violations, though some do.[17]

Finally, the retention of confirmation has resulted in confusion in the church over that rite's purpose and function. While the prayer book is clear that baptism is "full initiation" and that confirmation is "expected" but not required, the church has, in its canons, come to require confirmation before one is eligible for certain types of offices and roles. When resolutions to bring the canons into conformity with the prayer book came to General Convention in 2006 and 2012, these were rejected.[18]

One might reasonably argue, then, that the church is still in the process of living into the baptismal theology and liturgy of the 1979 prayer book. It has embraced the baptismal covenant with its emphasis on discipleship, and the concept of a baptismal ecclesiology with its empowerment of the laity. At the same time, it has struggled to adopt the liturgical norm of adult baptism, and it has resisted the implications of the precept that baptism is "full initiation."

## Possible Points of Revision

Should the General Convention authorize it to pursue a revision of the prayer book, the Standing Commission on Liturgy and Music will find suggestions already at hand. Proposals for adjustments to

---

17. Canon III.17.7 (*Constitution and Canons 2015*, 58).
18. Resolutions A042 and A044, *Journal of the 77th General Convention of the . . . the Episcopal Church 2012* (New York: General Convention Office, 2012), 689–90, 1034.

the baptismal rite fall into three broad groupings: those that would alter the existing structure of the rite, those that would rewrite the liturgy for theological reasons, and those that would add bits to the existing liturgy for political reasons.

Several scholars have suggested alterations to the structure of the present rite. Some have cited the baptismal covenant itself as posing difficulties, at least in its current location. Placed before the administration of the water, it appears to make the promises the contractual condition for baptism, rather than our human response to divine grace. Bryan Spinks at Yale Divinity School notes that this reverses the structure of Cranmer's baptismal rite, in which the administration of water was followed by instructions to the godparents on their duties, a sequence of "grace received followed by a response."[19] By contrast, he has labeled the covenant itself as "the self-conscious semi-Pelagian baptismal covenant."[20] To remedy this, the Church of England splits the Apostles' Creed from the behavioral promises (printed under the heading "Commission"), locating the former prior to and the latter after the administration of water.[21] One therefore professes faith, is baptized, and only then makes promises about behavior. While this does make clear that one is baptized without reference to one's conduct, dividing the creed from the behavioral promises is a rejection of the link

---

19. Bryan Spinks, *Reformation and Modern Rituals and Theologies of Baptism: From Luther to Contemporary Practices* (Aldershot: Ashgate Publishing, 2006), 175.
20. Pelagius was a fourth- and early fifth-century British monk who engaged in a literary debate with Augustine of Hippo about the degree to which humans were able to attain perfection. The term "pelagian" is used in theological debate to refer to those who emphasize human freewill over divine grace. See Bryan D. Spinks, "Cranmer, Baptism, and Christian Nurture; or, Toronto Revisited" *Studia Liturgica* 32 (2002): 109.
21. *Common Worship: Christian Initiation* (London: Church House Publishing, 2006), 69–73.

between faith and action that the framers of the 1979 prayer book were trying to promote. One might reasonably interpret the behavioral promises not as a precondition but as a sort of "informed consent": this is what Christian life entails, and it is the life into which one is about to be baptized—the covenant becomes an acceptance of what baptism means. Further, the scrutiny of candidates' behavior and belief was a hallmark of the early catechumenate; the baptismal covenant's focus on a candidate's manner of life was not entirely a twentieth-century innovation, for all the scrutiny and training in discipleship formerly happened prior to the liturgy itself. Finally, as Spinks notes, the current worship books of the Anglican churches in Australia, the West Indies, Kenya, and Ireland also follow the American pattern.[22] Moving the behavioral promises of the baptismal covenant to follow the administration of the water creates its own difficulties.

Some have also asserted that it would be desirable for the administration of water to happen in closer proximity to the profession of faith, as one finds in some early church liturgies. The candidate, in these examples, was asked, "Do you believe in God the Father?" and upon responding, "I believe," she was dunked; likewise, she was dunked upon affirming belief in the Son and the Holy Spirit.[23] One could, presumably, revive this pattern of an interrogative affirmation of faith, punctuated by the threefold administration of water. A different option, proposed by Bishop Neil Alexander, dean of the University of the South's School of Theology, would locate the covenant after the thanksgiving over the water and before the administration of the water, the pattern followed in the Canadian *Book of Alternative Services*, which places the affirmation of faith and behavioral promises in closer proximity to the water bath and may

---

22. Spinks, *Reformation and Modern Rituals*, 182.
23. Johnson, *Rites of Christian Initiation*, 88, 99.

partially address the concern raised by Spinks.[24] Neither structural adjustment, however, would locate the covenant entirely as a response to grace received, as *Common Worship* has done.

Some have suggested alterations to the language and imagery of the rite to respect the scruples of participants. Bryan Spinks has described some ecumenical efforts at devising a feminist rite, including some that substitute "Creator, Sustainer, and Redeemer" in place of the traditional Trinitarian formula drawn from Matthew. Spinks notes, however, that the principal goal of these rites has been avoiding "patriarchal" terminology, rather than mining the "rich womb/rebirth imagery of the Eastern rites" or other sources.[25] Within the Episcopal Church, a few congregations and clergy have taken upon themselves to rewrite portions of the liturgy. In 2009, a parish in Manhattan rewrote the presentation and examination of candidates and the prayer for the candidates to accommodate the scruples of non-Christian godparents.[26] (The prayer book itself presumes that the sponsors of a candidate will be themselves

---

24. J. Neil Alexander, "Christian Initiation: Ritual Patterns and the Future Shape of Revision," in *A Prayer Book for the 21st Century*, ed. Ruth A. Meyers (New York: Church Hymnal Corp., 1996), 23–28; *Book of Alternative Services of the Anglican Church of Canada* (Toronto: Anglican Book Centre, 1985), 156–60. Marion Hatchett endorsed this approach in "Unfinished Business in Prayer Book Revision," in Marshall and Northup, *Leaps and Boundaries*, 18. The Roman Catholic *Rite of Christian Initiation of Adults*, the Church of Ireland's 2004 prayer book, and the Evangelical Lutheran Church in America's 2006 worship book similarly locate their professions of faith after the Thanksgiving and before the bath, though there are no behavioral promises in those liturgies, thus sidestepping the "semi-Pelagian" character that Spinks notes. *Rite of Christian Initiation of Adults*, study ed. (Collegeville, MN: Liturgical Press, 1988), 130–43; *Book of Common Prayer* (Dublin: Columba Press, 2004), 362–65; *Evangelical Lutheran Worship*, leader's desk ed. (Minneapolis: Augsburg Fortress, 2006), 585–90.
25. Spinks, *Reformation and Modern Rituals*, 201–2.
26. "An Interfaith Baptism," https://www.facebook.com/note.php?note_id =253009651390&id=661228634 (accessed April 15, 2017).

Christian, and so one might argue that the pastoral situation that sparked the revision was the result of a misunderstanding of what godparents are intended by the book to be: mentors in the Christian faith and life, not family friends on whom the parents wish to confer peculiar honors). The Rev. Dr. Kevin Thew Forester, rector of a parish in Northern Michigan, rewrote the baptismal rite's presentation and examination of candidates, as well as the baptismal covenant, prayers for the candidates, thanksgiving over the water, and prayer for the gifts of the Holy Spirit that precedes the consignation. The revised rite avoids gendered language for the Trinity, but it also recasts the renunciations of Satan and the spiritual forces of wickedness, of the evil powers of this world, and of sinful desires that draw us from the love of God, instead offering promises to "let go" of self-deceit, fear, and anger.[27] Instead of the assertion, "I believe," the revised baptismal covenant has the candidate "place the trust of my heart" in God. In place of the petition, "Deliver *them*, O Lord, from the way of sin and death," the revised prayers for the candidates ask God to deliver the candidates from "anger, fear, and deceit." The conclusion of the revised Thanksgiving over the Water replaces the petition, "that those who here are cleansed from sin and born again may continue for ever in the risen life of Jesus Christ our Savior" to read "those who here are received into this household may continue for ever . . . ," suggesting a desire to avoid implying baptismal

---

27. See Bryan Owen, "'Buddhist' Bishop-Elect Revises Liturgy for Baptism" (April 24, 2009) http://creedalchristian.blogspot.com/2009/04/buddhist-bishop-elect-revises-liturgy.html (accessed June 19, 2018). See also the baptismal liturgy in Kevin Thew Forrester, *"My Heart Is a Raging Volcano of Love for You": Awakening to At-One-Ment Volume II: Liturgical Explorations Collects, Blessings, Litanies, Prayers & Eucharistic Prayers* (Leeds, MA: Leader Resources, 2011), 116–22. See also Frank Lockwood, "Believing Outside the Box?" *Arkansas Democrat-Gazette*, May 2, 2009, http://www.arkansasonline.com/news/2009/may/02/believing-outside-20090502/ (accessed April 17, 2017).

regeneration. Finally, in a revised prayer for the gifts of the Holy Spirit, rather than praying that God *grant* the neophyte "an inquiring and discerning heart" and "the courage to will and to persevere," the presider asks that the neophyte might *know* God as that selfsame heart and courage. Evil is displaced from this revision, as are disordered desires, and (to an outside reader) baptism is rendered as enlightenment, not cleansing from sin and rebirth. The revision of the baptismal rite was cited by several bishops who withheld consent to Thew Forrester's election as bishop of Northern Michigan.[28]

Rather than theological scruples, poor or incomplete catechesis of parents and sponsors prompted the development of the latest alternative texts in the Church of England. In response to a request from the Diocese of Liverpool to render the texts of the baptismal rite less opaque to those who are largely unformed as Christians, the General Synod authorized a 2015 addendum to *Common Worship*, "Christian Initiation: Additional Texts for Holy Baptism in Accessible Language." These texts use concrete language, eschew biblical imagery (such as "dying to sin and rising to new life" and

---

28. For some examples, see http://anglicancentrist5.blogspot.com/2009/04/tom-breidenthals-awesome-letter-and.html, http://anglicancentrist5.blogspot.com/2009/04/bishop-of-tennessee-explains-no-vote-on.html, http://anglicancentrist5.blogspot.com/2009/04/bishop-paul-v-marshall.html (accessed April 15, 2017). The same parish has offered a revised Eucharistic Prayer that did not conform even to the rather loose requirements of the "Order for Eucharist" in the prayer book, adapted instead from worship resources from Iona (St. Paul's Church, "Season of Advent," http://s3.amazonaws.com/dfc_attachments/public/documents/3154131/Advent_booklet_Year_B_111511.pdf [accessed April 17, 2017]; St. Paul's Church, "Season of Advent," http://s3.amazonaws.com/dfc_attachments/public/documents/3151013/Advent_booklet_Year_A_102010.pdf [accessed April 17, 2017]). The rector has published several Eucharistic prayers that similarly do not fit the "forms" to be used in the prayer book order, in some cases lacking an *epiclesis* and an oblation. Forrester, *"My Heart Is a Raging Volcano of Love for You,"* 129–33.

the deliverance of Israel from slavery in Egypt), avoid reference to the devil, and omit the Apostles' Creed. Finally, the alternative text eliminates the behavioral promises that had been part of the post-bath response by the neophyte in Common Worship.[29] The resulting liturgy is quite simplified, perhaps to the point of being "dumbed down," as its critics have asserted.[30] Pastoral necessity can be a compelling argument, but it is not clear to all whether it is better to jettison the old language and imagery (in all of its richness and complexity) in favor of a simplified, even impoverished text, or to engage in the sort of catechesis required to make the old terms comprehensible to new Christians.

Finally, some have suggested minor alterations to the existing baptismal liturgy to reflect particular concerns of groups within the church. In 2015, the General Convention referred to the Standing Commission on Liturgy and Music a resolution (C015), introduced by the Diocese of Connecticut, calling for a sixth question to be added to the covenant asking, "Will you cherish the wondrous works of God, and protect the beauty and integrity of all creation?" with the expected response, "I will, with God's help."[31] Six years earlier, a resolution (D005) that proposed an "alternative baptismal covenant" for trial use, including a sixth question addressing

---

29. *Christian Initiation: Additional Texts for Holy Baptism in Accessible Language*, https://www.churchofengland.org/prayer-and-worship/worship-texts-and-resources/common-worship/christian-initiation/christian; https://www.churchofengland.org/prayer-and-worship/worship-texts-and-resources/common-worship/guidance-on-using-the-alternative-baptism-texts. (accessed June 12, 2018).
30. Michael Nazir-Ali, "Why the CofE Must Abandon This Dumbed-Down Christening," http://michaelnazirali.com/articles/app/archive/01-2014/title/why-the-cofe-must-abandon-this-dumbed-down-christening (accessed April 17, 2017).
31. *Journal of the General Convention of . . . the Episcopal Church, Salt Lake City, 2015* (New York: General Convention, 2015), 841.

stewardship of creation, had been defeated outright.[32] The next revision of the prayer book, whenever it happens, will no doubt see efforts to include these and other concerns in any rewritten covenant.

Turning to ways that revision might encourage a more complete embrace of the ethos of the present book, confirmation and its cognates could be targeted for revision. *Prayer Book Studies 18* had proposed a single initiatory rite, of water bath/handlaying (with optional anointing)/first communion, reconstructing the early church's baptismal rite and reuniting the bits that had broken off as "confirmation" in the Middle Ages. The next draft liturgy, in *Prayer Book Studies 26*, had offered a repeatable rite in reaffirmation of baptismal vows, while keeping the unified baptismal rite. The eventual text in the prayer book offered a "confirmation" rite, with optional formulae for reception and reaffirmation, while retaining the unified baptismal rite and a rubric specifying that baptism is "full initiation," without the necessity of subsequent confirmation. While retaining the term "confirmation," with all the accompanying confusion from its historical origins, the 1979 Book of Common Prayer took into account the pastoral utility of a form for the public renewal of baptismal promises. Nevertheless, confusion has persisted in parts of the church about the relationship between confirmation and baptism. Ruth Meyers offered a solution in her study of the 1979 baptismal rite: stop using the formulae for confirmation and reception, and use only the (repeatable) reaffirmation formula in the prayer book's confirmation rite. That, together with dropping the terminology of "confirmation," would clarify what the church and candidate are doing in the liturgy.[33] This amounts to a return

---

32. *Journal of the General Convention of . . . the Episcopal Church, Anaheim, 2009* (New York: General Convention, 2009), 333–34.
33. Meyers, *Continuing the Reformation*, 247–48; see also Joe Goodwin Burnett, "Reconsidering a Bold Proposal: Reflections, Questions, and

to *Prayer Book Studies 26* and would provide for the pastoral need to ritualize a deepening or change in one's spiritual life, while at the same time avoiding confusion about the status of baptism as "full initiation." While this approach has a great deal to commend, it may prove politically impossible: when legislation to bring the canons into conformity failed at General Convention in 2012, it was because the modest changes involved were perceived by some as too threatening to what had been an emotionally significant ritual in their subjective experience. It is difficult to see a fruitful path toward revision of the confirmation rite itself, given that a mere adjustment to the canons was perceived as highly charged.

To encourage efforts to draw in and form adult converts, one might wish for the inclusion of the catechumenate in the prayer book itself, instead of in the *Book of Occasional Services*. This would mirror the place of the *Rite of Christian Initiation of Adults* (RCIA) in the Roman Catholic Church's liturgical texts. Yet RCIA itself has been only incompletely appropriated in its own church: its paradigm exists uneasily alongside the traditional initiatory model of the *Rite of Christian Initiation of Children*, and the use of RCIA has varied.[34] Both the Episcopal Church and the Roman Catholic

---

Concerns Regarding a Theology of Confirmation," *Anglican Theological Review* 88 (2006): 70–83; Ruth A. Meyers, "Fresh Thoughts on Confirmation," *Anglican Theological Review* 88 (2006): 321–40; Meyers, "Re-Imagining Confirmation," in *Signed, Sealed, Delivered: Theologies of Confirmation for the 21st Century*, ed. Sharon Ely Pearson (New York: Morehouse Publishing, 2014), 33–52. Burnett argues that the church should return to Meyers's proposal in *Continuing the Reformation*, while Meyers appears in her later work to argue for a repurposing of confirmation and reception alongside the rite of reaffirmation, as pastorally useful if theological clarity could be gained about its role relative to baptism.

34. Kavanagh, *Shape of Baptism*, 196–97; Paul F. X. Corvino, "The Postconciliar Infant Baptism Debate in the American Catholic Church," in Johnson, *Living Water, Sealing Spirit*, 333–35, 345–48; see also Aidan

Church looked back to pre-Constantinian models of Christian initiation, and therefore the catechumenate, because of a belief that the post-Constantinian circumstances of the church would parallel that period of the early church, with the rise of the "nones," who lack a religious identity; a corresponding separation of the church from the values of the former "cultural Christianity" of the postwar era; and finally an evangelization of adults as the church responded to its new circumstances. While the prevailing culture no longer promotes the Christian message and fewer adults claim any religious affiliation, the church has not been able to respond by sharing the good news on a wide and effect scale, as the meager results of the "Decade of Evangelism" and the "2020" efforts to increase church attendance suggest. Because the church's evangelistic efforts have not drawn in significant numbers, there is not a large supply of catechumens. As twentieth-century Roman Catholic liturgical scholar Aidan Kavanagh noted once, absent a successful and steady process of evangelization, the catechumenate will founder, with true catechesis replaced by mere "religious education."[35] Further, because the catechumenate was intentionally left to local leaders to adapt, without an off-the-shelf curriculum, and because it imagines at least several months of preparation before baptism, it requires a significant investment of time and energy by the clergy and laity in a parish. This suggests that it may be difficult to persuade the church to include the catechumenate in its prayer book, or if included, to put it into actual use. The church needs to reengage with the catechumenate, quite apart from the question of where its liturgical texts may be published.

---

Kavanagh, "Unfinished and Unbegun Revisited: The Rite of Christian Initiation of Adults," in Johnson, *Living Water, Sealing Spirit*, 259–73.
35. Kavanagh, "Catechesis: Formation in Stages," 37.

## Next Steps

It is significant that the baptismal rite in the prayer book has been largely immune to officially endorsed experimentation thus far (the activities of a few rogue parishes notwithstanding). The prayer book itself contains several *ordo* liturgies, directory-style outlines that provide a sketch of what a liturgy must include, with some boilerplate language required, but with great flexibility for local creativity. We see this, for example, in the Order for Eucharist, which provides the barest of outlines for the liturgy of the word and a "fill-in-the-blank" Eucharistic Prayer template, and in the Order for Marriage, which stipulates a common set of vows but otherwise supplies only an outline for the liturgy. Baptism, by contrast, has no *ordo* form in the prayer book. Similarly, trial use texts under the aegis of *Enriching Our Worship* have been produced for the Daily Office, the Eucharist, and most pastoral rites, but not for baptism. There seems to be a natural conservatism at work, because baptism is the sacrament from which the rest of our common life flows.

There is no clear groundswell of opinion demanding structural change to the baptismal rite, and one does not hear widespread complaint about its language and imagery. The few, unofficial revisions that wish to press beyond the 1979 text have gained limited support. Meanwhile, the appropriation of the 1979 prayer book's revolutionary baptismal theology has been partial at most. It may well be that the best approach to the baptismal rite is to do nothing to change it, but rather to encourage the clergy and laity to live into its theology more deeply.

# 6

# A Reflection on the Eucharistic Prayer in Light of the Possible Revision of the 1979 Book of Common Prayer

## JAMES W. FARWELL[1]

As we consider the possible revision of the Book of Common Prayer—a revision that *will* come, as it always has, sooner or later—there are a number of matters the church might consider with regard to the Eucharistic rites. Among them, we might consider altering the entrance rite so that the service could begin at the font with a remembrance of our baptism. Changes might be made to the instruction for Prayers of the People, that crucial intercessory response to hearing the gospel proclaimed, to encourage more winsome and heartfelt prayers for the needs of a world in travail. Better accommodation might be made there

---

1. The Rev. James W. Farwell, PhD, is Professor of Theology and Liturgy at Virginia Theological Seminary. This essay is an adaptation of the author's Inaugural Address to the seminary delivered in November 2015.

and elsewhere in the rite for the expression of genuine lamentation. We might consider a greater variety of Eucharistic prayers, drawing on the wide range of biblical imagery as yet untouched in liturgical language, crafting all of them on the West Syrian shape with which we are now familiar, but learning from the sheer elegance and rhetorical power of some of the prayers in the Lutheran and Presbyterian traditions, or in the books of our Anglican partners.[2] We might bring the rubrics of the prayer (requiring the presider to make something out of the words of institution with certain manual acts) into line with the guidelines of the International Anglican Liturgical Consultation[3] and with scholarly research about the shape of the prayer,[4] letting go of the Western idea that the prayer is basically a container for the priest to play-act the "last supper," rather than a post-resurrection meal in which the Spirit's power is invoked on the assembly and the gifts, making us witnesses of the mission of God through the crucified-risen One.

---

2. The West Syrian prayers associated with the churches in the regions from Antioch to Jerusalem were one among several early families of liturgies. They were known, among other things, for their Trinitarian structure (an opening section on creation addressed to the Father, a recitation of Christ's work of salvation, and petitions to the Holy Spirit) and for an invocation of the Holy Spirit (the epiclesis) over both the people and the bread and wine. Most of the Eucharistic Prayers in the Book of Common Prayer (1979) have a West Syrian structure. For more on West Syrian rites, see Frank C. Senn, *Christian Liturgy: Catholic and Evangelical* (Minneapolis: Fortress Press, 1997), 119–33.

3. David Holeton, ed., *Renewing the Anglican Eucharist: Findings of the Fifth International Anglican Liturgical Consultation* (Dublin: Grove Worship Series #135, 1995).

4. Thomas Talley, "The Structure of the Eucharistic Prayer," in Meyers, *A Prayer Book for the 21st Century*, 76–101.

## Saving the Incarnation

There are more issues that could be named, but the one I wish to single out here is the *significance of the Incarnation to our Eucharistic praying*. Specifically, it seems to me that it is time for us to write and to pray with Eucharistic prayers that make *more explicit reference to the life and ministry of Jesus of Nazareth* than our Anglican tradition has tended to do. I believe this is important because we need to "save the Incarnation" from our more-than-occasional tendency to submerge it into the atonement, to fixate on the cross to the degree that we detach it from Jesus' life-actions, experience, and practice. Particularly narrow construals of Anselm's forensic soteriology connected with a preoccupation with *post-mortem* destiny, represent the sort of fixated attachment to the significance of Jesus' death that I have in mind.[5] In the face of such narrow construals, I believe we must hold our attention on Jesus' life and death as a *whole reality*, as crucial to understanding just what it is that the resurrection seals, a resurrection into whose hope we are baptized. If religious ritual, as Michael Raposa notes, is "very much about how human beings pay attention," I am concerned for the way liturgy at every level draws our attention to Jesus, not only around the Word, but at the Table.[6]

What I propose to do in the following pages is to thicken this suggestion and illustrate what I mean, first by locating myself in a particular strand of Anglican theology; then by a selective walk

---

5. Anselm (1033–1109) was an eleventh–century theologian, monastery prior, and archbishop of Canterbury. His *Cur Deus Homo* (Why did God become human?) is a classic statement of penal substitutionary satisfaction for sin—the notion that by his undeserved death, Jesus Christ paid the penalty that we duly deserve for our sins.
6. Michael L. Raposa, "Ritual Inquiry: The Pragmatic Logic of Religious Practice," in *Thinking Through Rituals*, ed. Kevin Schibrack (New York: Routledge, 2004), 115.

through some historical and contemporary Eucharistic prayers; and finally with a few thoughts about additional benefits of this recommendation. I am hoping that regardless of whether the reader shares my particular brand of Anglican soteriology that he or she will consider the merits of attention to Jesus' life not simply in our reading and preaching, but also in our Eucharistic praying.

My perspective on the question of what is to be included in Eucharistic prayers is informed by my own long practice with the prayers; by my own study of the history and theology of the form; by my sense of what is distinctive in Anglican soteriology ("soteriology" is the understanding of the world's problem and its remedy by God in Christ, from the Greek *soter*, having to do with wholeness, healing, "salvation"); and perhaps even from my comparative work, including my interest in what Christian sacramental theology can learn from nondualist philosophies like those found in Advaita Vedanta and the Taoist-Buddhist tradition we know as "Zen." With regard to the latter, I find myself increasingly allergic to the preoccupation of Western logic with *binaries*, "either-or" distinctions that end up creating more problems than they solve. Is it the life or the death of Jesus that is crucial to our salvation? Would God's Word have become incarnate even if we had not sinned, or only because we did? How can Christ be "in" the sacrament and in all places as the Word through whom all was made? How can Jesus be both human and divine? Is salvation about the moral life, or is it about a gift of grace that morality cannot attain? These binaries with which Christian theology has been preoccupied, and many others like them, constitute a very long list. But theological thinking is the mind's act of prayer, and the object of that prayer is a Mystery; and that kind of thinking must be "both-and" rather than "either-or." The saved life, the life that flourishes is both a gift that cannot possibly be attained *and* the shape of a life that the giving makes possible. As both only make sense in the light of the other, the Eucharistic Prayer should attend to both.

The life of Jesus matters to our salvation. At least the Gospels think so, spending a substantial amount of time on Jesus' teaching and on the activities in which Jesus participated and which he initiated. It was Martin Kähler (1835–1912) who observed that each of the Gospels is a "passion narrative with an extended introduction."[7] I certainly have sympathy for the centrality of the passion in the Gospels, and I see the significance of the passion and death of Jesus to an understanding of salvation and its relationship to human suffering.[8] However, the meaning of his death cannot be understood outside of its connection to the whole of Jesus' life: his teaching, eating, healing, touching, being touched, preaching, praying, being baptized, being in conversation or arguing with religious leaders over the texts and ideas of the tradition in which he was embedded, and being in conversation with those considered outsiders by the temple leadership. His death on a cross doesn't make much sense on its own. I contend that the whole of the Gospels matters, because it is the whole of the life of Jesus, including but not limited to the cross, that matters to our salvation.

I am locating myself here in a long conversation among Christians about the relationship between Incarnation and Atonement. It is a complicated conversation because there is no neutral Christian term for the problem of existence and its remedy. Salvation, atonement, healing, redemption, illumination, and so forth are all already terms tilted in a certain direction, pushing one sense of the human problem forward over another, which recedes into the background. Although we have been preoccupied since the Middle Ages with a model of forensic justification for sin, there are

---

7. Marting Kähler, *The So-Called Historical Jesus and the Historic, Biblical Christ* (Philadelphia, Fortress Press, 1964), 80n11.
8. For an account of this relationship in connection with the liturgies of Holy Week, see James W. Farwell, *This Is The Night: Suffering, Salvation, and the Liturgies of Holy Week* (New York: T&T Clark, 2005).

many models not only of what we mean that God in Christ sets us right, but even if you put sin dead center in your soteriology, there are different models of that as well. The meaning of "salvation" is not a foregone conclusion but is funded by the many different metaphors and models in the Bible, from healing, to protection, consolation, illumination, liberation, and the conquest of death; and even the experience of deep recognition, of being truly seen and known, like the woman at the well in the fourth chapter of John's Gospel. Furthermore, immediate *experience* of the problem of existence is complex, and one has not brought the conversation about this to a conclusion simply by naming "sin"; consider, as just one example, the experience of *han*, that systemic suppression of the spirit that comes from being at the wrong end of racism and injustice, as the *minjung* Korean theologians have taught us. We deal not only with the effects of our sin or that of others, but with the way life that is difficult for no other reason than that, as Wendy Farley has explained so persuasively, the world is beautiful but also a tragically structured finitude.[9]

Neither Anselmian nor even Liberationist theologies are adequate to the full range of our predicament unless they make robust connection with the life, activities, and even in some sense the personality of the living Jesus of Nazareth. The cross is not a stand-alone transaction to which the life of Jesus was a preface, but rather a crescendo of a whole pattern of life marked by mutuality, compassion, deep insight into the heart, an understanding of the true purpose of the law, and generous self-offering, enfleshing a reign of God that is always larger or smaller or different than what we think it is. It is free; and it costs nothing less than everything we are. The cross of Jesus, planted in the middle of that life of the Incarnate Word, was a consummating symbol, a sacrament, if you like, of a

---

9. Wendy Farley, *Tragic Vision and Divine Compassion: A Contemporary Theodicy* (Louisville: Westminster/John Knox Press, 1990), 29.

*saving pattern of life* in which we see the consciousness of God and the courage, compassion, and forgiveness necessary to flourish in the context in which we find ourselves. I submit that living into that life, by the grace and wooing power of the God whose first word and last word are Love—entering into a discipleship of *metanoia* as we are drawn into that Life—is what we find *saving*.[10]

I did not invent this soteriological orientation. Its notes are sung in various forms and degrees of emphasis from Paul, Irenaeus (d. 202), and Athanasius (d. 373), through Abelard (d. 1142) and Duns Scotus (d. 1308), to Schleiermacher (d. 1834) and Rahner (d. 1984) and more, some of whom were convinced that the Incarnation of the Word of God would have happened regardless of whether human beings ever sinned. Most notably for me, a reverence for the Incarnation—perhaps for the Incarnation *as* Atonement—is in that strand of Anglican theology that we most often associate with the essays of *Lux Mundi* and its theological inheritors.[11] It is consistent with the Anglican Exemplarist tradition—a tradition in which the sacraments around which our worship is structured are not simply the reception of a grace coming from the cross but a *consent to our own participation, animated by the Spirit's action, in the divine life of God as it is revealed in the crucified and risen One*. I am suggesting that if we want to know what that *saved life* looks like, we will need to preserve and animate our memory of the person Jesus, and not just the memory of his death.

---

10. *Metanoia* [μετάνοια] is the Greek word for repentance, turning about, change of mind, and conversion. It has been preferred by many theologians in the past century as conveying a more active sense of change in direction of life than the English *repentance*, which is often understood simply as a mental process.

11. *Lux Mundi* (Latin, Light of the World) was the title of a set of English essays edited by Charles Gore and published in 1887. The essays embraced some elements of the emerging field of critical biblical scholarship.

## Eucharistic Praying

It is worth considering my proposal that we deepen our reference to the Incarnation in Eucharistic praying in light of some representative models of Eucharistic praying from the past. In the 1928 prayer book, when Morning Prayer was the norm on Sundays, the details of the life and ministry of Jesus were the focus of the Office readings, with the communion rite turning to his atoning death to complete the arc of his ministry. But the 1979 prayer book returns to an older tradition of a long and comprehensive Eucharistic Prayer that, in addition to whatever details of the life and ministry of Jesus are revealed in the lectionary for the liturgy of the Word, exhibits a scope that reaches from creation to the consummation of time. From the standpoint of structural and rhetorical analysis, as well as its liturgical theology, the Eucharistic Prayer is a summative moment in the liturgy. It typically offers a broad thanksgiving for what God has done for us—the content of which varies somewhat with the prayer and with the content of "proper prefaces" in the case of prayers that require them—and then invokes the Spirit's blessing on the life and work of the assembly, animated by the remembrance of Jesus. To what degree does this Eucharistic Prayer involve a focus on Incarnation as well as Atonement? Put differently, to what degree do Eucharistic prayers attend to the details of Jesus' life as much as to they do to his death?

In a 2016 essay in the journal *Liturgy*, I offered a somewhat more differentiated typology than I offer here of how this has occurred in Eucharistic prayers up to this point.[12] But for our purposes in this essay, let us say there are generally three categories into which these prayers fall. There are: (1) prayers in which the Lord's Incarnation is referenced as a fact, with no detail of what the Incarnate Lord did;

---

12. James Farwell, "Salvation, the Life of Jesus, and the Eucharistic Prayer: An Anglican Reflection and Proposal," *Liturgy* 31, no. 3 (2016): 19–27.

and (2) prayers in which, whatever the soteriological language of the prayer, there are direct references to Jesus' ministry, often as allusions to his characteristic behaviors. (3) There is a third category—Eucharistic prayers that make no reference to the Incarnation at all, either in fact or in the detail of Jesus' life, restricting their concern to Jesus' death. But as we will see, those involve a narrowing moment in Christian liturgical and theological history, concerned with a particular problem, which opens out again as we move into the modern period.

Looking to classical prayers, the first category is exemplified by the Eucharistic prayers known as the *Apostolic Tradition* and *Addai and Mari*.[13] Liturgical scholars now place the *Apostolic Tradition* as a layered product of roughly the third through sixth centuries.[14] A Eucharistic Prayer in the document contains a factual reference to the Incarnation but offers no details of the life and ministry of Jesus: "You sent him from heaven into the Virgin's womb, and . . . he was made flesh and was manifested as your Son. . . ."[15]

*Addai and Mari*, a rather early East Syrian prayer from perhaps the third century—interesting because of its apparent lack of the "words of institution" that typify Western prayers—contains a range of soteriological outcomes that are connected to a reference to the fact of the Incarnation. There is, however, no allusion to the details of Jesus' life and ministry: "For you put on our human nature to give us life through your divine nature; you raised us from our lowly state; you restored our Fall; you restored our immortality; you

---

13. The names of Eucharistic prayers are generally either given them directly or are drawn from larger documents in which they appear.
14. See chapter 10 of this volume for Bryan Spinks's discussion of the authorship and history of the text known as *Apostolic Tradition*.
15. Maxwell E. Johnson, ed., *Sacraments and Worship: The Sources of Christian Theology* (Louisville: Westminster-John Knox, 2012), 194.

forgave our debts; you justified our sinfulness; you enlightened our intelligence . . . conquered our enemies. . . ."[16]

The second category has a variety of interesting prayers in it, including the *Apostolic Constitutions*, the *Egyptian Anaphora of St. Basil*, and the *Alexandrian Prayer of St. Mark*. In the last of these, a text whose final form dates from roughly the fifteenth century but for which some early fragments exist, we see an interesting case in which the Intercessions within the prayer are constructed with an obvious allusion to the healing activities of Jesus, though without naming him specifically. The *Egyptian Anaphora of St. Basil*—the fourth-century foundation of the ecumenical modern prayer on which our Prayer D is based—goes beyond a simple reference to the Incarnation, albeit modestly and more thematically than descriptively: "He was made flesh of the Holy Spirit and of the holy Virgin Mary, and became man; he showed us the ways of salvation, granted us to be reborn from above. . . . He loved his own who were in the world, and gave himself for our salvation. . . ."[17] The *Apostolic Constitutions*, probably from the fourth century or a bit later, exemplifies this category: "He lived a holy life and taught according to the law; he drove away every disease and every sickness from men; he did signs and wonders among the people; he who feeds those who need food and fills all things living with plenteousness partook of food and drink and sleep; he made known your name to those who did not know it; he put ignorance to flight; he re-kindled piety; he fulfilled your will; he accomplished the work which you gave him."[18]

The third category of Eucharistic prayers generally developed when people became preoccupied with the interpretation of sacrifice or the relationship between the Eucharist and the all-sufficiency of

---

16. Johnson, *Sacraments and Worship*, 197.
17. Ibid., 206.
18. R. C. D Jasper and G. J. Cuming, *Prayers of the Eucharist: Early and Reformed* (New York: Pueblo, 1987), 109.

Christ's death. Historically, such prayers took some time to develop. These prayers were typical of the Protestant Reformation. The Eucharistic Prayer that Thomas Cranmer edited for the 1549 Book of Common Prayer, for example, makes no reference to Incarnation, much less any allusion to Jesus' life. This of course, with some incremental changes along the way, is the prayer we know all the way through to Rite I, Eucharistic Prayer I of the 1979 prayer book.

Many of the oldest and the newest Eucharistic prayers fall in category 1. They make reference to the fact of the Incarnation and move to the remembrance of this supper and his death. Among newer prayers, Rite II Prayer A in the 1979 Book of Common Prayer is an example. Prayer B, in contrast, is an interesting example of one that expands the range of soteriological tropes—we are in Christ made worthy, brought from error into truth; from sin into righteousness; from death into life—but it makes no reference to the specifics of Jesus' life.[19]

Prayer D is not ours only but is based on an international, ecumenical prayer built from the early Egyptian Basil and present in the Roman, Lutheran, Presbyterian, and other traditions. It falls in category 2 and makes the most specific reference to characteristic actions of Jesus in the 1979 Book of Common Prayer: Prayer D says of Jesus Christ, "Incarnate by your Holy Spirit, born of the Virgin Mary, he lived as one of us, yet without sin. To the poor he proclaimed the good news of salvation; to prisoners, freedom; to the sorrowful, joy. To fulfill your purpose he gave himself up to death...."[20]

Eucharistic Prayer 2 in *Enriching Our Worship 1* offers a similar and especially remarkable expansion of reference to the ministry of the human Jesus. The text reads:

---

19. Book of Common Prayer (1979), 361–63, 367–69.
20. Ibid., 374.

Living among us, Jesus loved us. He broke bread with outcasts and sinners, healed the sick, and proclaimed good news to the poor. He yearned to draw all the world to himself, yet we were heedless to walk in love. Then the time came for him to *complete upon the cross* the sacrifice of his life, and to be glorified by you.[21]

Here the cross is clearly positioned as the consummation of the whole life and ministry of Jesus. That is, in it the saving sacrifice of Jesus is presented as a pattern of life: breaking bread with outcasts and sinners, healing the sick, proclaiming good news to the poor, and dying for us.

There are some contemporary prayers beyond our own tradition that make robust reference to Jesus' life. I commend the Evangelical Lutheran Church of America, the Church of England, and the Presbyterian Church-USA for producing some of the most beautiful, elegant, and fulsome prayers in all their features. One particularly interesting example, written by Gail Ramshaw (ELCA) in response to a request from David Gambrell of the PCUSA's journal *Call to Worship*, and used in 2015 at the commemoration of St. Luke at the ELCA's Chicago headquarters, addresses all three persons of the Trinity. In the second clause in which the Son is addressed, the language is:

> Blessed are you, Jesus Christ, forgiving Savior, merciful Lord.
> We trust in your tender compassion.
> You are the good Samaritan, we the wounded traveler.
> You are the sweeping woman, we the lost coin.
> You ate with Mary, Martha, and Zacchaeus,

---

21. The Standing Liturgical Commission, *Enriching Our Worship 1: Supplemental Liturgical Materials Prepared by the Standing Liturgical Commission* (New York: Church Publishing, 1998), 61 (emphasis added).

and you filled Emmaus with your resurrection.
On the night before you died, you took bread....²²

The voicing of the prayer toward the persons of the Trinity has some precedent in the East Syrian tradition—the literary home of Addai and Mari—in which the presider addresses the second person of the Trinity. (The fully Trinitarian address is not unknown in Anglicanism either; see, for example, prayer 3 of the second communion rite of the Irish Book of Common Prayer 2004.)²³ The particular creativity of Ramshaw's prayer is in the deployment of the specific reference to some of Jesus' teaching in the form of metaphors, which, through direct address as prayer, fold us into the stories rather than simply alluding to them.

## Future Prayer Book Revisions

I hope that this brief review of the three identified categories of the Eucharistic prayer's patterns of Incarnational reference not only demonstrates the precedent for it in tradition but inspires the imaginations of those who might write Eucharistic prayers for the Episcopal Church in the future. To my earlier defense of why references to the life, teaching, and activity of Jesus in our Eucharistic remembrance are called for at Table as well as in Word, I add here a few final thoughts about the benefits of such a move in any future revisions of the Book of Common Prayer.

First, biblical studies of the last century have brought us renewed attention to the human Jesus. It is to such historical-critical work and analysis of the context of Jesus' ministry that we owe a renewed

---

22. Ramshaw made this version of the prayer available to the author. A slightly different version was published by Gail Ramshaw, "Eucharistic Prayer for Year C," *Call to Worship* 49, no. 1 (2015): 11.
23. Colin Buchanan, ed., *Anglican Eucharistic Liturgies 1985–2010* (London: Canterbury Press, 2011), 83.

understanding of the meaning of his teaching and his actions. Going deep into the exegesis of the Gospels can only deepen the language of prayer, engaging with the historical Jesus through scripture in that way, while treating Jesus as a trope or an abstraction in the language of our prayers is hard to justify. Of course, we attend to Jesus "in Word," but we also remember him "in Sacrament"; and if we are to remember him there, let us remember him well, for the shape of a human life lived in communion with God by which we measure our own.

Second, to pay attention to the specifics of Jesus' life is to be true to the Incarnational emphasis of the Anglican tradition rooted in theologians like Richard Hooker (1554–1600) and crystallized in *Lux Mundi* and beyond, and to take that emphasis even deeper.

Third, we have been moving ecumenically for some time toward models of liturgical celebration that link the elements of the Sunday liturgy more closely to lections for the day. The *Intercessions for the Christian People* was an example of this move with regard to Prayers of the People, and the ongoing work that Lutherans and Presbyterians do now to support the liturgical celebration, Sunday by Sunday, exemplify this as well.[24] There is no reason for us not to add to the repertoire of our Eucharistic prayers, built around a familiar shape like the West Syrian pattern, to do the same.

Finally, it is always of benefit to join to the necessity of ritual repetition a wise proportion of rhetorical variety to expand the spiritual and theological imagination of the assembly at prayer. There is no reason to worry that this will limit the dance across multiple narratives and symbols that is crucial to liturgical meaning making; there are plenty of other elements of the liturgy, fixed and otherwise, that will maintain that multivocal quality.

---

24. *Intercessions for the Christian People: Prayers of the People for Cycles A, B, and C of the Roman, Episcopal, and Lutheran Lectionaries*, ed. Gail Ramshaw (Collegeville, MN: Liturgical Press, 1990).

In conclusion, I suggest that we are at an inflection point in the Christian church when, remembering who we are again, our attention should return to what—or whom—we follow. It is to this renewed attention to Jesus that Michael Curry, our current presiding bishop, has been challenging us. And, as Herman-Emiel Mertens puts it, we follow "not the Cross, but the Crucified."[25] We are always, perhaps ever discovering this; and I believe that the writing and praying of Eucharistic prayers that draw our attention to the whole of Jesus' life, death, and resurrection, can only help us to remember again whose we are, and the nature of the mission in which we are called to participate by our manner of life.

---

25. Herman-Emiel Mertens, *Not the Cross, But the Crucified: An Essay in Soteriology* (Leuven, Belgium: Peeters, 1992).

# 7

# Calling Down the Holy Spirit

## A Consideration of the Implications of the Texts of the Epiclesis in the Episcopal Eucharistic Liturgies

### Amy C. Schifrin[1]

### The Work of the Spirit in a Divided World

O Holy Spirit, enter in,
And in our hearts your work begin,
And make our hearts your dwelling.
Sun of the soul, O Light divine,
Around and in us brightly shine,

---

1. The Rev. Dr. Amy C. Schifrin is the Associate Professor of Liturgy and Homiletics at Trinity School for Ministry. She is also Codirector of the MDiv program at Trinity and President of the North American Lutheran Seminary.

Your strength in us upwelling.
In your radiance
Life from heaven,
Now is given
Overflowing,
Gifts of gifts beyond all knowing.[2]

    Life in the Spirit is deeply hidden. It is impossibly hard for the world to see, because like a seed that falls into the ground, it is only known when it bears fruit. And given all the visible divisions, all the enmity between peoples within and without the church, from congregational squabbles to ecclesiastical sabotage, the world cannot see any unity, nor on its own is it capable of receiving a taste of the Spirit's good fruit.

    Rather than denying divisions of church life that existed even in the nascent church, the author(s) of the Johannine material in the New Testament recognized those divisions and understood the Holy Spirit as continually responding to them. The proclamation of the author(s) of the role of the Spirit was expressed in the bold clarity of a Trinitarian witness. The Son asks the Father, who sends the Spirit to serve as our Advocate and Guide. The Spirit, as the guarantor of the truth of the gospel, gives the power and grace needed to live through the most difficult of times, for it is the Holy Spirit who brings the unity that is essential for faithful witness to the reconciling and renewing work of Christ. All too often what we see and hear in both church and the everyday world lacks such a unifying bond, any sense of recognition of brotherhood and sisterhood, or simply of a common humanity created in God's image and likeness, let alone created to be vessels of God's

---

2. Michael Schirmer, "O Holy Spirit, Enter In," translated by Catherine Winkworth, from *Lutheran Book of Worship* (Minneapolis: Augsburg Publishing House, 1978), hymn 459, verse 1 (public domain).

love. In the Gospel According to St. John, we hear Jesus as he speaks to his disciples:

> "If you love me, you will keep my commandments. And I will ask the Father, and he will give you another Advocate, to be with you forever. This is the Spirit of truth, whom the world cannot receive, because it neither sees him nor knows him. You know him, because he abides with you, and he will be in you." (John 14:15–17)

Jesus explains further that the Spirit will validate his message: "When the Advocate comes, whom I will send to you from the Father, the Spirit of truth who comes from the Father, he will testify on my behalf" (John 15:26). The author of the First Letter of John picks up the same theme:

> This is the one who came by water and blood, Jesus Christ, not with the water only but with the water and the blood. And the Spirit is the one that testifies, for the Spirit is the truth. There are three that testify: the Spirit and the water and the blood, and these three agree. (1 John 5:6–8)

The witness we receive in the Johannine literature acknowledges the conflict between the spirit of truth and the spirit of error:

> They are from the world; therefore what they say is from the world, and the world listens to them. We are from God. Whoever knows God listens to us, and whoever is not from God does not listen to us. From this we know the spirit of truth and the spirit of error. (1 John 4:5–6)

This word about the Spirit is good news for this world, a world divided by conflict, violence, and mistrust, a world that is lost between "fake" news and bad news. The division, the necessary distinction between the spirit of truth and the spirit of error is in constant motion, like a current that runs far beneath the surface of a flowing stream. You might see that undercurrent, and you might not, but in the moment it takes for just one breath, you may find yourself pulled away from your intended destination, life lived in the power of the Spirit. The unfortunate truth is this, that the further we move away from one another, the more apt we are to be swept into the chaos that breeds hatred and disgust, the madness that explodes into contempt and warfare. When we lose sight of the common destination that God intends for humankind, we are unable to distinguish one spirit from another.

In the United States alone we are now culturally divided into eleven geographic/sociological regions, from "Yankeedom" to the Left Coast to the Tidewater to the Midlands.[3] People are desperate for an identity. Within each of these "existential" regions (regions with which people's identities are formed and normed) are economic variants, age variants, political variants, religious variants, educational variants, and cultural, historically ethnic, and racial variants. The continuum of rural, small town, suburban, and urban dwelling places means that children born the same day in two different places within the same country, and maybe even to parents within the same church body, may grow up to hate each other, or just as deadly, be apathetic toward one another, having no recognition that this person is neighbor.

What is so spectacular, however, is that underneath every fad and every division, every "ism" and every little tad of self-righteousness, every fear and every failure, every hushed duplicity and every false bravado, every wrong decision and every haughty glance, the One who created us is still at work in us, breathing the Spirit upon us and bringing us into the future that is binding and knitting us together through the grammar of a common liturgy that is our sacramental life. For while the Old Adam/Old Eve in each of

---

[3]. http://www.businessinsider.com/the-11-nations-of-the-united-states-2015-7 (accessed September 11, 2017).

us is still looking to go astray, still unable to trust, Jesus Christ who is life itself is bringing goodness where we on our own could never even imagine it.

The church is hidden in, with, and under a mix of peoples who make up a nation and who, for all intents and purposes, have no unifying metanarrative. As a nation we are a people without a sense that what is true for me is also true for you. The church herself, which has a metanarrative (God ruling by his Word, Jesus Christ risen from the dead), becomes increasingly hidden in this multivalent context, for the layers of human brokenness and division are like scales seared on our eyes, keeping us from seeing who we really are together as God's beloved creation. We remain sightless, until, like St. Paul, we are led by God's grace to a dirt-filled Damascus street where there a faithful, unassuming brother of the church prays, so that we may regain our true sight and be filled with the Holy Spirit (Acts 9:17). This is the work of the Triune God, Father, Son, and Holy Spirit, murderers (as we all are) dying to ourselves and coming to proclaim the sovereignty of Jesus, *He is the Son of God*. For until this world tastes death, it cannot hear such love.[4]

Alexander Schmemann, the great Orthodox theologian stated it clearly:

> The world rejected Christ by killing him, and by doing so rejected its own destiny and fulfillment. Therefore if the basis

---

4. "The point of [the law/gospel] distinction is once again the making public of the divine deed, making it hearable in a world that will not hear it. The distinction is made so that a new kind of speaking might be heard in this world: gospel speaking. . . . Proclamation, shaped by the theology of the cross, is governed by the distinction between law and gospel. This distinction comprehends the fact that publication of the electing deed cannot proceed directly to the world that crucified Jesus, but must bring it to an end." Gerhard Forde, "Called and Ordained," in *Lutheran Perspectives on the Office of Ministry*, ed. Todd Nichol and Marc Kolden (Minneapolis: Fortress Press, 1990), 122, 128.

for all Christian worship is the Incarnation, its true content is always the Cross and the resurrection. Through these events the new life in Christ, the Incarnate Lord, is "hid with Christ in God," and made into a life "not of this world." The world which rejected Christ must itself die in man if it is to become again means of communion, a means of participation in the life which shone forth from the grave, in the kingdom which is not "of this world," and which in terms of this world is still to come.[5]

As in the world before ultrasound, when we could not see the details of a child in the womb that was coming into this world, we receive our Lord in an incarnate promise: a promise that holds the power of life eternal, a promise that will crush the serpent's head, a promise that is hidden in the life of the baptized, a promise that the light will shatter the darkness, a promise that the leprosy that infects the human heart will be washed clean, until that great day comes when we "sing with all the saints in glory, the resurrection song."[6] And what is so stunning is that people who do evil to one another still are given this vision of the good, calling them to live in the light, to live as the light. This is the light to which Jesus called us in the Sermon on the Mount, the Paschal light from which our baptismal candles receive their flame: "Let your light shine before others, so that they may see your good works and glorify your Father in heaven" (Matthew 5:16).

---

5. Alexander Schmemann, *For the Life of the World* (New York: St. Vladimir's Seminary Press, 1973), 122.
6. William J. Irons, "Sing with All the Saints in Glory," in *With One Voice: A Lutheran Resource for Worship* (Minneapolis: Augsburg Fortress, 1995), hymn 691 (public domain).

This is the work of the Spirit, a ministry of reconciliation, where words of forgiveness break through that boulder stuck in our throats (that stone, too, needs to be rolled away), where we give not only the outgrown and outdated clothes to the Salvation Army, but we spend hours in what the world calls "leisure time" building furniture for the local homeless shelter or quilting for 1 of 19 million refugees, where we step out beyond our fear to see someone of a different race or socioeconomic class, or even a different religion, as beloved a child of God as we are. This is what the spirit of truth places before our hearts as we are faced with both our finitude and our complicity in another human being's pain and sorrow. And then . . . and then from our knees, we begin to love. Then we can participate in myriad expressions of service to the neighbor, joyfully—not because we have to, but because we want to. In our everyday vocational callings, that which the world calls our "professions," we work in personal and collective ways to treat everyone, absolutely everyone, with the dignity and respect befitting a child of God. Some of us may also do the most hidden work of renewing and creating systems that make life more joyous for people we will never meet. Your incarnate witness will serve as a word of law to those who do not care for their neighbor, but it will also be an embodied grace to those who receive it. Giving glory to our Father in heaven is always the work of the Spirit.

   Such a life does not call attention to itself and has no need to mimic a world that slathers its company name on its polo shirts and its favorite quarterback idol on its jerseys. Such a life has no need to succumb to a tribalism that seeks to destroy our true identity, the identity given to us when the water was poured and the word spoken—one Lord, one faith, one baptism—one God and Father of all (Ephesians 4:5). For such a life does not easily fall prey for those devilish forces that divide brother from brother, sisters and mothers, fathers and cousins all.

## A Spirit-Filled Life and the Sacraments

What does it mean for the baptized to live this life filled with the Spirit? To live the truth that is known by the Spirit, by the water and by the blood? The seventeenth-century hymn by Michael Schirmer with which this essay began (found in several contemporary hymnals, though not in those of the Episcopal Church), sings the hope of that life:

> Left to ourselves, we surely stray;
> Oh, lead us on the narrow way,
> With wisest counsel guide us;
> And give us steadfastness, that we
> May follow you forever free,
> No matter who derides us.
> Gently heal those hearts now broken;
> Give some token You are near us,
> Whom we trust to light and cheer us.[7]

The hope of the baptized in this day is to live filled with the Spirit of truth whom the world neither sees nor recognizes. Our corporate hope as members of congregations and of the larger configuration of Christians (i.e., the church catholic) is to be "called, gathered, enlightened, and sanctified" by the Spirit to discover the shape of a joyful obedience empowered by the Spirit.[8]

---

7. Schirmer, "O Holy Spirit, Enter In," hymn 459, verse 2. The hymn is also found in *Voices United: The Hymnal and Worship Book of the United Church of Canada* (Etobicoke, Ontario: United Church Publishing House, 1996), hymn 369.

8. As Martin Luther confessed in *Small Catechism*, when in 1529 he wrote in his explanation to the question of "What does this mean?" with regard to the third article of the Apostles' Creed, "I believe that by my own reason or strength I cannot believe in Jesus Christ, my Lord, or come to him. But the Holy Spirit has called me through the Gospel, enlightened me with his gifts, and sanctified and preserved me in true faith, just as he calls, gathers,

Such a declaration of this life-giving hope is a central theme in the *epiclesis* (Greek for "invocation"), the technical name given to the portion of the Eucharistic Prayer invoking the Spirit. Yet the manner in which these prayers are shaped is far from uniform. Over the last two thousand years there has been a long and rugged history of the role and placement of the epiclesis within the Eucharistic Rite.[9] At times the Spirit was called down upon the material gifts of bread and wine.[10] At other times the Spirit was called upon the persons in the assembly.[11] Many times the Spirit has ambiguously been called upon both, and on occasion, as in the *Apostolic Tradition*, that calling upon both was not only explicit but theologically pointed to show the "close relationship . . . between gifts transformed and the deepened unity of the church."[12] Sometimes the epiclesis preceded

---

enlightens, and sanctifies the whole Christian church on earth and preserves it in union with Jesus Christ in the one true faith. . . ." *The Book of Concord: The Confessions of the Evangelical Lutheran Church*, trans. and ed. Theodore G. Tappert (Philadelphia: Fortress Press, 1959), 345.

9. For a concise history of the epiclesis in another denomination with which the Episcopal Church is in full communion, see Maxwell E. Johnson, *The Church in Act: Lutheran Liturgical Theology in an Ecumenical Conversation* (Minneapolis: Fortress Press, 2015), 33–66.

10. For example, the Liturgy of St. John Chrysostom, which has been the "principal and normal rite of the Orthodox church" since about the year 1000, includes an epiclesis explicitly asking the Holy Spirit to change the elements into the body and blood of Christ but no parallel request that God the Father send down the Holy Spirit upon the assembly. See R. C. D. Jasper and G. J. Cuming, *Prayers of the Eucharist: Early and Reformed* (Collegeville, MN: Liturgical Press, 1980), 129, 133.

11. For example, the Egyptian Anaphora of St. Basil from the third or fourth century included a petition for the descent of the Holy Spirit upon the bread and wine as means to sanctify the assembly but no language at that point about the transformation of the elements into the body and blood of Christ. See ibid., 67–68, 71.

12. Kevin W. Irwin, *Models of the Eucharist* (New York/Mahwah: Paulist Press, 2005), 267.

the *verba* (the recitation of Jesus' words at the Last Supper: "Take, eat; this is my body," etc.) as in the 1549 Book of Common Prayer, and sometimes it followed.[13] By the time of the Reformation, the Roman Canon had no epiclesis within the Eucharistic Prayer (only in the offertory prayer) because the *verba* had taken on the consecratory function. So, as much as the reformers sought to change the shape and "sacrificial" direction of the canon, they kept the *verba* central as a consecratory proclamation.[14] In numerous Protestant expressions of the church, the Spirit was simply understood to be present when the *verba* flowed from the Proper Preface in this act of proclamation.[15] (This is a striking change between the 1549 and 1552 prayer books.) It is also important to note that the shape of the Eucharistic Prayers in the 1979 Book of Common Prayer as well as in other sacramentally centered denominational prayer and worship books did not occur in a vacuum. The work of Vatican II bore many fruits, including a clear epiclesis in the three new Eucharistic prayers that were authorized by the Roman See. Formal and informal conversations among liturgical theologians produced a flowering of such Eucharistic and particularly epicletic praying.[16]

---

13. For a clear ecumenical exposition of the position of the epiclesis, see Anne McGowan, *Eucharistic Epiclesis, Ancient and Modern: Speaking of the Spirit in Eucharistic Prayer* (Collegeville, MN: Pueblo/Liturgical Press, 2014).
14. Talley, "The Structure of the Eucharistic Prayer," 91.
15. In Luther's revision of the *Ordo Missae*, the *Formula Missae et Communionis* of 1523, the *verba* is still within a Eucharistic Prayer. Senn comments on the *Formula Missae*, "If this text of the institution narrative is compared with the text in the Roman canon, it will be seen that Luther has eliminated all extrabiblical words and phrases. . . . It should be noted that this institution narrative is still included within a Eucharistic prayer, since it is introduced by a dependent Qui-clause. This Eucharistic prayer concluded with the singing of the Sanctus." Senn, *Christian Liturgy*, 278.
16. A prime example of this recovery of the Eucharistic epicletic praying is Eucharistic Prayer D, which was created under the auspices of "an unofficial

In the case of the Episcopal Church in late twentieth- and early twenty-first-century North America, all the Eucharistic prayers currently authorized contain both a petition for the Spirit to fall upon the bread and wine, and a petition for grace for the gathered people, but the two are not always equal in emphasis and the role of the Spirit in the petition of the people is often muted. It behooves us to pay attention to both the individual texts as well as the placement of epicletic texts within the Eucharistic Rite, for what we believe about the church, i.e., our ecclesiology, flows from our understanding and enactment of the Eucharist, and our calling upon the Holy Spirit is the center of our obedient witness.[17]

In Eucharistic Prayers I and II, Prayer C (with its pre-verba epiclesis), and Forms 1 and 2 of the Book of Common Prayer (1979), there is no explicit invocation of the Spirit on the people, but the second petition is linked to the first by an affirmation that the cause of the grace given is the reception of the elements.[18] In Eucharistic

---

committee in 1974" and whose text "is drawn from early versions of the Anaphora of St. Basil and from Eucharistic Prayer IV in the Roman sacramentary because of its widespread use, its ancient roots, its broad scope, and its wide appeal in Eastern and Western Christianity." Philip H. Pfatteicher, *Commentary on the Lutheran Book of Worship: Lutheran Liturgy in Its Ecumenical Context* (Minneapolis: Augsburg Fortress, 1990), 181.

17. "Whether the invocation of the Spirit is or is not linked with the *anamnesis* is what gives a different shape to the two 'families' of Eucharistic prayer: the first with its *epiclesis before* the institution narrative, follows the 1549 model; the second, in the *epiclesis* follows that narrative and is associated with the *anamnesis*, follows the 'Scottish' model. The Institution narrative itself takes on a very different meaning in the two cases. When the *epiclesis* precedes the narrative, the words of institution take on a consecratory role, as they do in 1662, even when there is no *epiclesis* at all. When an *epiclesis* comes afterward, the institution narrative is actually part of the thanksgiving section." Ronald Dowling, "The Eucharist," in *The Oxford Guide to the Book of Common Prayer: A Worldwide Survey*, ed. Charles Hefling and Cynthia Shattuck (New York: Oxford University Press, 2006), 464–65.

18. Book of Common Prayer (1979), 335–36, 342–43, 371–72, 403–5.

Prayers I and II, the second petition is that the "partakers of this Holy Communion may . . . be filled with [Christ's] grace and benediction and made one body with him, that he may dwell in us, and we in him."[19] Prayer C expresses the hope that "the grace of this Holy Communion make us one body, one spirit in Christ, that we may worthily serve the world in his name."[20] However, this is clearly more a general supplication than a specific epiclesis.

Form 1 asks that God the Father "gather us by this Holy Communion into one body in your Son Jesus Christ. Make us a living sacrifice of praise."[21] We are to be *homo adorans*, the worshiping human, a clear word in concert with multiple Reformation catecheses, that our primary purpose is to give glory to God in all that we say and do. In Form 2 the petition is that the Father "grant that we who eat this bread and drink this cup may be filled with your life and goodness."[22] (This will be echoed theologically in Eucharistic Prayer B as the Spirit is called to unite us with Christ in his sacrifice for the purpose of making us acceptable through him.) Form B in *Enriching Our Worship* follows a similar pattern with the final paragraph asking God to "gather us by this Holy Communion into one body in the Risen One, and makes us a living sacrifice of praise."[23]

---

19. Ibid., 335–36, 342–43. Eucharistic Prayer II adds the phrase "also that we and all thy whole church" to emphasize the corporate nature of the prayer for the Spirit.

20. Prayer C also links the petition for the Spirit on the elements with a statement—not a petition—that those gathered have already been made "a new people by water and the Spirit"—i.e., through baptism. See ibid., 371–72.

21. Ibid., 403.

22. Ibid., 405.

23. *Enriching Our Worship 1*, 67. The Eucharistic Prayers in *Enriching Our Worship*, with their move to a more "gender-neutral language," lose the clarity that has preceded them linguistically throughout the Great Tradition. While every collect within the liturgy does not require a full Trinitarian expression in the naming of God, the sense that the assembly is calling upon the Father to send the Spirit is now ambiguous.

In each of these epicletic cries the gathered assembly hears a word to live a life worthy of the calling to which they are called, yet each epiclesis names the dimensions of such an obedient life with its own particular nuance. Thus, as these words become inscribed upon the hearts of the assembly over time, the baptized may come to know that serving in the world is a unifying force filled with the glory of God that comes from a sacrifice of praise.

Eucharistic Prayers A, B, and D follow a second pattern in which the petitions for the elements and for the people follow each other seamlessly. Eucharistic Prayer A clearly calls down the Spirit upon the Body and Blood and then calls upon the Spirit to open the hearts of those who will receive this holy meal in such a way, that as they go out into the world having been fed (by what has been deeply hidden amidst this world's despair and destruction), the Spirit will become known in the manner in which the baptized and fed now witness to the truth of God's everlasting love. This epiclesis expresses the unity of those who receive the sacrament in this day and all the faithful of every generation. Such a hopeful word is yet another way to speak of the foretaste of the Marriage Supper of the Lamb, where all the baptized will delight in the fullness of this eternal union.

> Eucharistic Prayer A:
> Sanctify them by your Holy Spirit to be for your people the Body and Blood of your Son, the holy food and drink of new and unending life in him. Sanctify us also that we may faithfully receive this holy Sacrament, and serve you in unity, constancy, and peace; and at the last day bring us with all your saints into the joy of your eternal kingdom.[24]

While neither Eucharistic Prayers B or D repeat the operative epicletic verb "sanctify," they each call down the Spirit upon the

---

24. Book of Common Prayer (1979), 363.

sacramental gifts and upon the people. In Eucharist Prayer B we ask the Spirit to join us to Christ's sacrifice, evoking the memory of what he has done on our behalf. Eucharist Prayer D reverses the order of the epiclectic sections, calling for the Spirit first upon the people and second upon the holy gifts, a subtle historical reminder that the calling of the Spirit upon the gifts occurs as a much later interpretive move in the history of the church. Unlike the previous epiclesis, Epiclesis D asks that the Spirit descend upon the people only for the purpose of showing that the Body and Blood of our Lord is truly the bread of life and cup of salvation. We ask for the Holy Sprit to come upon us for the express purpose of witnessing to the truth of who God is and how God has chosen to become known among us.

> Eucharistic Prayer B:
> We pray you, gracious God, to send your Holy Spirit upon these gifts that they may be the Sacrament of the Body of Christ and his Blood of the new Covenant. Unite us to your Son in his sacrifice, that we may be acceptable through him, being sanctified by the Holy Spirit.[25]
>
> Eucharistic Prayer D:
> Lord, we pray that in your goodness and mercy your Holy Spirit may descend upon us, and upon these gifts, sanctifying them and showing them to be holy gifts for your holy people, the bread of life and the cup of salvation, the Body and Blood of your Son Jesus Christ.[26]

Eucharistic Prayers 1, 2, and 3, and Form B in *Enriching Our Worship* (which lacks the clear Trinitarian address of Father, Son, and Holy Spirit) follow in similar linguistic manner, linking the two

---

25. Ibid., 369.
26. Ibid., 375.

petitions in the epiclesis and including an explicit reference to the Holy Spirit in each. Eucharistic Prayer 1, *Enriching Our Worship*, plays on the polysemy of "Body," in hopes that our everyday lives will reflect Christ's love for the world. Eucharistic Prayer 2, *Enriching Our Worship*, in a unique move, brings to mind the pouring out of the Spirit at the beginning of time and at the "birth" of the church. Eucharistic Prayer 3, *Enriching Our Worship*, continues that same Pentecost theme as it asks that we be filled with the Spirit's fire for the express purpose of a future being as a people of "hope, justice, and love."[27]

Eucharistic Prayer 1:
By your Holy Spirit may they be for us the Body and Blood of our Savior Jesus Christ. Grant that we who share these gifts may be filled with the Holy Spirit and live as Christ's Body in the world.[28]

Eucharistic Prayer 2:
Pour out your spirit upon these gifts that they may be the Body and Blood of Christ. Breathe your Spirit over the whole earth and make us your new creation, the Body of Christ given for the world you have made.[29]

Eucharistic Prayer 3:
Send your Holy Spirit upon us and upon these gifts of bread and wine that they may be to us the Body and Blood of your

---

27. The "justice" of "hope, justice, and love" may be received as a nod to those divisions that were mentioned in section I of this essay, since the ecumenical community is divided as it wrestles with the many distinctions that are manifest in the interpreting of both divine justice and human justice. A phrase such as "hope, mercy, and love" in any further revision might serve to be more inclusive.
28. *Enriching Our Worship 1*, 59.
29. Ibid., 62.

Christ. Grant that we, burning with your Spirit's power, may be a people of hope, justice, and love.[30]

Form B:
Sanctify them by your Holy Spirit to be for your people the Body and Blood of Christ.

*The Celebrant then prays that all may receive the benefits of Christ's work, and the renewal of the Holy Spirit.*[31]

## The Spirit of Truth and the Church

When we hear all these epicleses as if they were musical themes in a multimovement symphony, or we see these texts as pictures in a multidimensional collage, we begin to understand that we are still working out what has been prayed as far back as the *Apostolic Tradition*,[32] for this confluence of texts suggests an increasing clarity, a subnarrative within our metanarrative that proclaims that God, the Father of our Lord Jesus Christ, is the sender of the Holy Spirit to *establish our faith in truth*: the truth about who God is, from the beginning, Father, Son, and Holy Spirit, and how God acts; the truth about who we are and how we are called to live; and the truth about this world and the world to come, the truth about eternity, that is, the truth about the resurrection of the dead unto eternal life, that we *may enter* into it.[33]

---

30. Ibid., 64.
31. Ibid., 68.
32. In the model of Eucharistic prayer once attributed to Hippolytus, in the *Apostolic Tradition*, we pray in the epiclesis, "fill us with your Spirit to establish our faith in truth."
33. Suggesting new forms is beyond the scope of this essay, but a rereading of Frank Senn's "Toward a Different Anaphoral Structure," *Worship* 58 (July 1984): 346–58, may yet serve to open our theological imaginations.

If, indeed, Prosper of Aquitaine's gift to the church still holds true, *ut legem credendi lex statuat supplicandi* ("The law of praying establishes the law of believing"), then within the economy of a full Trinitarian language, it would be more than appropriate in any future revisions of the Book of Common Prayer to consider naming this multiplicity of works of the Spirit when the church at prayer calls for the Spirit to descend, sanctify, and unite. For as God the Father of our Lord Jesus Christ breathes out the Holy Spirit, the assembly breathes in this One, who is God's truth.

For the life of the church it is no small thing to live filled with the Spirit of truth whom the world neither sees nor recognizes. It is no small thing for a congregation, called, gathered, enlightened, and sanctified by the Spirit, to discover a joyful obedience empowered by the Spirit, to receive and to live out the Truth that is known by the Spirit, by the water and by the blood.

Every Lord's Day the baptized come to table and are joined in prayer for the Spirit to come upon these gifts of bread and wine, and to come upon those who have been assembled by the Spirit's own power. Within a continuum of ritual variations, our hearts and hands are made open so that we might become "living members of your Son our Savior Jesus Christ."[34] In some (often hidden) way, the Holy Spirit is always directing our attention to Christ, and it is in and through Christ that we are taken to the Father's heart.

The Eucharistic epiclesis is among the most paradigmatic expressions of the life and faith of the baptized. For as Christ himself is hidden in bread and wine, word and water, so the Spirit fills the assembly with the presence of the Triune God wherever that community is gathered: the living room in a house church, a stone and stained glass cathedral, an underheated city basement, or at the end of a gravel road in a white-walled church on the open prairie.

---

34. Postcommunion Prayer, Book of Common Prayer (1979), 365.

The Holy Spirit directs our full attention to Christ, who is, who was, and who is to come. When our attention is taken into the future that Christ is preparing for us, then, and only then, that future, that eternal love, happens now. For just as the Spirit descended upon Jesus as he came up from the River Jordan, and just as Jesus unrolled the scroll of the prophet Isaiah and proclaimed "The Spirit of the Lord is upon me," and just as Jesus breathed peace into the disciples who shivered behind a locked door, and just as you have been sealed with the Holy Spirit and marked with the cross of Christ forever, so now week after week, Sunday after Sunday, the Holy Spirit, whom you cannot see, but whose works you believe in—the communion of saints, the forgiveness of sins, the resurrection of the body and the life everlasting—the Holy Spirit is directing you to a Eucharistic life, a life in which we receive every breath with Thanksgiving. Our Lord Jesus says to us, "If you love me, you will keep my commandments." And he has commanded you to, "Do this in remembrance of me."

All those multiple contexts in which we live and move, but in which we do not have our very being, all those divisions are to be overcome, and indeed are overcome as the Holy Spirit directs us to receive the life of the resurrected Christ into our lives. In the words of Leo the Great, "The Spirit of truth breathes where he will, and each nation's own language has become common property in the mouth of the church."[35]

Hidden in the fragmentation of society and invading every subculture, the body of Christ sings Christ's resurrection song. Whether we wear the faded scrubs of an orderly at the county nursing home or the sleek Armani pinstripe as CEO of a Fortune 500 company, we are owned by neither one, but by Christ. Whether we are cooing homemade melodies of love in a baby's tiny ear

---

35. Leo the Great, Sermons 75.1-3, *Corpus Christianorum-Series Latina* 138A, 465–69, cited in Stephen Mark Holmes, *The Fathers on the Sunday Gospels* (Collegeville, MN: Liturgical Press, 2012), 166.

or singing lamentations as we caress the dying, it is the Spirit of truth witnessing to the eternal love of God for those whom he has made. Nothing can stop this love, "neither heights nor depths nor angels nor principalities, nor powers."[36] Nothing can stop this love because "Christ has died. Christ is Risen, Christ will come again."[37] We who once cried for his crucifixion, murderers all, have now met him at the cross, dragged by the Spirit of truth kicking and screaming in denial of our complicity of our sin, but in a breath—born up as on wings of an eagle by this same Spirit whom the Father has sent to carry us to the empty tomb. As St. Paul writes to the Corinthians, we are "always carrying in the body the death of Jesus, so that the life of Jesus may also be made visible in our bodies" (2 Corinthians 4:10).

## The Global Horizon and the Witness of Martyrs

There is, however, one place where we all too often painfully see this life being made visible. And it is a place to which we in the North American church need to pay attention. It is not within our national borders but on the global horizon that we see the most graphic and explicit scenes of what truth looks like. For the Spirit of truth is made visible for all the world to see in martyrdom. Twenty-one Copts beheaded, scores of Nigerian students mowed down, Iraqi Christians kidnapped and tortured, innocent young girls in nation after nation abducted and raped physically, emotionally, and spiritually, and then raped again and again and again: it is destruction and violation, defilement and desecration at every human level, and in this hell on earth these unsuspecting martyrs are speaking the truth, testifying with their whole body to the truth of who God is and whom God has made us to be, *homo adorans*, the worshiping

---

36. Author's paraphrase of Romans 8:30.
37. Eucharistic acclamation, Book of Common Prayer (1979), 363.

human, trusting his promise, *"I am the Lord your God,"* obedient to the command, "You shall have no other gods before me" (Exodus 20:2–3). Animated and empowered by the Spirit who is truth, martyrs incarnately speak Christ's essence, which is truth, "Father, forgive them; for they do not know what they are doing" (Luke 23:34). And speaking the truth about who God is, they simultaneously speak the truth about the world that God has made, and the truth about those upon whom the Spirit rests, the truth that God's mercy is greater than our damnable ways, God's forgiveness greater than any devil's temptation, and God's love even deeper than any mass grave. Death has no hold upon those in whom the Spirit rests, for the Spirit is testifying to the truth in the lives of those who look to the Lord for every breath.

The closing verse of Michael Schirmer's hymn, "O Holy Spirit, Enter In," sings this yearning for God into our hearts:

> O mighty Rock, O Source of life,
> Let your good Word in doubt and strife
> be in us strongly burning,
> that we be faithful unto death
> And live in love and holy faith,
> From you true wisdom learning.
> Lord, your mercy
> On us shower;
> By your power
> Christ confessing,
> We will cherish all your blessings.[38]

It is this vision that the Spirit breathes into the whole church, taking the resurrected life of Christ and giving it to us so that we may live faithfully in any and every context. We cannot fully imagine it, just as young soldiers cannot imagine how they would feel or

---

38. Schirmer, "O Holy Spirit, Enter In," hymn 459, verse 3 (public domain).

act when the Stryker in front of them hits an improvised explosive device and they find themselves hemmed in by enemy fire. None can imagine this, and all of us in some way or another are afraid that our fear would be greater than our faith, that we would be paralyzed, that we would capitulate, that we would submit to the evil that surrounds us, that we would seek to cling to this life more than to the promise of life eternal. But from the testimony of the martyrs we see and hear the same fullness of the Spirit who came to us in the waters, the same fullness of the Spirit, who in the words of the epiclesis in the document known as the *Apostolic Tradition*, "blesses us [God's] servants and [his] own gifts of bread and wine, so that we and all who share in the body and blood of his Son may be filled with heavenly peace and joy, and receiving the forgiveness of sins, may be sanctified in soul and body, and have our portion with all God's saints."[39]

God has breathed the Spirit on your hearts so that when faced with the fullness of the law, that is your death, you will be filled with the Spirit's gift of eternal truth and you will yet proclaim, "Accept these prayers and praises, Father, through Jesus Christ our great High Priest, to whom, with you and the Holy Spirit, your Church gives honor, glory, and worship from generation to generation. Amen."[40]

---

39. Eucharistic Prayer IV, *Lutheran Book of Worship* (Ministers Desk Edition), 226.
40. Eucharist Prayer C, Book of Common Prayer (1979), 372.

# 8

# "The Word of the Lord"

## An Examination of the Use of Lectionaries in the Episcopal Church

### Shawn O. Strout[1]

The reading of scripture in the liturgy extends back before the birth of the church into ancient synagogue practice as evidenced by reference to Christ reading from the prophet Isaiah on the Sabbath (Luke 4:17–20). Most liturgical scholars agree that the early use of scripture in the church was a form of reading known as *lectio continua*, in which a passage of scripture would be read from a book in the Bible at one liturgy and then continued at the next, marking the beginning and end of the reading in the manuscript itself. However, as the liturgical calendar expanded and the church's desire to coordinate the reading of scripture with the calendar grew, lectionaries began to develop. We do not have

---

1. The Rev. Shawn O. Strout is a PhD candidate in liturgical studies/sacramental theology at the Catholic University of America.

evidence of any lectionaries prior to the sixth century. However, scholars feel confident such lectionaries were in use by examining the homilies of earlier ecclesial figures.[2]

As the liturgical year became more complex, the lectionaries of the church also became more complex. In addition, nonscriptural readings from various ecclesial figures began to dominate within the lectionaries, so much so that by the sixteenth century, the preface to the 1549 Book of Common Prayer, which contemporary scholars believe was written by Archbishop Thomas Cranmer, explained:

> For the [ancient fathers] so ordred the matter, that all the whole Bible (or the greates parte thereof) should be read ouer once in the yeare, intending thereby, that the Cleargie, and specially suche as were Ministers of the congregacion, should (by often readyng and meditacion of Gods worde) be stirred up to godliness themselfes, and be more able also to exhorte other by wholsme doctrine, and to confute them that were aduersaries to the trueth. And further, that the people (by daily hearing of holy scripture read in the Churche) should continuallye profite more and more in the knowledge of God, and bee the more inflamed with the loue of his true religion. But these many yeares passed this Godly and decent ordre of the auncient fathers, hath bee so altered, broken, and neglected, by planting in uncertain stories, Legēdes, Respondes, Verses, vaine repeticions, Commemoracions, and Synodalles, that commonly when any boke of the Bible was begon: before three or foure Chapiters were read out, all the rest were unread. And in this sorte the boke of Esaie was begon in Aduent, and the booke of

---

2. Eric Palazzo, *A History of Liturgical Books from the Beginning to the Thirteenth Century* (Collegeville, MN: Liturgical Press, 1998), 83–91.

genesis in Septuagesima: but they were onely begon, and neuer read thorow.[3]

Cranmer sought to rectify what he saw as a departure from the true purpose of the lectionary—the stirring up to godliness of both the clergy and laity through reading and meditation on God's Word. Continuing the connection between the lectionary and the liturgical calendar, the preface again states:

> And for a readiness in this matter, here is drawen out a Kalendar for that purpose, whiche is plaine and easy to be understanded, wherin (so muche as maie be) the readyng of holy scripture is so set further, that all thynges shall bee doen in ordre, without breaking one piece therof from another. For this cause be cut of Anthemes, Respondes, Inuitatories, and suche like thunges, as did breake the continuall course of the readyng of the scripture.[4]

Thus, the preface establishes a strong connection between the ordered and continuous reading of scripture and the church's celebration of the liturgical year.

In this essay, I will examine the use of lectionaries in the Episcopal Church. I will accomplish this examination in three parts. First, I will offer a brief survey of the history of the use of lectionaries in the Church of England, as the predecessor to the Episcopal Church, and in the Episcopal Church leading up to the 1928 edition of the Book of Common Prayer. Then, I will look at the contemporary use of lectionaries in the Episcopal Church beginning with the revision of the Daily Office lectionary in 1945 and the

---

3. *The First and Second Prayer Books of Edward VI*, 3–4. The attribution of sole authorship of the preface to Cranmer is not unanimous; for a dissenting opinion, see Diarmaid MacCulloch, *Thomas Cranmer: A Life* (New Haven, CT: Yale University Press, 1996), 414.
4. Book of Common Prayer (1549), 4.

publication of *Lesser Feasts and Fasts* in 1963 along with their subsequent revisions, including *Holy Women, Holy Men*, and *A Great Cloud of Witnesses*.[5] I will also consider the Episcopal Church's authorization of the Revised Common Lectionary as the principle lectionary for Sunday Eucharistic liturgies.

As with all essays of a certain length, limits regarding scope are at play. Therefore, I will limit my examination to officially authorized liturgical books in the Church of England (only for historical context) and the Episcopal Church. Additionally, I will not address the use of scripture for what are sometimes called "occasional services" as these services are very specific in nature and do not tend to impact the church's use of the lectionary throughout the year. Lastly, I will not address the principles for inclusion in the *sanctorale* or sanctoral calendar, as that is a topic best addressed in an essay about the liturgical year.

## How Did We Get Here?

To understand Cranmer's reaction to the state of lectionaries in the pre-Reformation church in England, we must take a brief look at two important liturgical books at use: *The Sarum Breviary* and

---

5. *The Lesser Feasts and Fasts* (New York: Church Pension Fund, 1963); *The Lesser Feasts and Fasts*, rev. ed. (New York: Church Hymnal Corp., 1973); *The Lesser Feasts and Fasts*, 3rd ed. (New York: Church Hymnal Corp., 1980); *The Lesser Feasts and Fasts*, 4th ed. (New York: Church Hymnal Corp., 1988); *The Lesser Feasts and Fasts, 1991* (New York: Church Hymnal Corp., 1991); *The Lesser Feasts and Fasts, 1994* (New York: Church Hymnal Corp., 1994); *The Lesser Feasts and Fasts, 1997* (New York: Church Publishing, 1997); *The Lesser Feasts and Fasts, 2000* (New York: Church Publishing, 2000); *The Lesser Feasts and Fasts, 2003* (New York: Church Publishing, 2003); *The Lesser Feasts and Fasts, 2006* (New York: Church Publishing, 2006). Hereafter, I will refer to these editions by publication date and page number. *Holy Women, Holy Men* (New York: Church Publishing, 2010); *A Great Cloud of Witnesses* (New York: Church Publishing, 2016).

*The Sarum Missal.* "Sarum" in these titles refers to the "use" (i.e., the local adaptation of the Roman Rite) developed at Salisbury Cathedral in England. While the Sarum Use was not the only use in play in the pre-Reformation church in England, it was the most prevalent. In fact, G. J. Cuming states, "The overwhelming predominance of Sarum shows that, well before the Reformation, 'all the whole realm' was very close to having 'but one use.'"[6] Since a more detailed analysis of the other uses in the pre-Reformation church in England lies outside the scope of this essay, we will only consider the Sarum Use. As mentioned above, I will begin by looking at the use of the lectionary for the Daily Office tracing it through to the 1928 Book of Common Prayer and then for the Eucharist in a similar manner.

## The Daily Office

In the pre-Reformation church in England, *The Sarum Breviary* was the principal liturgical book in use for the Daily Office.[7] It provided for up to nine lessons per day, depending on the rank of the feast being observed. For example, the Feast of the Circumcision of Our Lord included a full set of nine readings. However, minor observances, like those for St. Felix or St. Maurice, only had three readings assigned to them. Using January as an example, we observe two important trends in the breviary lectionary. First, we observe the use of nonscriptural texts. In fact, for fifteen of the eighteen days that are feast days in January according to this breviary, a nonscriptural text is assigned for all the lessons for that day. For major feast

---

6. G. J. Cuming, *A History of Anglican Liturgy*, 2nd ed. (London: MacMillan Press, 1982), 14.
7. *Breviarium ad Usum Insignis Ecclesiae Sarum*, ed. Francisci Procter. [Cantabrigiae]: typis atque impensis almae matris Academiae Cantabrigiensis, 1879, section A2; hereafter *Sarum Breviary* followed by section or page number.

days, an additional brief passage from one of the Gospels was also assigned for the seventh lesson. These nonscriptural texts range from homilies such as Augustine's Sermon 220 on the Octave of the Innocents to legends such as the Legend of Felix on his feast day. Second, we observe that the only days on which scripture is assigned are the Epiphany of the Lord and the First and Second Sunday after Epiphany. Furthermore, these scripture passages are very brief, only several verses, and not continuous from day to day but only across the nine lessons for that particular day.[8] Thus, a faithful adherent of the Daily Office in the pre-Reformation church in England would be exposed to very little scripture and with very little consistency.

Cranmer's lectionary for the Daily Office in the 1549 Book of Common Prayer radically changes this approach. The instructions for the new calendar make this change abundantly clear:

> THE olde Testament is appoynted for the first Lessons, at Matins and Evensong, and shal bee redde through every yere once, except certain bokes and Chapiters, whiche bee least edifying, and might best be spared, and therfore are left unred.... The newe Testament is appoynted for the second Lessons, at Matins and Evensong, and shalbe red over orderly every yere thrise, beside the Epistles and Gospelles: except the Apocalips [i.e., Revelation], out of the whiche there be onely certain Lessons appoynted upon diverse proper feastes.[9]

In addition, the 1549 Book of Common Prayer substantially reduced the number of feast days found in the sanctoral calendar (i.e., the calendar assigning lessons for individual saint's days). The only saints commemorated in the entire *sanctorale* are the conversion of St. Paul in January; the Purification of Mary and St. Matthias in February; the Annunciation in March; St. Mark the Evangelist

---

8. Ibid., A2, *Januarius*.
9. *The First and Second Prayer Books of Edward VI*, 9.

in April; Ss. Philip and James in May; St. Barnabas the Apostle, and the Nativity of St. John the Baptist and St. Peter in June; Mary Magdalene and St. James the Apostle in July; St. Bartholomew the Apostle in August; St. Mathew and Michael and All Angels in September; St. Luke the Evangelist, and Ss. Simon and Jude in October; All Saints and St. Andrew the Apostle in November; and St. Thomas the Apostle, St. Stephen, St. John the Evangelist, and the Holy Innocents in December.[10] Thus, except December and June, no month has more than two saints' days in it. This radical reduction in the sanctoral calendar allowed the 1549 Daily Office lectionary to be almost a true *lectio continua*, working its way through the Hebrew Scriptures, Psalms, Epistles, and Gospels with little interruption.

This *lectio continua* through scripture continues through the 1552, 1559, and 1662 editions of the Book of Common Prayer in the Church of England, as well as the 1789, 1892, and 1928 editions of the Book of Common Prayer in the Episcopal Church. The main difference between these various editions for the Daily Office occurs with propers (designated lessons, collects, and prefaces for particular days) for feast days. With only limited exceptions, the 1549 Book of Common Prayer does not include special propers for the major feast days assigned. Instead, the *lectio continua* proceeds uninterrupted. The 1552 Book of Common Prayer does introduce twenty-one propers for feast days, as well as Wednesday through Saturday before Easter and Monday and Tuesday after Easter. It also eliminates the feast of St. Mary Magdalene in July.[11]

The 1559 edition of the Book of Common Prayer does introduce an important difference by scheduling nonsequential proper lessons for the reading of the Daily Office on Sundays, as well as raising the number of proper lessons for feast days to thirty-three

---

10. Ibid., 9–20.
11. Ibid., 341.

and providing four proper lessons for the Psalms on Christmas, Easter, Ascension, and Whitsunday.[12] The 1662 edition of the Book of Common Prayer initially increases the number of proper lessons to eighty-nine, not including Sundays. However, the English revision of the lectionary of 1922 reduces the number to five feast days plus Holy Week, Easter Week, and Monday and Tuesday after Whitsunday.[13] The early editions of the Book of Common Prayer (1789, 1892, and 1928) for the Episcopal Church inherit the *lectio continua* of their predecessor editions from the Church of England for the lectionary of the Daily Office. The propers for Sunday continue, and the propers for feast days and other observances expand and contract only slightly in each edition.[14]

Thus, the various editions of the Book of Common Prayer in the Church of England and the Episcopal Church have held true to the original principle of *lectio continua* with few interruptions for feast days for the Daily Office. When we remember that the typical Sunday service consisted of Morning Prayer, Litany, and Antecommunion or Communion on select Sundays, the special propers for Sundays made sense for the experience of the average worshiper on a Sunday morning.[15] This *lectio continua* provided the practitioner of the Daily Office with a solid foundation in scriptural reading throughout the year.

---

12. John E. Booty, ed., *Book of Common Prayer 1559: The Elizabethan Prayer Book* (Washington, DC: Folger Shakespeare Library, 1976), 27–33.
13. "The 1662 *Book of Common Prayer*," https://www.eskimo.com/~lhowell/bcp1662/info/calendar.html (accessed March 20, 2018).
14. See "1789 U.S. Book of Common Prayer," http://justus.anglican.org/resources/bcp/1789/BCP_1789.htm; "The 1892 U.S. Book of Common Prayer," http://justus.anglican.org/resources/bcp/1892/BCP_1892.htm; and "The 1928 U.S. Book of Common Prayer," http://justus.anglican.org/resources/bcp/1928/BCP_1928.htm (all accessed March 20, 2018).
15. Standing Liturgical Commission, *Prayer Book Studies VII*, 4.

## Eucharist

Unlike *The Sarum Breviary* with its numerous lessons, *The Sarum Missal* provides only two passages from scripture for every mass celebrated. It does not include any extrascriptural readings as found in the breviary. However, the large number of feast days does not allow for a continuous reading of scripture in the Eucharist any more than it did for the Daily Office.[16] *The Sarum Missal* and *Breviary* were unique in that they observed the universal feasts of the Roman calendar but also added far more local feasts than other uses had added. In fact, the calendar was so complicated to read that an additional liturgical book, nicknamed "the Pie," had to be employed by local priests to figure out which commemoration to celebrate on which day.[17] Thus, the sanctoral calendar in the pre-Reformation church in England almost obliterated the *temporale* (the temporal calendar with lessons specified according to the Church Year) entirely, including Sundays. The effect this had on the lectionary was to create a very haphazard reading of scripture. There was no continuity to the reading.

Again, the 1549 edition of the Book of Common Prayer sought to rectify this haphazard approach. As mentioned above, the size of the sanctoral calendar was greatly reduced, which created simplicity to the lectionary. However, the proper lessons for the Eucharist did not follow a *lectio continua* as in the lectionary for the Daily Office. One logical explanation for this inconsistency in continuity would be the reality that Morning Prayer was said every Sunday as the first service, with the Litany and Ante-Communion or Holy Communion following. Thus, the Sunday worshiper was already receiving a continuous reading of scripture through Morning Prayer. A rubric did

---

16. J. Wickham Legg, ed., *The Sarum Missal* (Oxford: University Press, 1969), xxi–xxxii.
17. Archdale A. King, *Liturgies of the Past* (Milwaukee, WI: Bruce Publishing Company, 1959), 315.

exist for those communities that had Eucharistic services during the week: "Ye muste note also, that the Collect, Epistle, and Gospell, appoynted for the Sundaie, shall serve all the weeke after, except there fall some feast that hath his propre."[18] This trend would continue for all subsequent editions of the Book of Common Prayer in both the Church of England through 1662 and the Episcopal Church through 1979. The number of commemorations for saints changed slightly. The 1549 edition had nineteen. The 1552 edition removed one, St. Mary Magdalene. The 1789 United States edition had twenty-one and then added one (Transfiguration) in 1892.

Thus, we can see that the strong emphasis on lectionary usage in the early prayer books of the Church of England and the Episcopal Church was in the Daily Office. We would expect this emphasis given the liturgical experience during that time. Weekly Eucharistic celebrations began to gain momentum with the second generation of the Oxford Movement in the nineteenth century. However, it would not be until the 1979 revision of the Book of Common Prayer in the Episcopal Church that the Eucharist would be described as ". . . the principal act of Christian worship on the Lord's day and other major Feasts. . . ."[19] Nonetheless, we will see that an emphasis upon the Eucharist begins to develop before 1979, at least in terms of the lectionary, if not in actual parish practice.

## What Are We Doing Now?

Following its final adoption of the 1928 edition of the Book of Common Prayer, the General Convention of the Episcopal Church created a "Standing Liturgical Commission," and charged it with the "preservation and study [of the] the liturgical experience and scholarship of the Church [in] all matters relating to the Book of

---

18. *The First and Second Prayer Books of Edward VI*, 8.
19. Book of Common Prayer (1979), 13.

Common Prayer [with the idea of] some possible further use." That body, which was renamed the "Standing Commission on Liturgy and Music" in 1997, continues to meet and has been the vehicle for a sustained and scholarly dialogue on the current and future shape of the liturgy ever since.[20] This dialogue took many shapes, but most notably it took the shape of the *Prayer Book Studies* series. This series laid the groundwork for the future 1979 revision of the prayer book. In addition, the General Convention of the Episcopal Church approved an alternative calendar for optional use in 1963 called *Lesser Feasts and Fasts*. This publication and its subsequent editions had a profound impact upon the sanctoral calendar as we will see below. The Eucharistic lectionary was also affected first by the 1979 revision of the prayer book and then by the later adoption of the Revised Common Lectionary. As we will see, these changes have provided far more options for lectionary usage but, arguably, far more complexity.

## *The Daily Office*

The lectionary for the Daily Office first underwent a revision in 1945. This revision did not affect the structure of the lectionary, but it did significantly affect the ordering of the readings. The lectionary of 1928 (and all previous editions) began with Genesis chapter one in Advent for Morning Prayer and I Kings for Evening Prayer. Then, with minimal interruptions, it proceeded through the books of the Hebrew Scriptures in a mostly ordered fashion. The second reading would alternate between an Epistle reading for Morning Prayer and a Gospel reading for Evening Prayer to vice versa in other months.

---

20. Edwin Augustine White and Jackson A. Dykman, *Annotated Constitution and Canons Adopted for the Government of the Protestant Episcopal Church in the United States of America, Otherwise Known as the Episcopal Church, Adopted in General Conventions, 1789–1979*, 2 vols. (New York: Church Publishing, 1981), 1:456–58.

Nonetheless, it followed a fairly, although not perfectly, consistent pattern through the Epistles and Gospels.[21]

The 1945 edition of the Daily Office lectionary changed the ordering significantly. For example, the lectionary in Advent begins with Isaiah, and it does not reference Genesis until the week after Septuagesima Sunday (the ninth Sunday before Easter, one of the three Sundays in a season of pre-Lent, which was dropped in the 1979 revision). Another significant change affected the Psalter. Instead of reading the Psalter through every month, chapters were assigned for each service each day.[22] Thus, we see what appears to be a shift toward a more thematic reading with the lessons being somewhat associated with the liturgical year and the psalms corresponding more closely to the lessons assigned.

The 1979 edition of the Book of Common Prayer would include a much more substantial structural change to the lectionary for the Daily Office. *Prayer Book Studies 27*, published in 1973, provided the first rationale for a revision of the Daily Office including its lectionary:

> The lectionary now presented to the Church is based upon the new arrangement of the Church Year, as set forth in *Prayer Book Studies 19* and reprinted in *Services for Trial Use*. It differs from the prayer book lectionary particularly with regard to Sundays, where the Office Readings were thematically related to the prayer book Epistles and Gospels; but the difference extends also to the weekdays, as a result of the suppression of the Season of Pre-Lent, and a corresponding increase in the length of the Season after Epiphany.... Unlike the eucharistic

---

21. "The 1928 U.S. Book of Common Prayer," http://justus.anglican.org/resources/Book of Common Prayer/1928/Lectionary_1928.pdf (accessed March 20, 2018).
22. Ibid.

lectionary for Sundays, which is arranged in a three-year cycle, the proposed lectionary follows a two-year cycle.[23]

Thus, one of the major changes to the Daily Office lectionary is the move from a one-year cycle of readings as found in the 1928 edition to a two-year cycle of readings in the 1979 edition. The first cycle, Year One, begins on the First Sunday of Advent preceding odd-numbered years, while the second cycle, Year Two, begins on the First Sunday of Advent preceding even-numbered years.[24]

Another major structural change was the move from four readings per day to only three readings per day. The option is given that all three readings may be read if the Office is prayed only once per day. If the Office is prayed twice per day and two readings are desired at both times, then the reading from the Hebrew Scriptures of the alternate year is used.[25] The 1979 edition of the prayer book does not provide a rationale for this substantive structural change. However, *Prayer Book Studies 27* would seem to offer a glimpse at a rationale when it states,

> On all Sundays, however, and on major Holy Days, the Psalms and Lessons appointed for the Eucharist may be substituted for those cited in the following tables. If desired, all three Eucharistic lections may be read at the Office. One or both of the Psalms appointed for the Eucharist may be used, and when only selected verses are cited in the Proper, the entire Psalm, or a longer portion of the Psalm, may be used.[26]

---

23. Episcopal Church, Standing Liturgical Commission, *Prayer Book Studies 27: The Daily Office Revised* (New York: Church Hymnal Corp, 1973), VI–VII.
24. Book of Common Prayer (1979), 934.
25. Ibid.
26. *Prayer Book Studies 27*, 84.

On weekdays, the reverse was possible. As *Prayer Book Studies 27* explained:

> A further factor in the case of weekdays is the permission given in *Services for Trial Use*, pp. 242 and 245 to use the Daily Office in the place of the Ministry of the Word at the Eucharist. In order that advantage may be taken of this possibility on weekdays, a passage from the Gospels is included as one of the Readings for each day, and the Gospel reading is available for use at either Morning or Evening Prayer, depending on the time of the Eucharistic celebration.[27]

Thus, we see a desire for interchangeability between the lectionary for the Daily Office and the lectionary for the Eucharist. The rubrics in the 1979 edition do not include either of these statement from *Prayer Book Studies 27*, though they are constructed in a manner that would permit them. The rubrics "Concerning the Lectionary" direct that "the Psalms and lessons appointed for the Sundays and for other major Holy Days are intended for use at all public services on such days, except when the same congregation attends two or more services. Thus, the same Lessons are to be read at the principle morning service, whether the Liturgy of the Word takes the form

---

27. The idea for use of the Daily Office lectionary for weekday celebrations of the Eucharist came from the ecumenical British Joint Liturgical Group, which provided the structural model—but not the actual lessons—for the Episcopal Church's Daily Office lectionary. The Joint Liturgical Group suggested that "in churches where it is customary to have a daily Eucharist it would be possible to use Year 1 for the Office and Year 2 for the Eucharist, both in the same year; then in the following year, the two cycles could be transposed." The Church of England did not adopt this provision in its 1980 *Alternative Service Book*. The American Book of Common Prayer 1979, however, allows use of the Daily Office lectionary on weekdays, when Daily Office is used as the liturgy of the word. See *The Daily Office by the Joint Liturgical Group* (London: SPCK, 1968), 36; *Prayer Book Studies 27*, viii; and Book of Common Prayer (1979), 36, 74.

given in the Holy Eucharist, or that of the Daily Office." In addition, the 1979 edition does permit the Office to be used for that portion of the Eucharist prior to the offertory, and, when this is done, there is no prohibition against following the advice of *Prayer Book Studies 27* and using the office's lectionary on weekdays.[28]

In addition to this possibility of great interchangeability, the Daily Office lectionary in the 1979 edition of the prayer book increases the sanctoral calendar. The 1945 edition had nineteen fixed feast days, while the 1979 edition raised that number to thirty-one with an additional seven propers for the eve of significant feast days.[29]

## The Eucharist

While the changes to the lectionary for the Daily Office were substantial, the changes to the lectionary for the Eucharist were even more so. Due to the complexity of these changes, I will address three separate, yet interweaving units within the Eucharistic lectionary: the Sunday lectionary, the weekday lectionary, and the sanctoral lectionary.

The Sunday Eucharistic lectionary went through its first major revision in the 1979 edition of the prayer book. All previous editions utilized only two readings for the Eucharist. The first reading was typically from the Epistles but occasionally came from the Hebrew Scriptures. The second reading was always a selection from the Gospels. In addition, the lectionary cycle was only one year.[30] With the 1979 edition, two major structural changes occurred. First, the readings increased from two to three readings. Now,

---

28. Book of Common Prayer (1979), 36, 888.
29. Ibid., 996–1000.
30. "Collects, Epistles, and Gospels to Be Used Throughout the Year," http://justus.anglican.org/resources/Book of Common Prayer/1789/collects_epistles_gospels_1789&1892.htm (accessed March 20, 2018).

the first reading was typically from the Hebrew Scriptures (except in Eastertide when it would come from the Acts of the Apostles). The second reading was from the Epistles, and the third reading was from the Gospels. In addition, though, the cycle of readings increased from one year to three years.[31] Considering that the 1979 edition of the prayer book describes the Eucharist as ". . . the principal act of Christian worship on the Lord's Day and other major Feasts . . ." and the older pattern of Morning Prayer preceding Ante-Communion or Holy Communion was fading away, this new lectionary greatly increased the exposure of the Sunday worshiper to scripture.

However, another change would come. In 2007, the General Convention of the Episcopal Church authorized the Revised Common Lectionary to replace the lectionary found in the prayer book effective Advent 2007 with a provision for continued use of the previous lectionary until Advent 2010.[32] The Revised Common Lectionary is a product of two ecumenical bodies, the North American Consultation on Common Texts and the International English Language Liturgical Consultation. They first produced a lectionary in 1983 based on the Roman Lectionary for Mass of 1969. They then revised and republished it in 1992.[33] Like the prayer book Eucharistic lectionary, the Revised Common Lectionary provides three readings over a three-year cycle. The first reading from Advent 1 through Trinity Sunday was selected to match thematically with the Gospel. However, after Trinity Sunday through Christ the King Sunday, the Revised Common Lectionary provides two tracks for the first reading and responsorial psalm. The first track

---

31. Book of Common Prayer (1979), 888.
32. General Convention, *Journal of the General Convention of . . . the Episcopal Church, Columbus, 2006* (New York: General Convention, 2007), 466.
33. Consultation on Common Texts, "The Revised Common Lectionary," http://www.commontexts.org/rcl (accessed March 20, 2018).

is a somewhat continuous reading through passages in the Hebrew Scriptures independent of the Gospel reading. The second track attempts to retain the thematic harmony between the first reading and the Gospel reading.[34] Thus, the choices for readings from the Sunday Eucharistic lectionary have increased from two readings to three readings with a psalm in the 1979 Book of Common Prayer and then to the potential for four readings plus two psalms in the Revised Common Lectionary. This change both widens choices and increases complexity.

A weekday Eucharistic lectionary outside of the sanctoral calendar did not exist for the Episcopal Church until *Lesser Feasts and Fasts 1973*, which added "The Collects, Psalms, and Lessons for the Weekdays in Lent" only for the season of Lent. It consists of two psalms, a lesson from the Acts of the Apostles, and a lesson from the Gospel According to John.[35] *Lesser Feasts and Fasts 1994* then added, "The Weekdays of Advent and Christmas until the Baptism of Christ." The first lessons come from Isaiah, Sirach, and 1 John.[36] *Lesser Feasts and Fasts 1997* then adds two additional weekday Eucharistic lectionaries, "A Six-Week Eucharistic Lectionary with Daily Themes and Suggested Collects" and "A Two-Year Weekday Eucharistic Lectionary *(Adapted from* The Book of Alternative Services *of the Anglican Church of Canada).*" Two daily readings are provided. The Two-Year Weekday Eucharistic Lectionary does provide a more extensive range of scriptural readings.[37] These weekday lectionaries compare almost identically with only small variations

---

34. Consultation on Common Texts, "The Revised Common Lectionary," http://www.commontexts.org/wp-content/uploads/2015/11/RCL_Introduction_Web.pdf, 3 (accessed March 20, 2018).
35. *Lesser Feasts and Fasts 1973*, 19–32.
36. *Lesser Feasts and Fasts 1994*, 19–26.
37. *Lesser Feasts and Fasts 1997*, 467–98.

in the verse numbers assigned to *The Lectionary for Mass* from the Roman Missal.[38]

The sanctoral calendar experienced a very significant change beginning in 1963 with the publication of *Lesser Feasts and Fasts*. Initially, the desire to provide additional propers for minor feast days (also known as "black letter days") was to allow for greater variety in the lectionary during the week when the propers for Sunday were simply repeated unless there was a major (or "red letter") feast day. *Prayer Book Studies XII* suggested an additional forty fixed days and twenty-eight days having to do with Ember and Rogation Days and Octaves of Easter and Whitsunday with full propers.[39] With the publication of *Lesser Feasts and Fasts* in 1963, the number of commemorations went up to 136.[40] That is a 523 percent increase in commemorations. This number would continue to increase substantially with future editions of *Lesser Feasts and Fasts*, eventually leading to a total of 305 days of commemoration celebrating the lives of 345 saints in *Holy Women, Holy Men*. Chart 1 graphically displays this substantial increase in the *sanctoral* calendar.

This increase in the sanctoral calendar has an equal impact on the Eucharistic lectionary during the week, but not on Sundays as none of these commemorations may replace the Sunday liturgy or any other principle feast day.[41] If a community were to choose to commemorate all the feast days found in *Holy Women, Holy Men*,

---

38. Catholic Church, *Lectionary for Mass: English Translation Approved by the National Conference of Catholic Bishops and Confirmed by the Apostolic See; Bible Texts from the Jerusalem Bible* (New York: Benziger, 1970), 232–650.

39. Episcopal Church, Standing Liturgical Commission, *Prayer Book Studies XII: The Propers for the Minor Holy Days* (New York: Church Pension Fund, 1958), 39–41.

40. *Lesser Feasts and Fasts 1963*.

41. Book of Common Prayer (1979), 15–18.

## Chart 1
### Number of Days of Commemoration & Saints

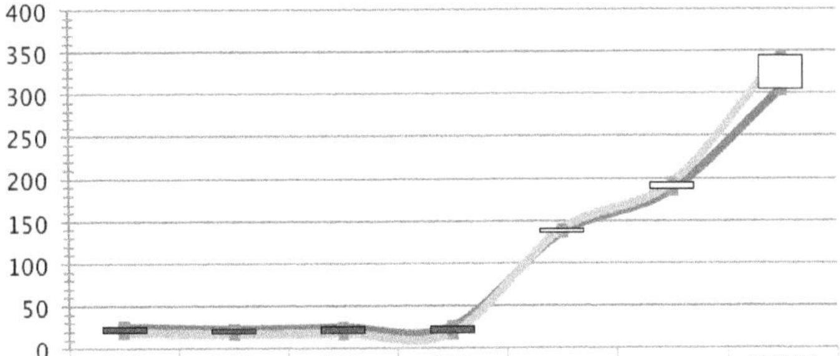

| | BCP 1662 | BCP 1789 | BCP 1892 | BCP 1928 | LFF 1963 | LFF 2006 | HWHM 2010 |
|---|---|---|---|---|---|---|---|
| # of Days of Commemoration | 26 | 23 | 25 | 26 | 136 | 187 | 305 |
| # of Saints | 19 | 17 | 18 | 18 | 140 | 195 | 345 |

the range of scriptural exposure would be greatly limited as indicated by charts 2, 3, and 4.

As stated above, the changes in the lectionaries of the Episcopal Church since 1928 have offered both greater choices and greater complexity. The lectionary for the Daily Office now permits the worshiper to select from among three readings for the day. However, if the worshiper chooses to pray both Offices and desires two lessons at each Office, then the worshiper must select a fourth reading from the lectionary of the alternate year. Furthermore, the readings in the Daily Office follow a more thematic pattern than the semi-continuous pattern of earlier editions of the prayer book.

The Eucharistic lectionary now has the greatest number of choices and the greatest complexity. The current Sunday Eucharistic lectionary authorized in the Episcopal Church is the Revised Common Lectionary, which has a three-year lectionary and provides two alternate tracks for the first reading and responsorial psalm from the Sunday after Trinity to Christ the King Sunday. Only principal feast days can intrude upon a Sunday, however. The

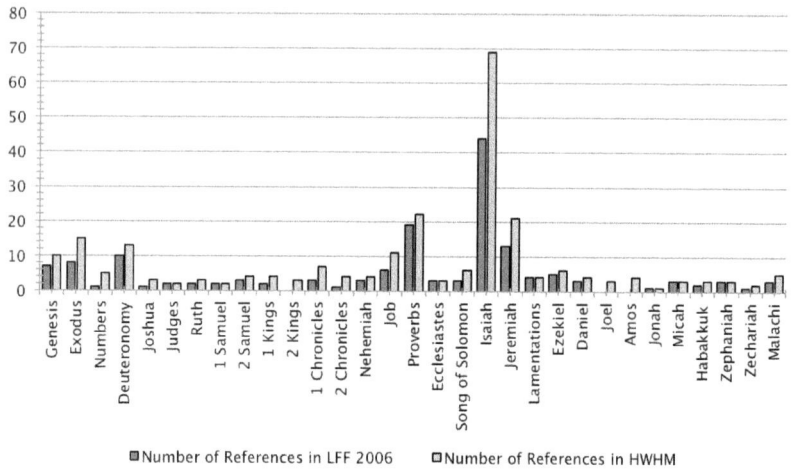

**Chart 2**
**Number of OT References in LESSER FEASTS AND FASTS 2006 and HOLY WOMEN, HOLY MEN**

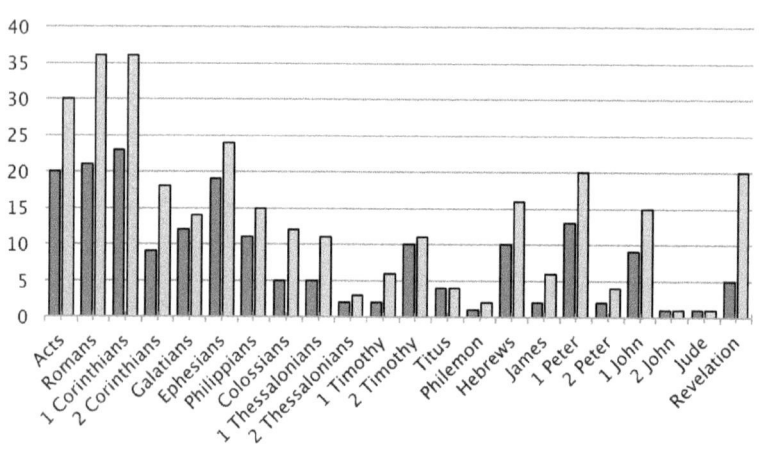

**Chart 3**
**Number of Epistle References in LESSER FEASTS AND FASTS 2006 and HOLY WOMEN, HOLY MEN**

## Chart 4
### Number of Gospel References in LESSER FEASTS AND FASTS 2006 and HOLY WOMEN, HOLY MEN

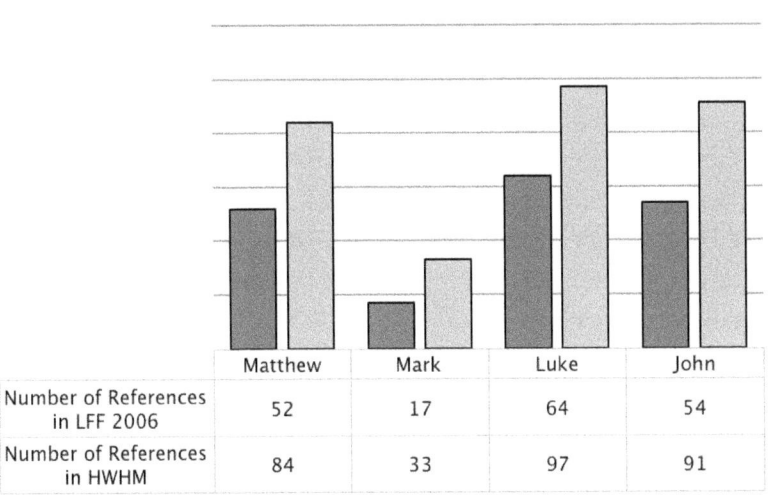

|  | Matthew | Mark | Luke | John |
|---|---|---|---|---|
| Number of References in LFF 2006 | 52 | 17 | 64 | 54 |
| Number of References in HWHM | 84 | 33 | 97 | 91 |

weekday Eucharistic lectionary is the most complicated lectionary. The worshiper must select from four weekday lectionaries depending upon the liturgical season and choice of theme or sequence. Then, with 305 days of commemoration proposed in *Holy Women, Holy Men*, the worshiper would have a separate proper for nearly each day of the year.

The recent publication of *Weekday Eucharistic Propers* helps organize these lectionaries. It has three sections. The first is the proper lessons, and sometimes full propers, for the seasons of Advent, Christmastide, Lent, Eastertide, and the two-year and six-week weekday lectionaries for the rest of the church year as found in *Holy Women, Holy Men*.[42] The second section includes the propers

---

42. *Weekday Eucharistic Propers* (New York: Church Publishing, 2017), 3–117.

for the sanctoral cycle. These propers come from the Common of Saints in the Book of Common Prayer (1979), as well as New Common of Saints, including a Common of Artists, Writers, and Composers, Common of the Blessed Virgin Mary, Godbearer, Common of Prophetic Witness in the Church, Common of Prophetic Witness in Society, and Common of Scientists and Environmentalists.[43] The final section is propers for Various Occasions from the Book of Common Prayer (1979) as well as new propers including Care of God's Creation, Goodness of God's Creation, On the Occasion of a Disaster, On the Anniversary of a Disaster, Reconciliation and Forgiveness, and Space Exploration.[44] While this resource helps organize the various lectionaries into a single volume, it does not answer the important questions regarding priorities, especially concerning the sanctoral cycle. *Lesser Feasts and Fasts* 2006 remains the official sanctoral calendar of the Episcopal Church as *Holy Women, Holy Men* and *A Great Cloud of Witnesses* have been approved only as resources. The SCLM cannot determine the status of these various resources, only General Convention can.

## Where Do We Go from Here?

The current state of the lectionaries in the Episcopal Church is a far cry from the simplicity desired in the preface to the 1549 Book of Common Prayer. Although one does not need the equivalent of the Pie to determine the proper commemorations and their readings yet, one can imagine such a need if further complexities are introduced. Would such further complexities serve the needs of the church? To answer that question, one must first consider the purpose

---

43. *Weekday Eucharistic Propers*, 122–35 for the Book of Common Prayer (1979) Commons and 136–41 for the new Commons.
44. *Weekday Eucharistic Propers*, 142–74 for the Book of Common Prayer (1979) various occasions and 175–80 for the new various occasions.

of the lectionary. Is its purpose to provide a semicontinuous reading of scripture for the edification of the personal worshiper? Or is its purpose to provide thematic readings for the indicated liturgical contexts? The answers to these questions will greatly determine future reforms of the lectionaries. I will not attempt to answer these questions, as they require the discernment of the entire church. However, to provide some avenues for reform, I will offer three possible approaches: reduction for simplicity, focus on a single challenge at a time, or a complete overhaul. None of these approaches is without benefits and challenges.

*Reduction for Simplicity*

The simplest, but by no means easiest, solution to the current complexity of the lectionary is to reduce it. The most effective lectionary currently in use that could fit most of the needs of the liturgical rites would be the Daily Office lectionary. It provides three lessons that could be used for the Eucharist. It has propers for the principle feast days and even some vigil observances. The minor feast days could return to using the propers of the day or Common of the Saints as suggested in *A Great Cloud of Witnesses*.[45]

The benefits of this approach include the simplicity of a single two-year lectionary with additional propers for special occasions. Furthermore, the readings in the lectionary would retain their own internal harmony. They also follow a semicontinuous reading of scripture. If a more thoroughly continuous reading of scripture was desired, the lectionary from the 1928 Book of Common Prayer could be revived.

However, several challenges exist with this option. First, this option would uncouple the Episcopal Church from the ecumenical Revised Common Lectionary during a time when greater

---

45. *A Great Cloud of Witnesses*, XIII–XIV.

ecumenical engagement is occurring. Furthermore, communities that pray both Offices and the Eucharist daily would not have sufficient lessons even when using the lessons from the alternate year. At least one lesson would have to be sacrificed. Finally, this approach does not allow for the lessons to speak most directly to the liturgical event, particularly the saint being commemorated.

## Focus on a Single Challenge at a Time

Another approach is to focus on a single challenge at a time. The members of the SCLM appeared to haven taken this approach with its publication of *A Great Cloud of Witnesses*, focusing first on the challenge of the complexity of the current sanctoral calendar and its impact on the weekday Eucharistic lectionary. By removing propers for each commemoration and encouraging the use of the weekday Eucharistic lectionaries and/or Common of Saints as found in *A Great Cloud of Witnesses*, the SCLM is focusing on that single challenge first.

The benefit of this approach is that it allows the church to consider a single issue deeply. It also avoids a simple, but perhaps unnuanced, approach to the problem. As shown above, the sanctoral calendar has had the biggest impact upon the lectionary of all other components. Focusing on this challenge first allows the church to decide the relative importance of the sanctoral calendar in its life, at least in terms of the lectionary.

This approach also involves challenges. First, by focusing on a single challenge at a time, the church may lose sight of the big picture. Will challenges met with one lectionary then pose new challenges for other lectionaries? If the church discerns that the primary purpose of the lectionary is to provide thematic readings for the liturgical event rather than a semicontinuous reading of scripture, these challenges are not as important. However, if the church discerns the opposite priority, they pose a greater problem.

The SCLM's Blue Book Report submitted early in 2018 suggests, moreover, that members of the commission may be of mixed minds about the direction taken in 2015. Rather than suggesting that *A Great Cloud of Witnesses* or some edited version of that document replace *Lesser Feast and Fast 2006* as the church's official sanctoral calendar—as the SCLM had done in 2015—the 2018 SCLM report suggested retaining *A Great Cloud of Witnesses* as a volume of local celebrations (for which no propers for new individuals would be suggested) and creating a *Lesser Feasts and Fasts 2018* that would contain multiple new additions (for which propers were suggested).

## Complete Overhaul

The final approach would be a complete overhaul of the lectionaries. This would include the lectionaries for the Daily Office, Sunday Eucharist, weekday Eucharist, and the sanctoral calendar. Again, the primary purpose for the lectionaries would need to be clearly discerned to provide guiding principles for the overhaul.

The benefits of this approach would include a comprehensive lectionary reform. With the experience of past lectionary reforms, this approach could produce more simplified and yet also robust lectionaries for the church's use. It would provide an integration to all the church's liturgical services through its lectionaries.

However, the challenges are great. The first and greatest challenge is the time, effort, and resources needed for such a complete overhaul. Does the church have the needed resources now? Also, this overhaul would remove the Episcopal Church from the ecumenical Revised Common Lectionary as with the simplified approach. In addition, given the Episcopal Church's lifelong tension between Catholic and Protestant theologies, could the primary purpose of the lectionary be discerned?

## Conclusion

The lectionaries of the church are an important tool for the church. Whether they are meant to provide continuous formation in scripture or the scriptural context for a liturgical event, they are still necessary. The current trend of greater complexity with the lectionaries does not seem sustainable unless the church intends to reach the point of its medieval predecessors. Therefore, some type of reform is necessary. The best approach to that reform, however, may still need to be discerned, though perhaps by the time of the publication of this essay the 2018 General Convention will have made progress in that direction.

# 9

# Burial Rites

## Patrick Malloy[1]

Religion, it has been said, is the human response to the problem of death, and, indeed, death stands at the heart of the Christian proclamation. The Christian narrative hinges on a specific death, God's saving response to it, and the hope that all humanity will share in the glory of the Risen Christ. In the face of human death, Christianity holds forth the life revealed in Jesus and offers it as the antidote, as Paul says, to the sin of Adam by which all die.

But how the resurrection of Jesus is brought to bear upon the death of others has never been settled in Christianity. "What must I do to be saved?" has for much of Christian history been translated as, "What must I do to transcend death as Jesus did?" The conquest of death is but one aspect of a full Christian understanding of salvation, but it is central. Historical-critical biblical scholars suggest that it is the key piece, the cornerstone, of the entire Christian

---

1. The Reverend Canon Patrick Malloy, PhD, is the Sub-Dean at the Cathedral Church of St. John the Divine in New York City. From 2009 to 2015, he was the Professor of Liturgy at the General Theological Seminary.

narrative. The Gospels cannot be read as history in the modern sense but, rather, must be understood as reflections on the life of the historical Jesus viewed through the lens of the church's experience of the risen Christ. The church's experience of the resurrected Jesus shaped the hermeneutic that produced the Gospel narratives and, consequently, the hermeneutic for properly understanding the received texts. The believing reader, like the biblical writers, views the life of Jesus, including his death, from the safe vantage point of death overcome.

The Christian narrative's claim is that God, in conquering the mortality of the One, made the victory available to all. How, though, is death conquered for those who came before Jesus in history and, more to the point, how is it solved for those who have come since? How is it conquered for us and for those whom we love who are torn from our embrace by death? What must those after Jesus' glorification do to share in the power of his resurrection? And what, exactly, is this risen life of which Jesus is the first fruits? Concern for such questions have informed the shaping and revising of the burial office in the various editions of the Book of Common Prayer.

## The Reformation and the First Books of Common Prayer

The question of how one merits a share in Jesus' conquest of death and the "mechanics" of what happens to a human being after death was so integral to the debates of the sixteenth-century Reformation that it is reasonable to view the entire Reformation as a revolution in the Christian understanding of the afterlife and the criteria by which a person can attain eternal blessedness. Whether, for example, faith or works saves—a central Reformation debate, if not *the* central one—is precisely the question of how one achieves eternal joy and escapes eternal damnation. The famous argument over the sale of indulgences but, more to the point, the view of the afterlife upon which indulgences were predicated, brings us again to the problem of death and speculation about how to solve it. So, too, does the question of whether the Eucharist may be celebrated to the benefit of the dead. It would be impossible to review any of the great debates of the sixteenth century and not come eventually to the question of what the afterlife is like and how one can move toward it with hope. Even the question of the nature of the ordained ministry comes around to this question. Is the ordained minister a sacrificing priest, making offerings for the living and the dead, or are the dead beyond the reach of the living, ordained or not?

In most of the reformation churches, prayer for the dead (and even more, prayer *to* the dead, that is, to the saints) was not only rejected but also systematically suppressed. The Church of England in Article XXII of the Thirty Nine Articles taught officially and succinctly, "The Romish Doctrine concerning Purgatory, Pardons, Worshipping and Adoration, as well of Images as of Relics, and also Invocation of Saints, is a fond thing, vainly invented, and grounded upon no warranty of Scripture, but rather repugnant to the Word of God."[2] With this one sentence, the English Church dismantled (or at least tried to dismantle) a great deal of the medieval sacramental system and condemned a key medieval enterprise: prayer to the dead.

More than that, it remapped the afterlife. Purgatory, once imagined as so real that Dante devoted a third of his trilogy to it and described it in topographic detail, was reduced to no more than an illusion. In an age when the reality of Purgatory was as certain as, in our age, the reality of Antarctica, the claim that it simply does not exist was revolutionary. And in an age when Christian piety centered on praying and doing good works for the dead, it must have created utter disorientation among believers. To think, in medieval terms, of one's loved ones suffering a temporary fiery purgation

---

2. Book of Common Prayer (1979), 872.

would have given birth to anxiety, but probably even more anxiety would have come from the Reformation claim that you can do absolutely nothing to care for the dead whom you love, nor, after your death, can those you leave behind do anything for you.

Some have argued that denying the reality of Purgatory, which would seem to preclude prayer for the dead, did not really preclude anything in the English Church. In an earlier draft of Article XXII, prayer for the dead was explicitly rejected, but that clause was stripped out before the final version was authorized.[3] This suggests that not all those in authority, whether ecclesiastical or civil, objected to praying for the departed. Indeed, prayer for the dead seems to have continued in England to the present age, even if in unauthorized ways, and so throughout the Anglican Communion.

It has also been argued that the burial office in the prayer book, in all of its editions, actually has always contained prayers for the dead, but it is hard to see where. Even if Article XXII does not absolutely and explicitly preclude prayer for the dead, the prayer book eventually did abandon it.

The prayer book's burial office, like many of its rites, moved edition-by-edition from reflecting the medieval theology to imposing the Reformation consensus. The 1549 Book of Common Prayer, the first prayer book, included a funeral Eucharist and psalms to be said as "suffrages" for the dead. Both were excised from the second edition of the prayer book in 1552.

Comparing the 1549 and 1552 texts for the casting of earth upon the body, for example, further shows the significant shift between these two editions. In the 1549 version, the priest says, "I commend thy soul to God the Father Almighty, and thy body to the

---

3. A compact discussion of the history of prayer for the dead among post-Reformation Anglicans, which provides evidence that it was never forbidden, is given in: Paul A. Welsby, "Prayer for the Dead," *Theology* 69, no. 552 (June 1966): 244–51.

ground, earth to earth, ashes to ashes, dust to dust. . . ." The 1552 version has only, "Forasmuch as it hath pleased Almighty God of his great mercy to take unto himself the soul of our dear brother here departed: we therefore commit his body to the ground, earth to earth, ashes to ashes, dust to dust. . . ."[4] The first text is addressed to the deceased, while the second to the liturgical assembly. Too, the earlier text commends both the (soul of the) dead person to God and the body to the ground, while the later commends only the body to the ground. The line between the living and the dead is drawn more clearly in the later text, and the notion of intercession or action on their behalf is rejected by omission. American editions of the Book of Common Prayer from 1789 to 1928 added an eschatological reference to the committal, which made it clear that the line between the living and the dead would remain until Christ's second coming "in glorious majesty to judge the world," at which point the "the earth and the sea shall give up their dead" and they would join the living for final judgment and reward or punishment.[5]

Both 1549 and 1552 include the Kyrie and the Lord's Prayer in the burial office, but then the two diverge. The earlier book moves to a series of versicles and responses that are an unambiguous prayer for the dead. "Enter not, O Lord, into judgment with thy servant / for in thy sight no living creature shall be justified. From the gates of hell / deliver their souls, O Lord." The later book, however, removes all of this.[6]

---

4. The First and Second Prayer Books of Edward VI (London: J. M. Dent & Sons, Everyman's Library, 1910), 424–25.
5. Book of Common Prayer (1928), 333.
6. The one collect in 1552 that is taken by some to be an oblique prayer for the dead can be read that way only with a greatly nuanced and, I would suggest, biased hermeneutic. The collect's petition is: ". . . that it may please thee of thy gracious goodness shortly to accomplish the number of thine elect, and to haste thy kingdom, that we with this our brother, and all other departed in the true faith of thy holy name, may have our perfect consummation

## The 1928 Books of Common Prayer

Liturgy, as powerful as it is, cannot by fiat conquer long-standing cultural patterns and primal urges. The human desire and—one could argue—the Christian impulse to pray for the dead was, indeed, not conquered by the 1552 rite. Unofficially, it seems never to have stopped, and eventually it entered again into the official prayer of the church. The American 1928 prayer book reintroduced prayers for the dead in an ambiguous prayer near the end of the burial office that the dead person might "go from strength to strength in the life of perfect service." The petition concerning the dead in the Prayer for the Whole State of Christ's Church in the Eucharist, which had previously simply blessed God for the example they had provided, was reworked along similar lines, asking God to "grant them continual growth in . . . love and service."[7] Neither prayer was entirely clear about when this growth was to take place—after the anticipated return of Christ on the last day or at some point between death and resurrection.

Two new prayers in the graveside service included petitions for the dead in more traditional terms, although only as an option. After the Lord's Prayer in the burial office, the minister was instructed to say one or more of three collects. Two were from Cranmer's 1552 rite, but now a new collect was added before them:

---

and bliss, both in body and soul, in thy eternal and everlasting glory." This asks, in a general way, for the consummation of the eschatological hope and presumes the salvation of the elect, among whom it hopes the deceased is numbered. It does not ask that the deceased be so numbered but wishes for it. Moreover, this text cannot be seen in isolation from the other texts in the burial rite. The changes between 1549 and 1552 are all in one direction, and it would be hard to understand why every other allusion to prayer for the dead was excised if this collect is, in fact, that very thing. Cranmer's intention was to suppress, at least in the liturgy, prayer for the dead.
7. Book of Common Prayer (1928), 74–75, 332, and Book of Common Prayer (1892).

O God, whose mercies cannot be numbered; Accept our prayers on behalf of the soul of thy servant departed, and grant *him* an entrance into the land of light and joy, in the fellowship of thy saints; through Jesus Christ our Lord. *Amen.*[8]

This collect was also included with the set of propers (a collect, lessons, and in some cases a proper preface) for use with burial, which was added in the 1928 prayer book.[9] A new fourth prayer was also added at the beginning of the optional prayers printed following the blessing.[10] Like the new collect before the blessing, this addition was an unapologetic prayer for the dead.

These prayers were not required, so the entire burial office could be celebrated with only the petition about going from "strength to strength." Still, the insertion of the two new prayers in the graveside service and the possible use of one of them in a celebration of the Eucharist show a marked departure from Cranmer's program and a return to the pre-Reformation and, in truth, the primitive practice of praying for the dead.

In the same year, 1928, a new edition of the prayer book was proposed for the Church of England, not to replace but to enrich the 1662 book, the edition then in force.[11] More than three-fourths of the members of the church's governing bodies—like the General Convention of the Episcopal Church—accepted it. Parliament, however, rejected it, largely because the objections of the dissenting one-fourth, representing both the Catholic and Evangelical wings, were so strong. So the 1662 book—whose burial office was like that

---

8. Book of Common Prayer (1928), 334.
9. Ibid., 268–69.
10. Ibid., 335–36.
11. Had the book been approved, it would have been subtitled, "The Book of 1662 with Additions and Deviations Approved in 1928." See *The Book of Common Prayer with the Additions and Deviations Proposed in 1928* (Oxford: Oxford University Press, n.d.), v.

of 1552 except for the insertion of two psalms after the body was borne into the church—remained and remains the official liturgy in England. Yet, the 1928 proposed English Book of Common Prayer reflected a marked shift. It reappropriated even more prayer for the dead than the Episcopal Church's 1928 edition. The text for when earth is cast upon the body, for example, was not the 1552 version but a modest reworking of the 1549, which not only committed the body to the earth, but also commended the person to God. The versicles and responses were returned to their place after the Lord's Prayer and, as in the American book, a prayer specifically for the dead person was included as an option among the collects.[12]

In addition to the book's prayer for the dead, also striking was its acknowledgement of the Communion of Saints within the burial rites. After the burial collects, the collect for All Saints' Day was given as an option, as was a collect that referred to the church as "those who believe and trust in the Communion of Saints."[13] The line between the living and the dead, drawn in 1552 and still solid in the 1662 book, was being erased.

In Cranmer's 1552 Book of Common Prayer, perhaps the most revolutionary move had been the suppression of the funeral Eucharist. In the English proposed 1928 prayer book, a rubric referred to "a special celebration of the Holy Communion on the day of the Burial" and provided texts for it. It allowed for the collect for Easter Even and a number of lections, which highlighted the hope of new life through the Paschal Mystery of Christ. If the 1549 Book of Common Prayer was a bridge to move Anglicans from medieval to reformation religion, the 1928 prayer books, both in the United States and in England, were meant to walk Anglicans at least partway back. Unlike the medieval funeral texts, however, which took a rather pessimistic view of the afterlife and focused on the "day of

---

12. Ibid., 478–81.
13. Ibid., 481.

wrath," the texts that were emerging in the Anglican Communion emphasized the "sure and certain hope of the resurrection to eternal life through our Lord Jesus Christ."[14] Undeniably, this was a return to the most ancient Christian attitude toward death. This rehabilitation of ancient burial customs and notions of the afterlife did not arise in a vacuum. The force of the nineteenth-century Oxford Movement, along with the subsequent Cambridge Movement and the work of the so-called ritualists, began the recovery of aspects of Christian belief and practice, which the proponents of these movements claimed had been wrongly jettisoned at the Reformation. Prayer for the dead was central to what they believed the church had unwisely discarded. "Recovery" is not quite the right word, though. *Doctrine in the Church of England: The Report of the Commission on Christian Doctrine Appointed by the Archbishops of Canterbury and York in 1922* admitted that "the practice [of praying for the dead] has never entirely died out in the Church of England."[15] While especially the Evangelical members of the church had consistently condemned it, and the prayer book itself did not allow for it, the instinct to pray for the dead had not been conquered and had never gone unexpressed.

More than movements in theology and Anglican liturgical style, however, set the stage for prayer for the dead to come into plain sight in the liturgy. *Doctrine in the Church of England* admits that terrible losses "in times of great distress, such as those of war," had moved the church from treating prayer for the dead as a matter for theological debate to seeing it as a matter of pastoral exigency.[16] The unimaginable number of deaths in the Boer War (1899–

---

14. Ibid., 478; and Book of Common Prayer (1928), 333.
15. Commission on Christian Doctrine, *Doctrine in the Church of England (1938): The Report of the Commission on Christian Doctrine Appointed by the Archbishops of Canterbury and York* (London: SPCK, 1938), 215.
16. Ibid., 216.

1902) and World War I (1914–1937) had made acute the yearning of the English heart to intercede on behalf of the dead. This instinct could not be dismissed as heretical or impious, especially when, as the document claimed, such prayer had really always been part of English church life. More significantly, it had been universally practiced since at least the second century.

The document's theological statement about prayer for the dead is worth quoting, since it steers a classically Anglican middle path between the Roman notion of a punitive purgatory and the Protestant notion of a static afterlife.[17]

> All Christian prayer aims at being prayer that God's will may be done; Prayer for the Departed is not, any more than any other prayer, an attempt to persuade or suggest to God some action that was not already His will to take. If there is any such fellowship of living and departed as Christians have always believed, and if the thought of growth and of purification after death is not to be dogmatically excluded, there is no theological objection in principle to Prayer for the Departed. The question of the safeguards that may wisely be imposed in any given circumstances belongs to the realm not of theology, but of pastoral exigency.[18]

---

17. The following section of the Commission's report, however, dealt not with differences between Rome and the Protestants of the Reformation but between what it identified as the "traditional" and "Evangelical" view ("a particular Judgment immediately after death, the general Judgment at the general Resurrection," with the understanding that "the period of open choices closes with death") and a Liberal universalist position ("a general expectation of further opportunities [after death] of grace for all" with the hope that no "soul will suffer final loss"). See ibid., 216–18, and subsection (1) "The Question of Who Can Be Saved" in the final section of this chapter.

18. Commission, *Doctrine*, 216.

Here, the transforming process a Christian experiences after death is imagined, not as punishment, but as growth and purification. The use of the word "growth" to describe the experience of the saints after death will echo in the minds of Episcopalians since it is how the catechism of the 1979 prayer book justifies prayer for the dead: the church prays for them as they continue their growth into the fullness God intends for them.[19]

At least as striking as the defense of prayer for the dead in *Doctrine of the Church of England* is its positive attitude toward prayer *to* the dead. "The Communion of Saints," the document says, "is apprehended as a fellowship of mutual intercession," where all pray to God on behalf of all the others, but it goes further. Just as importantly, "it is impossible to declare that departed saints cannot hear our prayers, and we therefore must not condemn as impossible direct address to them as a private practice, provided this be to ask for their prayers whether for ourselves or for others; anything other than this seems to us both perilous and illegitimate. But also it is impossible to have well-grounded assurance that the saints hear us, so that direct address to them may well be thought inappropriate in the official worship of the Church."[20] This balance between defending private prayer to the dead and rejecting public prayer to them shaped the English proposed 1928 book. Even as it included prayer *for* the dead, it never prayed *to* them.

Despite Parliament's rejection of the proposed 1928 prayer book, it was used in many English parishes. Many bishops authorized it in their dioceses as what we would call "supplemental texts," and to this day the proposed 1928 book is sometimes used. When next the English Church set out to renew the liturgy, it did so in accordance with the 1975 Worship and Doctrine Measure, which had been negotiated with the Parliament. According to the measure, the

---

19. Book of Common Prayer (1979), 862.
20. Commission, *Doctrine*, 214–15.

church created not a new edition of the prayer book, which would have required state approval, but *The Alternative Service Book 1980* (ASB).[21] This book, as well as the more recent *Common Worship*, does not supplant the 1662 Book of Common Prayer. The 1662 book remains the Book of Common Prayer of the Church of England. English Anglicans, however, are free to use these alternative resources in place of the 1662 book (in the same way that American Episcopalians, with the permission of the diocesan bishop, can use the *Enriching Our Worship* materials), and they commonly do. The funeral services in both books show all the marks of the proposed 1928 book, and enrich it with an extensive collection of lections, psalms, collects, and other material. It is virtually impossible to celebrate these rites without praying for the dead. So, despite the rejection of Parliament in 1928, the intent of the burial office in the Proposed 1928 Book of Common Prayer has gained official status.

## The Book of Common Prayer (1979)

In the American 1979 Book of Common Prayer and, by extension, the supplemental materials that have followed it, the journey begun in both England and the United States has progressed. In the 1979 book, while we find the texts and emphases of the classically Protestant 1552 Book of Common Prayer, we see as well the tradition-rooted and Catholic texts and emphases of the 1549 Book of Common Prayer. The 1979 rites to mark death, however, are not merely an amalgamation or a compromise between two competing views. They are the ritual embodiment of a theology that

---

21. The preface to the new liturgy explained that "this new book of services is the first fully authorized alternative to the Book of Common Prayer. Under the terms of the 1975 Worship and Doctrine Measure, from which services now derive their legal status, the Book of Common Prayer retains its authority as a doctrinal standard." See "Preface," in *The Alternative Service Book 1980* (London: Hodder and Stoughton, 1980), 10.

transcends sixteenth-century polarities by drawing freely upon what is primitive and what is new. The 1979 prayer book notes, "The liturgy for the dead is an Easter liturgy. It finds all its meaning in the resurrection. Because Jesus was raised from the dead, we, too, shall be raised."[22]

Easter liturgy, of course, is baptismal liturgy. The entire season of Lent builds toward the baptisms at the Great Vigil of Easter, and the entire fifty days of Easter are a prolongation of that single baptism-focused night. Saying that the burial liturgy is an Easter liturgy means that the "baptismal ecclesiology" central to the 1979 Book of Common Prayer is fully expressed in the burial rites, especially when options provided within the rites and the material in *Enriching Our Worship* are fully exploited. The rites are not the recapturing of bits and pieces of old liturgies but the expression of the 1979 prayer book's coherent baptismal theology.

In the catechism's treatment of "The Christian Hope," the question is asked, "Why do we pray for the dead?" The answer is reminiscent of the 1922 doctrinal statement of the English Church.

> We pray for them, because we still hold them in our love, and because we trust in God's presence those who have chosen to serve him will grow in his love, until they see him as he is.[23]

The afterlife of "those who have chosen to serve" God is imagined as growth, not stasis.[24] Since God is infinitely more than mortals (even mortals who have moved into "the greater life"), it is not unreasonable to see the afterlife, not merely as growth, but as eternal growth. Always there is more to "see" of the Infinite One, even

---

22. Book of Common Prayer (1979), 507.
23. Ibid., 862.
24. See note 16. The 1979 catechism presumes an essential choice for God before death, and does not make the universalist assumption that "the period of open choices" extends into the afterlife.

unto eternity. So the church on earth can rightly pray for those in every age who have died, even those who are unknown to us and unnamed, even those who died millennia ago.

## Ecumenical and Inter-Anglican Developments

The rites related to death in the 1979 Book of Common Prayer must be understood not only in light of the history out of which they emerged and the theological threads that weave through the entire prayer book, but also the ecumenical conversations that have brought the churches well beyond the controversies and struggles of the sixteenth century. Methodist Geoffrey Wainwright of Duke University, considering rites at the time of death, writes:

> The dialogues between Lutherans and Roman Catholics clearly manifests a considerable convergence in positions, which may perhaps be extended also to other Protestants if Lutherans can now be viewed as pioneers in the reconciliation of divergences which found their sharpest historical expression around the person and reforming intentions of Martin Luther.[25]

Wainwright goes on to admit that at least three areas of prior disagreement need further clarification: purgatory, indulgences, and canonization. Still, as he earlier says, a liturgical consensus seems to be further ahead than a theological one. The rites used by the various churches look more and more alike, which Wainwright speaks of as the *lex orandi* (the patterns of liturgical prayer) getting a head start on the *lex credendi* (the standards of belief).[26] It is

---

25. Geoffrey Wainwright, "The Saints and the Departed: Confessional Controversy and Ecumenical Convergences," *Studia Liturgica* 34 (2004): 83.
26. For a further exploration of the role of liturgy in ecumenism, see Geoffrey Wainwright, *Doxology: The Praise of God in Worship, Doctrine, and Life* (New York: Oxford University Press, 1980), 287–323.

not clear whether this is an unfortunate use of the liturgy to gloss over real theological differences or the prayerful instincts of God's people leading the way into theological agreement. In the meantime, however, as the answer waits to be revealed, it is undeniable that customs once quite common among Roman Catholics, and less public but still common among many Anglicans, are being commended to mainline Protestants through the official liturgical books of their denominations.

In many Protestant liturgical books that have been produced in the last decades, for example, Cranmer's prayer for casting earth upon the body, which in the 1549 version commended both the dead person to God and the body to the ground, but in the 1552 version mentioned only the body, appears in its original form. In no less surprising a place than the American Presbyterian *Book of Common Worship*, the text is:

> In sure and certain hope of the resurrection to eternal life, through our Lord Jesus Christ, we commend to almighty God our brother/sister N., and we commit his/her body to be returned to its elements, ashes to ashes, dust to dust.
>
> Blessed are the dead who die in the Lord, says the Spirit. They rest from their labors, and their works follow them.[27]

The Book of Common Prayer 1979 version is not exactly this. Missing in the Presbyterian form is the phrase "earth to earth," and the Aaronic blessing that caps the Book of Common Prayer text is replaced by Revelation 14:13. Undeniably, though, this is a prayer for the dead person. In the Presbyterian book, texts like this appear elsewhere in the funeral rite. In the proper funeral Eucharistic Prayer—a remarkable thing in itself, since it suggests a funeral

---

27. *Book of Common Worship* (Louisville: Westminster/John Knox Press, 1993), 941.

Eucharist—immediately after the epiclesis (of the assembly and the elements), comes a *memento* of the dead:

> Remember our brother/sister N., whose baptism is now complete in death. Bring him/her, and all who have died in the peace of Christ, into your eternal joy and light.[28]

Echoing in this Presbyterian prayer is the embolism for the deceased inserted into Eucharistic Prayer II at Roman Catholic funerals:

> Remember N. In baptism he (she) died with Christ; may he (she) also share his resurrection when Christ will raise our mortal bodies and make them like his own in glory.[29]

We see, then, a blurring of the sharp liturgical lines drawn at the Reformation across the denominations.

The 2006 *Evangelical Lutheran Worship*, like its predecessor, *Lutheran Book of Worship* of 1978, duplicates the Book of Common Prayer text for the casting of the earth, "In sure and certain hope," making only one change in the later edition. It renders "The Lord make his face to shine" as "The Lord's face shine," clearly to avoid the masculine pronoun. It also indicates that the sign of the cross is to be traced over the body at the words, "give *her/him* peace." *Evangelical Lutheran Worship*, far more than any edition of the Book of Common Prayer, suggests specific manual acts in all its liturgies.[30]

Most Anglican churches today, like the Episcopal Church and the Church of England, use the 1549 text, but the Church of New

---

28. Ibid., 932.
29. *The Roman Missal*, trans. International Commission on English in the Liturgy, first typical edition, no. 105. This was the approved English translation when the Presbyterian book was published.
30. *Evangelical Lutheran Worship* (Minneapolis: Augsburg Fortress, 2006), 673; and *Lutheran Book of Worship* (Minneapolis: Augsburg, 1978), 213.

Zealand has edited it in a way not seen before in the Common Prayer tradition. In the *New Zealand Prayer Book*, the text is addressed to the dead person *by name*.

> Now therefore, N., we commit your body to be buried/cremated, earth to earth, ashes to ashes, dust to dust; in the sure and certain hope of the resurrection to eternal life in Jesus Christ our Lord.[31]

The retrieval of ancient elements and attitudes and the growing ecumenical convergence, however, are neither seamless nor complete. Some churches, both Anglican and not, continue not to pray for the dead during funeral rites, and certainly they do not pray *to* them. The introductory notes for "A Funeral Service" in *A Prayer Book for Australia*, an "alternative service book" for the Anglican Church of Australia, are noteworthy for what they do *not* say.

> Human beings have sensed the mystery of death, and the pain of grief, since time immemorial. Every society has developed rites to mark the passage from life through death, and to commemorate the dead. Today we do this through the funeral service, and the rites by which we lay a person's body to rest.
>
> The wounds of grief need time and care to heal. The funeral may help this process, by enabling us to acknowledge our loss, give thanks for the life of the person who had died, make our last farewell, and begin to take up life once more.[32]

These introductory comments go on to affirm that the church does all of this in light of the Paschal Mystery of Jesus, the source of Christian hope. What is never suggested, however, is that the

---

31. *New Zealand Prayer Book/He Karakia Mihinare o Aotearoa* (Auckland: William Collins, 1989), 837.
32. *A Prayer Book for Australia* (Alexandria, NSW: Broughton Books, 1995), 771.

funeral as a rite is a prayer *for* the dead person, and the texts that follow confirm that it is not.

Compare this to the American prayer book which, while eloquently affirming that Christian funerals are, at their core, an affirmation of the hope brought to birth by the resurrection of the Lord Jesus—"an Easter liturgy [that] finds all its meaning in the resurrection" (507)—also asserts unequivocally that "prayer, including the Lord's Prayer, is offered for the deceased" (506) as well as for those who mourn.[33] The funeral in the Australian book is clearly celebrated only for the living, while the funeral in the American book is celebrated for the living and the dead.

This divergence can be found in the Protestant as well as the Anglican world. The *Book of Common Order of the Church of Scotland*, for example, like the American Presbyterian *Book of Common Worship*, is intended for Calvinists. Yet, the Scottish book, unlike the American one, includes not one prayer for the dead, praying only for comfort for the mourners and trust in God, in thanksgiving for the resurrection of Jesus and the hope it offers, and in gratitude for the life of the one who has died.

In the same way, the Lutheran Church-Missouri Synod, unlike the Evangelical Lutheran Church in America, does not include prayer for the dead in its funeral rite, and quite intentionally. This is not merely an argument from silence. *Lutheran Worship* (2006) borrows texts from the American Book of Common Prayer, but it excises any phrases that suggest prayer for the dead. (The American Book of Common Prayer is not copyrighted, so material from it can be copied and printed by others at will.)

The theology of the 1979 Book of Common Prayer, then, assumes that orthodox Christians may and even should pray for the dead. This is embedded in a far greater assumption of the prayer book: one that runs through every rite. All the baptized are joined in a

---

33. Book of Common Prayer (1979), 506–7.

single Body, members of one Communion, and so are never separated from one another, not even by death. The baptismal ecclesiology of the 1979 book and its vision of the *ecclesia*—those called out of the world and into the life of the Risen Jesus—lead almost inevitably to the assurance that prayer for the dead is as natural for Christians as prayer for the living.

The funeral rite in the prayer book, however, cannot be reduced to this one point. To celebrate a funeral well, Episcopalians must recognize the fullness of the prayer book rite's vision and give it ritual shape. Because the rite is often misunderstood, they must realize what it is *not*, as much as what it is.

## The Pastoral Theology of the Burial Office in the 1979 Prayer Book

*The Question of Who Can Be Saved*

Like all Christian liturgy, the funeral is above all else a celebration of the presence of the Risen One in the midst of the church by the power of the Spirit. In the funeral liturgy, the church focuses particularly on the "sure and certain hope of the resurrection to eternal life" that Jesus' presence among the saints brings to them. The Christian funeral does not deny that others may also transcend death, but it does not presume it. Universalism—the belief that all are saved simply by virtue of existing, and that God grants eternal life along with mortal life—is not the orthodox Christian claim and it is not presumed in the prayer book's rites of burial. Eternal life, the hope of every Christian, is a free gift of God. It is not a human right. This baldly stated fact runs afoul of a great deal of modern thinking, but it is, nonetheless, the immemorial teaching of the church. *"Lex orandi legem credendi statuat,"* famously said Prosper of Aquitaine. What the church believes and what it does in its liturgy are mirror images of one another, and so the liturgy does not proclaim universal salvation, since that is not the teaching of the church, nor has it ever been.

That is not to say that the church categorically believes that there are people who will not be saved. The church, at its best, does not presume to speak for God. God saves whom God saves, by whatever means God wills. While not denying God's absolute freedom to save everyone, however, the church does not speak for God and assert that God *will* save everyone. The church has the right only to proclaim the gospel it has received: that in Christ Jesus, God has overcome death, and that in baptism, God gives to Christians a share in the death and resurrection of Christ, a free and underserved gift. That is the only gospel the church has received and the only one it has a commission to proclaim. It is not an arrogant claim. It does not deny that God can save those who are not Christians, and it does not even assume that God will save all Christians. In fact, the Book of Common Prayer funeral certainly does not assume that God will save the person who has died. It merely affirms what the church does know: that in baptism, Christians become heirs of the promise of eternal life, but it is an inheritance that can be accepted or rejected.

There is another reason, though, that in the burial rite the church cannot declare what those outside the church can expect after death. Christians in modern times have accepted that we cannot presume to speak for those who are not of our number without falling into a sort of Christian imperialism: an imposition of our views on others. Interreligious and ecumenical dialogue has called the church to hold fast to what it has received but not to impose it on others, nor to discount the fervently held beliefs of others. There are a great many people who do not believe in the afterlife, at least not in the way Christians understand it, and among them are fervently religious people. To proclaim in our rites that, in effect, they have got it all wrong is not the same thing as proclaiming what we ourselves believe. Members of Eastern religions, for example, conceive of the afterlife in terms of reincarnation. To suggest in our liturgy that, in fact, the God of Jesus Christ will usher them at death into the risen life made manifest in Jesus is presumptuous and disrespectful. Even among Jews, the notion of an afterlife is hardly universal. Many devout observant Jews see a person's legacy—good deeds and progeny—as the fulfillment of life and do not expect to personally transcend death. The New Testament records a running argument among the Jews about whether the dead will be raised, and that argument continues. A Christian funeral that tells Jewish visitors that they will, indeed, not only be raised up, but also that they will be raised up because of Jesus, would be a gross example of religious inhospitality. To even tell them that they will survive death in some vague, universal way that they emphatically deny would also be inhospitable and profoundly disrespectful.

Even some religions that have their roots in Christianity and claim, in fact, to *be* Christian, do not share the view of the afterlife held forth in the American prayer book. Mormons, for example, expect to inherit planets in the afterlife and to be charged with procreating and filling them. Jehovah's Witnesses deny explicitly that human beings have immortal souls and teach that at death, a person ceases to exist. Only in the *parousia* will the saved gain a share in Christ's risen life, and, essentially, all of them will be Jehovah's Witnesses. The rest will be obliterated entirely. And then there are those thoughtful a-religious people who believe that there is neither God nor afterlife. In the modern age, we have learned (from the errors of our ancestors) that all of those people deserve our respect. The gospel demands that we respect them.

Our funeral rites are a celebration of what we have come to believe and the proclamation of the hope to which we hold fast, not an arrogant assertion that others, including our guests, will find out in the end that we were right all along, and they were mistaken. In an assembly made up of people of various views—and that is what nearly any assembly for a funeral will be—to say, "We trust that just as God raised Jesus from the dead, so God will bring to life those who have died with Christ in baptism," may to some of them seem like nonsense. No matter. It is, in fact, what Christians believe, even if other fine and bright people think it is delusional. To say, though, to that same assembly, "We know that God will raise every single human being into the glorious life of Christ, and that includes you, whether you believe it or not" is another thing altogether. It is arrogant, inhospitable, and beyond our purview.

## The Subject of the Funeral Liturgy

Often, printed orders of worship at funerals call the rite, "A Celebration of the Life of" the dead person. That is not at all what an Episcopal funeral is. An Episcopal funeral—certainly a funeral celebrated according to the 1979 prayer book—is "A Celebration of the Life of Jesus" in whom alone we have hope. At a funeral, the church looks for signs of Jesus' life manifest in the life of the deceased, and looks, too, with hope to the day when the dead person, along with all who believe, will be called forth from death. The death of a particular person, then, is an occasion for reclaiming hope and reasserting faith, for looking for signs of Jesus' action in our own time and among our own people, and for beseeching God for rest and resurrection, not just for the one who has died, but for the whole church. In all of this, the focus is never diverted from Jesus.

This presents the church with an often-difficult challenge, because in focusing on Jesus, the church cannot ignore the person who has died. The funeral does not celebrate death as an abstraction: a fact of the universal human condition. It celebrates an actual death. Just as the church's hope is rooted, not in an abstract theological proposition that God raises the dead, but in the historical and specific resurrection of the man Jesus, so the celebration of a funeral is rooted in the church's hope that God will raise this specific person to life.

Furthermore, what the church hopes for the one around whose remains it gathers, it hopes for the entire church and each of its members. Every funeral, then, calls the Christians who celebrate it to encounter in a most undeniable and unavoidable way that all people die, but at the same time, it holds out for them what they already know: that God "has given us the victory through our Lord Jesus Christ." Just as at every baptism the members of the assembly vicariously relive their own immersion in the waters of baptism and pledge again to live out the grace God freely gave them at the font, so at funerals the members of the assembly proleptically come to their own death, remember that God has made them heirs of eternal life, and so recommit themselves to live here-and-now as if they are in the Reign of God because, indeed, they are.

To reduce all of this to celebrating the life of a dead person is to squander a tremendous pastoral opportunity.

### *The Criteria By Which Eternal Salvation Is Gained*

The Reformation's battle over how a person is saved was not a new battle. In essence, it was the Pelagian controversy.[34] Are we saved by what we do, or by a free and unrestrained act of God? Which comes first: our efforts or God's grace? Out of the church's wrestling with that question came Prosper's dictum, now so often quoted by Anglicans: how we pray is evidence of what we believe.

That is not because the church takes its theories and translates them into prayers. It is because, as Prosper saw it, the church's prayer is organic. It develops in response to the church's ongoing experience of God. In our own day, this dynamic brought prayer for the dead back into the Book of Common Prayer tradition.

---

34. Pelagius was a fourth- and early fifth-century British monk who engaged in a literary debate with Augustine of Hippo about the degree to which humans were able to attain perfection.

When the church paid attention to how people, in response to the experience of God in their lives, actually prayed, it saw that they were, in fact, praying for the dead. Since the church could find nothing in the scripture, the tradition, or simple logic to discount this instinct among Anglicans—but, in fact, saw good support for it—the church accepted it as authentic. Gradually, then, prayer for the dead was restored to the official prayer of the church. So how we pray is at least one sign of what we truly believe, and what we truly believe is shaped by how we pray. The two are in a dialogical relationship.

Prosper used the prayer of the church to counter the view of Pelagius (that salvation begins with the good works of humans to which God responds with saving grace). He pointed out that the church, in its liturgy, asks God to bring unbelievers to faith. In other words, in its liturgy, the church expresses its instinctual awareness that God's grace comes first, and human faith and works follow. By "reading" the liturgy, Prosper concluded that Pelagius was wrong. Human action—whether thoughts or deeds—does not come first in the dance. God's action comes first, and the human person follows.

One of the dangers of funerals, and especially of eulogies (which are not mentioned or envisioned in either the two funeral rites or the funeral order in the Book of Common Prayer), is that they can easily focus on the good works and wonderful traits of the dead person, rather than the Paschal victory of Jesus that was manifest in the person. This creates the incorrect impression—the Pelagian impression—that we save ourselves by thinking the right things or doing the right things, when, in fact, the tradition assures us that we are saved by accepting God's free gift of grace and responding to it. God always leads the dance.

The pastoral implications are innumerable. Perhaps most important is that it is entirely unnecessary, potentially misleading, and pastorally dangerous to "canonize" a dead person. The truth is, some of those whose remains arrive at the doors of our churches are strangers to us. We do not know the sorts of lives they lived. Some others—and perhaps most others—were not stellar examples of the Christian life but were as sinful as most of us are, and we know it as the coffin or the urn appears before us. And, of course, there are those whom we did know and who were exemplary Christians. If funerals are concerned with the good deeds of the one who has died, the presider and especially the preacher cannot win. Funerals can easily become public statements about who the good Christians were and who were not really so good, and that can be communicated as much by what is not said as by what is.

In some cases, the basis for what is said will be hearsay; in others, truths stretched so far as to be lies; and in others, apologies and excuses for the unfortunate behaviors of a person whose complex motivations we cannot possibly understand. And then there will be those whom we know well and can praise without effort. By doing that, however, the presider and preacher will risk advancing a Pelagian view of salvation, and if people are paying attention, funeral-to-funeral, the minister will risk causing great offense and pain. "She did not speak so well of my father when he died," a member of the assembly might think, "so does that mean that my father was not a good Christian?" Someone else might think, "He said such amazing things about that other woman at her funeral, but he is not saying nearly so much to praise my wife. Are other people picking up on this?" And then there will be those blatantly untrue claims that the dead person was exemplary, which can be as dangerous as holding up to ridicule the person's imperfections. People have wandered away from the church for less. There is, too, the temptation to say more about the wealthy and the famous who have died, simply because more about them is publicly known, and that is perhaps the worst temptation of all. It suggests, even if unintentionally, that money and fame matter in the church, even in death. Nothing could be further from the gospel and nothing could so easily destroy pastoral relationships and congregational health.

Among mainline Christians, there is legitimate disagreement about exactly how and by what criteria God welcomes the dead into eternal blessedness. There is no disagreement, however, about this: human beings cannot earn their salvation. If one imagines a God whose essential property it is to condemn, the human inability to save the self is a reason for despair, but if one imagines a God whose essential property it is to forgive and love, there is reason for hope, because God can save us even if we are not model citizens. The God of Jesus Christ, and the God spoken of and spoken to in the Book of Common Prayer funeral rites, is the latter. Episcopal funerals proclaim the saving power of God manifest in the resurrection of Jesus and known to the church in the Spirit present in its midst. They do not proclaim the virtues or enumerate the flaws of the person who has died.

### The Normative Assembly at Funerals

The second note in the "Concerning the Service" section of both burial rites in the prayer book is pivotal but largely ignored. "Baptized Christians are properly buried from the church. The service should be held at a time when the congregation has opportunity to be present."[35] What this rubric says, in brief, is that the death of a Christian is an event in the life of the church. It is not a private or family moment. Episcopalians have made great strides in realizing that baptism is an ecclesial event—an event in the life of the church—and our liturgies both show and reinforce it. While baptisms still are sometimes celebrated privately, they are mostly celebrated, as the prayer book directs, "within the Eucharist as the chief service on a Sunday or other feast."[36] While the same vision stands behind the rubric that intends funerals to be public events

---
35. Book of Common Prayer (1979), 468, 490.
36. Ibid., 298.

in the life of the community—in the community's worship space and in the community's presence—especially the second half of the directive is rarely observed. We have not done as well with funerals as we have with baptisms.

Most Episcopal congregations are small enough that most members know and regularly interact with one another. We do have some very large churches, but they are an anomaly. When one of us dies, the other members of the parish cannot ignore it. It says everything about who we understand ourselves to be that our prayer book explicitly directs that we, as a community, bury our dead and support the grieving family and friends. When someone dies whom we do not know, however, it is still our vocation to gather around the remains and comfort the mourners. We are joined to them in baptism, and while close personal relationships make the bond more obvious, they do not make it more real. In death as in life, we are all one in Christ Jesus.

The normative assembly for an Episcopal funeral, therefore, is the entire parish or a significant part of it. The intent of the funeral rubric is the same as the baptismal rubric that calls for the rite to be celebrated at the principal weekly service. The parish should be there. That, however, would require us to alter how and when we celebrate funerals. During the workday, most people cannot come to the church for a funeral, and yet that is when most of our funerals are held. The evening would be a more reasonable time, making it possible for far more members of the parish to assemble. Undeniably, evening funerals are not what people expect, and it would require both catechesis on the nature of Episcopal funerals and gradual formation until the practice would seem natural. It can be done, though, and it has.

Faulty but common assumptions about funeral directors would give us an easy excuse for not even trying to make the change. Since Jessica Mitford published *The American Way of Death* in 1963, the church has often claimed that funeral directors have a stranglehold on how we mark death, but they do not. I can speak now only about my own experience, but in a decade as rector of a parish that celebrated not only the funerals of its members but also the funerals of many of those who died in the care of the church's AIDS ministry, not one funeral director ever argued about the parish's custom of holding funerals in the evening, and none ever charged the family one cent more. The parish and the funeral directors forged a good working relationship. In the evening, not only are most adults home from work but children are home from school. This allows congregations to introduce children to the fact of death in a way that makes it seem both natural and sacred, and begin to form in them a commitment to care for the dead, to honor their bodies, and, with the rest of the community, to support those who mourn.

## The Tone of Funerals and the Other Rites at the Time of Death

The prayer book envisions funeral liturgies that are, at the same time, joyful and sorrowful. The joy is a response to the hoped-for entry of the dead person into "the nearer presence of our Lord," and the sorrow is a sympathetic identification with the mourners, among whom all the members of the congregation often may be counted.[37] Holding the Christian middle ground between a plastic happiness that pretends that death is not anguishing and a despair that assumes that death is not conquered requires an attitude of hope. To craft and preside over a rite that gives shape to that hope demands of liturgical ministers great skill and sensitivity.

The Paschal Triduum—the three-day liturgy that runs from sundown on Maundy Thursday to sundown on Easter Sunday—is a model of how to hold anguish and joy in tension. While in practice the prayer book rites for these days are sometimes treated as if they

---

37. Book of Common Prayer (1979), 507.

are independent rites, they are actually only one. A common way of explaining this is that they are three movements of one symphony or three acts of one play. They are not three independent rites. That is why the proper liturgies of Maundy Thursday evening and Good Friday do not end with dismissals. They simply stop, the assembly disperses, and then, one day later, it comes again to the same place to, in a sense, engage the next movement or act. Just as themes repeat in well-crafted theater and music, with echoes of what will come later heard early on and resonances of what has been repeating near the end, so is the Triduum. The Maundy Thursday liturgy is about glory: the glory of humble service and self-giving. The Good Friday liturgy is about triumph: the triumph of Jesus even in his crucifixion. The Easter liturgy is about death and life meeting at the tomb. Paul, in the passage from Romans 6, read every year at the Vigil, makes it clear that baptism is not just about rising but about *dying* and rising. So even at the Easter Vigil we see death, not just life. We see it, though, as Christians see it: full of hope. And so, throughout the Triduum, we look from various angles at the one truth: that for the Christian, joy and sadness can and must coexist in the face of death and never give way to frivolous denial or faithless capitulation.

The hymn "Lift High the Cross" is a fine example of this dynamic tension and is a perfect hymn for the Great Vigil of Easter. The cross is not a mournful thing but a "triumphant sign." Every Christian, newborn in the font, "bears on the brow the mark of him who died." This is an allusion to the signing of the forehead of the newly baptized ones, marking them "as Christ's own forever," a signing that the assembly would just have witnessed. The cross, then, is not absent from the Easter celebration, nor is resurrection absent from Good Friday. Jesus was "once lifted on the glorious tree," not the shameful tree. The Good Friday liturgy is rich with images of triumph and victory. John's account of the Passion is read, for example, because of all the Passion accounts, it shows most clearly that even in his suffering and death, Jesus was strong and powerful. The collect, too, that ends the Solemn Collects in the Good Friday segment of the Triduum liturgy is the very opposite of mournful. It asks that all people might see that "things which were cast down are being raised up, and things which had grown old are being made new."[38] Sandwiched between the proclamation of the Passion and the presentation of the cross, this collect makes a clear point: what may look like failure and death is not that at all, if only we would have the eyes to see. That is how the funeral liturgy can be both sorrowful and joyful simultaneously.

The prayer book funeral, then, will find its fullest expression in congregations that understand the interpenetrating of death and life that the Triduum celebrates. A key step in celebrating funerals well is celebrating the Triduum well. Because all baptisms echo the Easter Vigil, another key to celebrating funerals well is celebrating every baptism well. Conversely, by celebrating every funeral well, a congregation will be prepared to celebrate baptisms well and the Triduum well. And since every Sunday celebrates in a restrained way what Easter celebrates with an intensity that could only be generated once a year, a congregation that celebrates Sunday well will be prepared for the Triduum, baptisms, and funerals.

The tone of the Book of Common Prayer funeral rite cannot be set just at funerals. It is the tone of the Paschal Mystery, which is the dynamic of Christ's glorification through self-emptying. If that tone permeates the entire life of the congregation, both in the liturgy and beyond it, it will naturally permeate its funerals. If not, it will be almost impossible for its funerals to hold in tension the sorrow and the joy that are both authentic Christian responses to death.

---

38. Ibid., 280.

## Revision in Future Editions of the Book of Common Prayer

The place of religion in most cultures has shifted greatly since the 1979 prayer book was published, and so has the place of funerals. "The formula for human funerals was fairly simple for most of our history: by getting the dead where they needed to go, the living got where they needed to be. By acting out the necessary tasks to rid ourselves of dead human bodies, we came to understand the meaning of death."[39] Now, however, the presence of a body, even of cremated remains, has become less and less common at rites for the dead. In some parts of the United States, it is virtually unheard of. Funeral Director Thomas Lynch suggests that Jessica Medford and other critics of his profession object not only to its oddities and excesses but also, and even primarily, to its role in making it possible for the dead to come to their own funerals. The victory of these critics of the funeral industry, Lynch claims, is actually a defeat. It is a symptom of a cultural and religious urge away from incarnationalism and a subsequent glorification of "less embodied, more free-flowing forms of spirituality."[40]

Any thought of prayer book revision that does not take seriously this cultural transformation would be, at best, futile. It must be taken seriously so that the church will not unthinkingly fall prey to it but can, instead, be a prophetic witness against it. The history of the prayer books' rites for the dead is proof that cultural evolution and liturgical revision are not distinct. Indeed, were it not for shifts in British attitudes toward death in the early twentieth century, the church may never have seen the retrieval of prayer for the dead and the creation of rites that lead with "sure and certain hope" rather

---

39. Thomas G. Long and Thomas Lynch, *The Good Funeral: Death, Grief, and the Community of Care* (Louisville: Westminster John Knox, 2013), 54.
40. Ibid., 97.

than pessimism and fear. Yet, not all cultural trends surrounding death call the church to its best self. "Faith is now most at home speaking only of inward spiritual things, sentiments confined to the tiny tableau of the soul and psyche. It will not speak boldly of the embodied human being who ate and drank and loved and sinned and hoped and wept and whose life and very body are not carried forth as an offering to God, but rather more meekly of 'memories we will always have,' or the 'grief that may last for a night but vanishes in the morning,' of 'the laughter she will leave with us forever' and 'the inspiration of his life.'"[41] If Lynch is right, then the body-positivity and incarnational faith that permeates the prayer book and Anglican spirituality is what is really at stake in our funeral rites.

The prayer book presumes the presence of a person's body at a person's funeral. It presumes the presence of the bodies of the living, too, as one last time we bring into the house of the church what we knew of a person. While, in fact, this is less and less common, the church would do well to retain it as the norm and, perhaps, to expand explanatory notes "Concerning the Service" to emphasize the dignity and sacredness of the human body, both in life and in death.

Any revision of the texts themselves should follow the lead of *Enriching Our Worship*.[42] This collection truly enriches the prayer book rites while maintaining their ethos. They are characterized by joy but embrace a healthy and holy grief.[43]

Future revisions of the burial office should be made with a sensitivity to the relationship of the funeral gathering to the great Paschal victory of Christ over death, while retaining the marks of his

---

41. Ibid., 102f.
42. Standing Commission on Liturgy and Music, *Burial Rites for Adults Together with a Rite for the Burial of a Child: Enriching Our Worship 3* (New York: Church Publishing, 2006), 66–69.
43. Book of Common Prayer (1979), 507.

suffering. A future revision might, for example, incorporate prayers from the Triduum that speak directly of Christ's death and resurrection (rather than indirectly by focusing on what Christ will accomplish for the one who has died) and expand the lessons to include accounts of Christ's resurrection. The delivery of eulogies at Episcopal funerals, something not envisioned by the prayer book but perhaps so ensconced now as to be almost inevitable, could be moved, for example, to before the service proper begins. A rubrical note would clarify the nature of a funeral sermon—to proclaim Christ's death and resurrection as the grounds for our common hope.

Minor changes could be made to encourage a wider gathering of the church at the time of funeral. The opening rubric about holding the service "at a time when the congregation has opportunity to be present" might, for example, be expanded to mention that an evening is an appropriate time for such an assembly.[44] It might even draw a parallel between baptism and funerals as two actions, not of a private or familial group, but of the whole church.

There is much to commend in *Enriching Our Worship 3*'s Rite for the Burial of One who does not Profess the Christian Faith. Such a rite will be increasingly necessary as traditional religiosity continues to decline in the culture. Often those who have no faith and no relationship to the church turn to us for guidance and assistance at the time of death. The danger of such rites, however, is that in the name of offering comfort, they sometimes not only proclaim God's mercy but also promise salvation. This kind of universalism can then drift into our rites for believers. In place of the proclamation of salvation through faith and baptismal grace, there can come a bland optimism and even a suggestion that a relationship with Jesus and the church is not the source of Christian hope. This would be a case of the culture not calling the church to a deeper engagement with its true self but a drift away from it.

---

44. Ibid., 490.

# 10

# The Apostolic Tradition and Liturgical Revision

### Bryan D. Spinks[1]

Educated people in the Western world living in 1929 were taught that there were eight planets in the solar system. Then in 1930 a ninth was discovered, Pluto. Thereafter all well-educated people knew there were now nine planets. Until 1992 no one questioned the status of Pluto, but following the discovery of several objects of similar size, its status began to be questioned. In 2005 after the discovery of Eris, which is more massive than Pluto but not a planet, Pluto's status was changed, and it has been reclassified as a dwarf planet. To those of us who are not astronomers, the difference might not seem obvious, but for the scientific community, the solar system once more has eight planets, and Pluto is something else. In the course of time many discoveries have been hailed as new game-changing accomplishments and regarded as new assured facts. However, even in scientific fields

---

1. Bryan D. Spinks is the Bishop F. Percy Goddard Professor of Liturgical Studies and Pastoral Theology at the Yale Divinity School.

that are rigorous and detail oriented, theories are proven wrong, and what was regarded as an assured fact comes to be acknowledged as a mistake.[2]

And so what has all this to do with liturgy and liturgical revision? Liturgical scholarship as it is understood today is a relatively young scientific discipline and was developed by the German scholar Anton Baumstark in the early twentieth century.[3] His method has been called the comparative method, because that is how it worked. Texts of Eucharistic prayers, or collects, or baptismal rites from the different classical churches (Catholic and the Eastern churches) were compared to see what they have in common and to see how they developed. It worked with certain rules and on the whole many hypotheses emerged which have stood the test of time.

Out of this comparative method came what was regarded as a remarkable discovery and the answer to a centuries-old problem. It was the "discovery" or "recovery" of a supposed lost church order that contained liturgical texts called the "Apostolic Tradition" and was attributed to St. Hippolytus, Bishop of Rome in the early third century.

In 1551, during the time when Archbishop Thomas Cranmer was finishing his 1552 Book of Common Prayer, a headless statue was discovered in Rome by the papal architect Pirro Ligorio. Although no name appeared on the statue, the plinth did have inscriptions of what were titles of works, and some of these were known to be titles by Hippolytus. The inference was that the statue was of Hippolytus and all his books were listed on the plinth.

---

2. Charles Q. Choi, "Dwarf Planet Pluto: Facts About the Icy Former Planet," *Space.com*, http://www.space.com/43-pluto-the-ninth-planet-that-was-a-dwarf.html (accessed July 22, 2015).
3. Anton Baumstark, *Comparative Liturgy*, trans. F. L. Cross (Westminster, MD: Newman Press, 1958, original 1939); Baumstark, *On the Historical Development of the Liturgy*, trans. Fritz West (Collegeville, MN: Liturgical Press, 2011, original 1922).

Amongst the titles on the plinth were "Apostolic Tradition" and "Concerning Charisms," but no such works by Hippolytus were known. The statue was repaired, given a head suitable for this third-century saint, and placed in the Vatican.

In the early twentieth century, German scholar E. Schwartz and British scholar R. H. Connolly had started a painstaking comparison of some ancient church orders, associated with Egypt and Syria, and Ethiopia, and also a Latin version in Verona.[4] The comparison would be rather like comparing the Gospels of Matthew, Mark, and Luke, where there are common features and where Mark seems to have been used by the other two. However, there are also common elements in Matthew and Luke, and scholars have isolated this material and called it "Q," *Quelle*, source—a common source. St. Mark's Gospel actually exists, but Q is only known by scholarly reconstruction. Schwartz and Connolly apparently began their investigations independently, but it is now known that they were in contact about their mutual work and findings. They noted that in the *Epitome* of the fourth-century *Apostolic Constitutions*, which has material from a common source, which one might call the "liturgical Q," some of the ordination material is attributed to Hippolytus, and that another document with common material is called the *Canons of Hippolytus*. They also found reference to "gifts" and "the apostolic tradition," and so by arguing backward concluded that the underlying common source was by Hippolytus, and represented the "missing" works listed on the plinth of the statue. By extracting the common material, the likely original work could be reconstructed. Important critical editions were prepared by leading liturgical and classical scholars of the early twentieth century: Dom

---

4. Eduard Schwartz, *Über die Pseudoapostolischen Kirchenordnungen* (Strasbourg: Truner, 1910); R. H. Connolly, *The So-Called Egyptian Church Order and Derived Documents* (Cambridge: Cambridge University Press, 1916).

Bernard Botte (French Roman Catholic), Dom Gregory Dix (English Anglican), and Burton Scott Easton (American Episcopalian).[5] The "liturgical Q" was regarded as an ancient liturgical source, c. 215, by Bishop Hippolytus, representing Roman use, and crucial for understanding the evolution of liturgy in the West. Dom Gregory Dix had written in 1937:

> Here from the pen of a disciple of St. Irenaeus is what claims to be an accurate and authoritative account of the rites and organization of the Church as the men of the later second century had received them from the sub-apostolic age.... It represents the mind and practice not of St. Hippolytus only but of the whole Catholic Church of the second century. As such it is of outstanding importance.[6]

The Roman Catholic scholar, Bernard Botte, wrote of the anaphora or Eucharistic Prayer: "It is certainly one of the oldest examples of Christian prayer literature so it is hardly surprising that when the liturgical reform was initiated, consideration was given to restoring to use this admirably simple prayer."[7] For reasons never fully explained, it seemed that the liturgical revisers of the 1960s onward took it for granted that this document carried an authority that made it a foundational text for revision. It was regarded

---

5. Bernard Botte, *La Tradition Apostolique de Saint Hippolyte: Essai de Reconstitution* (Münster: Aschendorff, 1963); Gregory Dix, *Apostolike Paradosis: The Treatise on the Apostolic Tradition of St. Hippolytus* (New York: MacMillan, 1937); Burton Scott Easton, *The Apostolic Tradition of Hippolytus* (New York: MacMillan, 1934).
6. Gregory Dix, ed., *The Treatise on the Apostolic Tradition of St. Hippolytus of Rome, Bishop and Martyr*, second edition with preface and corrections by Henry Chadwick (London: published for the Church Historical Society by the Society for Promoting Christian Knowledge, 1968), xi, xliv.
7. Bernard Botte, "The Short Anaphora," in *The New Liturgy: A Comprehensive Introduction*, ed. Lancelot Sheppard (London: Darton, Longman and Todd, 1970), 194–99.

as going back behind the Reformation debates and divisions, and offering an early third-century blueprint for twentieth-century liturgical revision. In the Roman Catholic reforms, the Eucharistic Prayer of Hippolytus was the foundational text for Prayer II of the new missal, and the ordination prayers were used for the revised ordination rites. In the Church of England's 1980 *Alternative Services Book*, Hippolytus was the basis for Eucharistic Prayers 1, 2, and 3. In the Episcopal Church's 1979 Book of Common Prayer, it was foundational for Rite II, part of Great Thanksgivings A and B; and—following the Roman Catholic reforms—the ordination prayer for bishops was used in the Episcopal ordination rite. The Eucharistic Prayer found its way into the *Lutheran Book of Worship* altar book. In addition, the American Book of Common Prayer (1979), the Canadian *Book of Alternative Services*, and the English *Common Worship* all followed Hippolytus in dividing the question about the Apostles' Creed in the baptism office into three questions and responses.[8]

One of the puzzles of the influence of this text at the time was why it was assumed—and never fully explained or justified—that supposed third-century liturgical texts should be appropriate for the twentieth century. Why were the prayers in this text more suitable than fourth-century texts or texts from other epochs? One argument that was put forward was that the era of Christendom was over, and in the culture of twentieth-century secularism, the pre-Christendom or pre-Constantinian forms of liturgy were more

---

8. Earlier prayer books took several different approaches: the celebrant recited the entire Apostles' Creed and asked for assent (English 1662 Book of Common Prayer), the priest and congregation recited the creed together as a whole (Canadian 1962 Book of Common Prayer), or the celebrant asked whether the person believed "all the Articles of the Christian Faith, as contained in the Apostles' Creed" (American 1928 Book of Common Prayer). Apostolic Tradition had divided the Creed into separate questions about belief in the three persons of the Trinity.

appropriate and suitable.⁹ The assumption that pre-Constantinian Roman culture was analogous with twentieth-century secularism is highly questionable, as is the implicit belief that the post-Constantinian Church represented a considerable discontinuity with church practice prior to that epoch. Whatever else liturgical history illustrates, one lesson is that worship never seems to revert to a past but is reformed to suit the needs of present circumstances.

The other puzzle was that the Anaphora in this text appeared only in the Verona Latin and the Ethiopian Church Orders. What the text says is that this is the type of Eucharistic Prayer that a bishop might author or recite *at his ordination*. In other words, no claim is made that this was typical of Sunday Eucharistic Prayers, but rather, it was appropriate for the special occasion for *episcopal ordinations*. Yet it became the basis for ordinary Eucharistic celebrations.

However, a much more serious problem has been that more recent scholarship has brought into question the whole integrity of the so-called Apostolic Tradition. The distinguished Italian archaeologist Margherita Guarducci seriously challenged the 1551 identification of the statue with Hippolytus. Looking at the original drawings from the period it was clear that the statue was in fact of a female, and so certainly not bishop or any other third-century Hippolytus! Perhaps the most damaging critique was the large tome by Cambridge scholar Allen Brent. Accepting that the statue was in fact that of a woman, he noted that none of the documents identified by Schwartz and company carried the title "Apostolic Tradition," and that names associated with Church Orders are ciphers.[10] Brent went on to examine the rest of the Hippolytus Corpus, concluding

---

9. For example, Daniel B. Stevick, *Baptismal Moments, Baptismal Meanings* (New York: Church Hymnal Corp., 1987), 227–34.
10. Allen Brent, *Hippolytus and Roman Church in Third Century: Communities in Tension Before the Emergence of a Monarch-Bishop* (Leiden: E. J. Brill, 1995).

that it derives from a time when a monarchical bishop emerged in Rome, replacing the older polity of churches each having presbyter-bishops. The statue of a woman, so he argued, was a corporate icon of the distinctive community that had achieved a continuing influence under the pseudonym of Hippolytus, and which contained at least two authors.

As for the liturgical Q, Brent opined that the assumption of an autograph named "Apostolic Tradition" that once existed as the work of a single, "real" author is chimerical. Paul Bradshaw, a British scholar of liturgy who for many years was a member of the faculty at Notre Dame, has suggested that while some elements in this document may be of the early third century, as a living document it probably reached its present state in the early fourth century—the period in which Christianity was finally legalized in the Roman Empire—and has a variety of layers of material reflecting different times and community practice.[11] This has been reiterated and examined in more detail in a commentary on "Apostolic Tradition" by Bradshaw, his Notre Dame colleague Maxwell Johnson, and Emory professor L. Edward Phillips.[12] English liturgical scholar Alistair Stewart-Sykes, even though arguing for a mid-third-century redaction, also concedes that there is more than one layer of material in the rite.[13] Although the prayer has archaic fea-

---

11. Paul F. Bradshaw, "Redating the Apostolic Tradition: Some Preliminary Steps," in *Rule of Prayer, Rule of Faith: Essays in Honor of Aidan Kavanagh, OSB*, ed. Nathan Mitchell and John F. Baldovin (Collegeville, MN: Liturgical Press, 1996), 3–17.
12. Paul Bradshaw, Maxwell Johnson, and Edward Phillips, *The Apostolic Tradition: A Commentary* (Minneapolis: Fortress Press, 2002). See also Paul F. Bradshaw, *Ancient Church Orders*, Alcuin Club/Group for Renewal of Worship Joint Liturgical Study 80 (Norwich: Hymns Ancient and Modern, 2015).
13. Alistair Stewart-Sykes, *Hippolytus: On the Apostolic Tradition* (New York: St. Vladimir's Seminary Press, 2001). For the problem in a wider context, J. A. Cerrato, "The Association of the Name Hippolytus with a Church

tures—Jesus is described as child and the angel of God's will—it also has features that suggest a fourth-century date, particularly the inclusion of the words of institution within the prayer. Paul Bradshaw has noted that references to the words of institution in Justin and many other documents seem to be from a catechetical rather than a eucharistic context. The inclusion of the institution narrative within a Eucharistic Prayer would appear to be a fourth-century development. It would seem, therefore, that the liturgical Q may be a fourth-century creation looking back in time to an imagined third-century ideal. However, the material—and the prayer—continued to have a life as living texts as it was redacted and adapted in subsequent Church Orders. Whatever else may be said of the Eucharistic Prayer, and probably the ordination material too, it is not the universal liturgy of Rome in 215 CE. It is the imagined past of one particular community in Rome that may have been Syrian or Egyptian in ethnicity.

In other words, like the planet Pluto, the so-called Apostolic Tradition is not what scholars of the twentieth century thought it to be, or perhaps wanted it to be. Perhaps the revisers genuinely felt that a third-century text from Rome, going behind the Reformation disputes, would give some sort of liturgical unity and ecumenicity. The state of liturgical scholarship at present suggests that this is in fact a pseudo-document, representing no single tradition, certainly not all things Roman circa 215, and having no real authority than that which anyone would like to give it. As Robert Morgan and John Barton, authors of a late-twentieth-century volume on biblical interpretation, said of interpreting biblical texts:

> The balance of power and moral rights then shifts to the interpreters. They are the masters or judges of meaning now, for

---

Order Now Known as *The Apostolic Tradition,"* in St. Vladimir's *Theological Quarterly* 48, no. 2 (2004): 179–94.

better or worse. The interpreters are never mindless servants of the text, or midwives at the birth or communication of meaning. They are human agents with their own aims, interests, and rights.[14]

It is not that liturgical scholars deliberately mislead or cannot offer helpful suggestions for revision and reform. What is important to understand is what it is from our present conscious and unconscious agendas that help us to privilege one liturgical era or tradition over another. In the meantime, Pluto is not a planet and Apostolic Tradition is not an ancient liturgical text by Bishop Hippolytus of Rome circa 215.

In practical terms this means that we ought not to use a presumed—and now questioned—antiquity and authenticity to bracket 1979 prayer book texts from "Hippolytus" from the possibility of future revision. There seems no valid reason to give these texts some privileged status. They need to be examined, preserved, revised, or deleted on the same grounds as other texts. The liturgical Q is not an error-free window into the use of the early church.

Perhaps the most glaring example of the use of the liturgical Q is in the 1979 ordination services. The revisers of the ordination office made some positive theological improvements in the 1979 prayer book revision, including an expanded role for the people and a revision in the texts for consecration so as to drop a medieval presumption that ordination was a gift from the bishop rather than a grace bestowed by God. However, following the Roman Catholic Church's new ordination rite for bishops, the Episcopal Church utilized the corresponding prayer found in Hippolytus, on the grounds that it embodied the practices of the early church in Rome.[15] Other

---

14. Robert Morgan and John Barton, *Biblical Interpretation* (New York: Oxford University Press, 1988), 6–7.
15. See further in Paul F. Bradshaw, *Rites of Ordination: Their History and Theology* (Collegeville, MN: Liturgical Press, 2013), 185.

Anglican provinces, by contrast, had built upon the ordination rite of the Church of South India, and the proposed British Anglican-Methodist ordinal of 1968.[16] In the latter rites, the servant role of bishops is stressed, and the sole high priest is Christ. By contrast, by using Hippolytus (translation by Harry Boone Porter), the Episcopal bishop is "one with the apostles," on whom God is requested to pour out "the power of your princely Spirit," and he or she may "exercise without reproach the high priesthood to which you called him/her." In place of servant and *kenosis* (Greek for self-emptying, used of Christ in Philippians 2:7) of other Anglican provinces, we have a concept of a prince bishop and high priest. Not only are these concepts theologically questionable, but given that Hippolytus is not at all what the compilers of the Episcopal rite thought the document to be, this requires a wholesale revision. An appeal to the liturgical Q no longer holds theological or historical weight.

---

16. Bryan D. Spinks, "An Unfortunate *Lex Orandi*? Some Comments on Episcopacy Envisioned in the 1979 ECUSA Ordinal," *Journal of Anglican Studies* 2 (2004): 58–69.

# 11

# Has the Time Come for Hymnal Revision?

## WILLIAM BRADLEY ROBERTS[1]

### Recent Historic Practices and the Current Mandate

After the American 1928 Book of Common Payer was authorized by the Episcopal Church's General Convention, the church waited another fourteen years for the appearance of a new Episcopal hymnal. *The Hymnal 1940*, named for the year of its authorization by General Convention, was published in 1943, finally providing the church with a new, official hymnal for the first time since 1916.

Because of worldwide calamities in the 1930s, one can easily imagine the reasons for a fourteen-year lapse between the 1928 Book of Common Prayer and the *Hymnal 1940*. A general, global economic depression kept individuals and societies focused on the basic necessities of life. In addition, the menacing, encroaching

---

[1]. The Rev. William Bradley Roberts, DMA, is Professor of Church Music and Director of Chapel Music at the Virginia Theological Seminary.

Third Reich provoked widespread anxiety and fear. As important as the liturgy and music of the church might have been, issues of survival and safety easily claimed priority.

Since the Anglican Church in the United Kingdom does not have an authorized hymnal, the relationship between the Church of England's Book of Common Prayer and liturgical music resources is less collaborative. In the American Episcopal Church and some of its affiliates, however, the relationship between the two documents—prayer book and hymnal—is vital and essential.

The 78th General Convention of the Episcopal Church (Salt Lake City, 2015) passed resolutions that directed the Standing Commission on Liturgy and Music to present a plan (at the 79th General Convention, Austin, 2018) for revision of the Book of Common Prayer as well as the hymnal.[2] Though little urgency marked the language of the mandate, it carried at least the implication that the needs of the worshiping church warranted revision.

## New Hymns from Various Sources

Episcopal hymnody over the years since the *Hymnal 1982* has not been static but to the contrary has exhibited robust expansion. Supplements have appeared—*Simplified Accompaniment Edition*; *Lift Every Voice and Sing*; *El Himnario*; *Crowning Glory*; *Wonder, Love and Praise*; *Voices Found*; *Music by Heart: Paperless Songs for Evening Worship*—that amply demonstrate that the Standing Commission on Church Music (and, after the 1997 General Convention, the combined Standing Commission on Liturgy and Music) has sensed a keen need for expanded music resources over the past three decades.

---

2. Resolution 2015-A169 and Resolution 2015-D060, General Convention, *Journal of the General Convention of . . . The Episcopal Church, Salt Lake City, 2015* (New York: General Convention, 2015), 886–87, 941.

In addition to these official supplements, many unofficial documents appeared, resulting in an ever-widening corpus of congregational song. The proliferation of unofficial materials was so rapid, in fact, that the Standing Commission on Church Music, in the period from 1992 to 1994 when I was its chair, concluded that any attempt by the commission to monitor and/or regulate local songbooks would be an exercise in futility. Despite the denomination's declining population, the expansion of the church's song indicates an ever-expanding vitality in worship, at least in some quarters. Perhaps this is best seen in the widening cultural diversity of the Episcopal Church. The Diocese of Los Angeles, for example, speaks and sings its worship in ten languages, a fact that would astonish our forebears from the era of the 1928 Book of Common Prayer and the *Hymnal 1940*.

Not only have new discoveries arisen from diverse cultural groups within the Episcopal Church, but also hymnists and composers have continued the prolific creation of new hymnic materials. It is indicative of God's grace and generosity that these poets and musicians continue to be inspired by God to write new hymns and tunes, and that they respond faithfully and creatively. The so called "Hymnal Explosion," begun in the 1960s in Great Britain and the United States, has never really come to a halt.

In addition, other denominational hymnals subsequent to the *Hymnal 1982* have created (or discovered) new hymnody, later adopted by Episcopal congregations. Just as the *Hymnal 1982* lent new congregational song to other denominations, so has the flow been reciprocal. Our Episcopal hymnody has been vastly enriched by the contributions of other denominations.

## To Press Forward or Not?

This Niagara of hymnic material might be seen in and of itself to warrant production of a new Episcopal hymnal immediately (whether paper, electronic, or some combination), making new hymnody available as soon as possible. While resource-size and corporate-size parishes might easily locate these new materials on their own, congregations with limitations in finances and personnel are less likely to do so. Does this need indicate a new hymnal? If fresh, inspired, and life-giving song is being created, doesn't the church want to disseminate this song as soon as possible? Even though the church is faltering in some places, isn't it imperative to spread the Spirit's life-giving song from vibrant worshiping communities to struggling ones? If poets and composers are creating wonderful new congregational song, shouldn't we reward their efforts and encourage others to do the same?

In other words, does the Episcopal Church need to produce a new hymnal with all deliberate speed? Perhaps. But evidence points more clearly to a process that is at once carefully considered and skillfully coordinated.

## Hymnal Survey

A survey[3] by the research department of Church Pension Group in 2009 demonstrated that a large number of people (particularly young adults) were opposed to the production of a new hymnal. In this author's opinion, the survey was limited in some respects, and that skewed its results. Following is one respect in which the survey fell short.

While baby boomers might insist that music of a folk or rock style is required to reach young people, my experience over the past decade with young seminarians suggests otherwise. I cannot attest to the trends in other denominations (where "Popular Religious

---

3. https://www.cpg.org/linkservid/57003D75-DA12-05B2-F4FFD5819BE00E5A/showMeta/0/?label=Hymnal%20Revision%20Feasibility%20Study (accessed March 21, 2017).

Song," a term coined by Dr. Carol Doran, might have a strong appeal), but among young adults in the Episcopal Church there is a pronounced attraction to music that is steeped in mystery and transcendence. Even young adults who love rock music repeatedly attest in seminary classes that they do not want this style of music in worship.[4] Their deep response to Gregorian chant, for example, indicates young adults who yearn deeply for the numinous. This is not to deny the effectiveness of Popular Religious Song in some quarters. It is to say, however, that mystery is a vital component in the worship lives of young Episcopal adults. For example, weekday Evening Prayer at Virginia Theological Seminary is student led, and exhibits a different style and flavor each night. At the time of this writing, Choral Evensong consistently draws the largest number of students.

Parishioners of Episcopal parishes (as well as seminary students) probably remain unaware of the proliferation of new hymnody that is firmly rooted in the church's tradition. When questioned about new congregational song, therefore, they are most likely to assume this refers to Popular Religious Song. Whereas Popular Religious Song has its strong adherents, the young adults I describe above are more passionate about the church's traditional song. Because the Church Publishing survey might not have made apparent the repertoire of a prospective hymnal, my own theory is that young adults (again, the demographic group expressing the most vociferous opposition) spoke out against a new hymnal.

I suggest, therefore, that a new hymnal that brought to light new (and newly discovered) hymnic material in traditional musical language, as well as the classics of our faith, might be remarkably appealing to young adults (as well as to other groups who voted against a new hymnal in the survey). Another carefully considered survey

---

4. For a fuller discussion, see the introduction to William Bradley Roberts, *Music in Vital Congregations* (New York: Church Publishing, 2009).

might yield nuanced results to inform the Standing Commission on Liturgy and Music.

## Taking Cues from Book of Common Prayer Revision

Still, a far more significant factor suggests forestalling a new hymnal: the need to wait for prayer book revision. *Hymnal 1982* editor Raymond F. Glover (1928–2017) called the hymnal "the Companion to the Book of Common Prayer." If that is the case, and I believe it is, then one can't design a hymnal without first knowing the shape, substance, and theological content of the prayer book it intends to serve.

We have only to look at the changes in language and theology of the church's prayer from the Book of Common Prayer (1928) to the Book of Common Prayer (1979) revision to observe its influences on the *Hymnal 1982*: a stronger emphasis on Eucharistic liturgy, a widespread appeal for public baptism in the presence of the gathered community ("Will you who witness these vows do all in your power to support *these persons* in *their* life in Christ?"), a balance of penitence and joyful discipleship ("Deliver us from the presumption of coming to this Table for solace only, and not for strength; for pardon only, and not for renewal."), a move from parishioners engaging in private worship in public to worshiping as a corporate body that recognizes and celebrates the presence of other believers ("The peace of the Lord be always with you."), and a measured—though not extensive—attempt to broaden liturgical language to become more gender inclusive ("to us and to all whom you have made").[5] *The Hymnal 1982* responded to and reflected these changes among others.

Besides these issues of theology and anthropology, there were more literal language changes in the Book of Common Prayer (1979)

---

5. Book of Common Prayer (1979), 101, 303, 360, 372.

that required specific adjustments in the words of the hymnal: the newly translated texts of service music (the Ordinary of the Mass and the canticles, for example). Had musical settings of these texts been composed before the completion of the Book of Common Prayer (1979), they would have been rendered immediately obsolete, because they wouldn't have accommodated the new language. Likewise, prudence demands that new musical settings of liturgical texts in our time be delayed until prayer book language is settled.

While musical settings of the liturgy need to wait on a possible revision of the Book of Common Prayer, the collection of new hymnic materials need not be deterred. In fact, a broad collection of hymns and hymn tunes could begin very soon. Pulling the most-used items from the supplements, looking to the hymnals of other denominations, and searching through the vast contributions of poets and composers over the past three decades, one could find a wealth of new hymnic materials. Surveying congregations to determine which hymns are regularly sung would identify the active repertoire.

## The Abiding Legacy of the *Hymnal 1982*

Inevitably, some tunes in the *Hymnal 1982* will fall by the wayside. This certainly happened when the *Hymnal 1940* was revised. Whereas two-thirds of the hymns in the *Hymnal 1982* derived from the commonly used hymns of the *Hymnal 1940*, fully one-third were dropped. Every hymnal worth its salt has some cutting-edge material. As a foundation officer once told me, "We figure that if we're not making some mistakes, then we're not taking enough risks." Some hymns gain widespread usage and remain in the repertoire, but others decline in usage and are dropped, a natural and unavoidable process. Though we might suppose that our standard, traditional hymnody forms a closed canon that has remained consistent for centuries, comparing the past three Episcopal hymnals will reveal a continually shifting canon. When one browses through the *Hymnal 1916*, for example, there are many hymns and tunes that are unfamiliar, even to a seasoned hymn singer.

If the church decides to proceed with hymnal revision, it cannot move forward without acknowledging the Herculean accomplishments of the *Hymnal 1982*. New "classics" were added ("Lift high the cross" to the tune *Crucifer*); more American hymnody was included ("Come, thou fount," *Nettleton*; "How firm a foundation," *Foundation*; "Amazing grace," *New Britain*); a number of African American spirituals were newly published ("Let us break bread together on our knees," "Go tell it on the mountain"); and hymnody from Africa ("Jesu, Jesu") and Latin America ("Duérmete, niño lindo"), from Asia ("For the bread which you have broken," *Beng-Li*), and from the charismatic movement ("Seek ye first," "I am the bread of life") first found its way into an Episcopal hymnal in the *Hymnal 1982*. New additions also included ancient Greek and Latin hymns, often translated into English by members of the Hymnal 1982 committee ("Father we thank thee who hast planted," by F. Bland Tucker; "Redeemer of the nations, come," Charles P. Price). Texts and tunes, newly created for the *Hymnal 1982*, have become standard hymnody ("Like the murmur of the dove's song," *Bridegroom*; "O day of peace that dimly shines," *Jerusalem*). The latter two texts were penned by the Rev. Dr. Carl P. Daw Jr., a member of the Hymnal 1982 committee, who went on to become the leading American hymnist of his generation.

The *Hymnal 1982*'s accomplishments are myriad. Whenever it is revised, the new editorial committee will stand on the shoulders of the creators of the *Hymnal 1982* and its editor Dr. Raymond F. Glover.

# 12

# The Style and Format of the Book of Common Prayer

### Robert W. Prichard[1]

The members of the Standing Liturgical Commission who guided the General Convention in the adoption of the 1979 Book of Common Prayer were not only interested in improvements, expansion, and corrections to the contents of the liturgical texts that they had received from the previous edition of the prayer book; they were also interested in considering ways in which the format and the appearance of the Book of Common Prayer might be improved. This is hardly surprising, given the moment in which they were engaged in their work. The last third of the twentieth century was marked by a revolution in graphic design. As Gavin Ambrose and Paul Harris explain in *Fundamentals of Graphic Design*, photocomposition and digital technology led to "an explosion of the number of typefaces available due to the relative ease,

---

[1]. The Rev. Dr. Robert W. Prichard is the Arthur Lee Kinsolving Professor of Christianity in America and Instructor in Liturgics at the Virginia Theological Seminary.

speed, and cost of storing them compared to traditional type creation techniques."[2] It was no longer necessary to create fonts (the medium used to print texts in various typefaces) in hard metal. The available typefaces expanded exponentially from a limited number that had increased only slowly over the centuries. This was a moment in which graphic designers and those who appreciated their work were willing to consider new possibilities.

This willingness to experiment with style was evident in *The Liturgy of the Lord's Supper* (1967), *Services for Trial Use* (1971), and *Authorized Services 1973*, the three trial liturgies that preceded the *Proposed Book of Common Prayer* (1976), which on second adoption by the General Convention became the Book of Common Prayer (1979). The preface to *Services for Trial Use* was quite clear about the intention to consider new possibilities:

> It will be seen that the services are printed in very different style of layout and typeface. The reason for this is the pages which follow are, for the most part, reproduced from the pages of Prayer Book Studies. The Standing Liturgical Commission considers that the format of the service is no less a matter of experimentation than the rites themselves. It hopes that the comments of church members will help the Commission to decide in which of the several styles a future revised Book of Common Prayer should be printed.[3]

All three of the trial use volumes abandoned the Janson typeface in which the standard edition of the 1928 Book of Common Prayer had been printed. They did differ with one another, however. *The Liturgy of the Lord's Supper* made wide use of Baskerville typeface,

---

2. Gavin Ambrose and Paul Harris, *Fundamentals of Graphic Design* (New York: Bloomsbury Publishing, 2008), 35.
3. *Services for Trial Use: Authorized Alternatives to Prayer Book Services* (New York: Church Hymnal Corp., 1971), vii.

which would later be used for the *Hymnal 1982*.[4] *Services for Trial Use* was printed in a serif typeface but employed a sans serif typeface in some notes, titles, and headers.[5] *Authorized Services 1973* was most clear about the typefaces used; a note on the last page of the pew edition identified nine different ones used in five different combinations: Melior and Helvetica (Calendar); Mallard, Oracle, and Univers 65 (Holy Baptism); Caledonia and Optima (Holy Eucharist); Mallard and Univers 65 (Morning and Evening Prayer); and Baskerville and Spartan (Psalter).[6]

*The Liturgy of the Lord's Supper* and *Services for Trial Use* followed the Standard Book of 1928 in printing rubrics in red.[7] *Authorized Services 1973* dropped the use of red for rubrics in Baptism, Noonday Prayers, and An Order of Service for the Close of the Day (Compline). All three trial liturgies followed the 1928 printing convention of indicating congregational response in two

---

4. For a discussion of typefaces in use in the Episcopal Church, see Adam Michael Wood, "Episcopal Church Fonts," http://progressivesolemnity.org/2015/05/08/episcopal-fonts/ (accessed February 13, 2017).
5. The tails at the ends of letter stokes in some typefaces are known as serifs. Sans serif typefaces lack such tails.
6. The note on typefaces was not included in the expanded edition. See *Authorized Services 1973*, pew edition (New York: Church Hymnal Corp., 1973), 462.
7. The Book of Common Prayer is not copyrighted and is printed by multiple publishers. Church Publishing, however, prepares a "Standard Book of Common Prayer," to which all other editions are to be compared by the Custodian of the Book of Common Prayer. If all is in order, the Custodian issues a certificate indicating the book conforms to the Standard Book and is therefore appropriate for use. The canon on the standard edition (Canon II.3 in the 2015 numeration) was revised in 1892 to say that use of either red or black rubrics would constitute conformity to the standard edition. The rubrics in the Standard Book of 1928 were in red; most pew editions had black rubrics. See Society of Archbishop Justus, "The 1928 Book of Common Prayer: The Standard Book," http://justus.anglican.org/resources/bcp/1928Standard/Standard.htm (accessed October 12, 2017).

different ways: by printing the people's response in italics or by using small print designations to identify speakers.[8]

The text in all three books was justified on left and right margins, with an important exception. The International Consultation on English Texts, a gathering of representatives from the Roman Catholic Church and from many English-speaking Protestant denominations, agreed on common language for certain key liturgical texts. These were printed in *Prayers We Have in Common* (1970) with phrase-length lines rather than with right justification. This formatting was copied in the three Episcopal trial liturgies.

Consultation with the Roman Catholic Church may have been the reason for an anomaly that appeared in *Authorized Services 1973*. An Order of Service for the Close of the Day (Compline), a service that had appeared in *Service for Trial Use*, abandoned what Daniel Berkeley Updike, the graphic designer of the 1928 prayer book, had identified as the chief feature that distinguished Anglican from Roman Catholic liturgical printing. Updike had written that the "Anglican use in printing these official prayer books differs from the Roman use only in minor details, the chief of which is its employment of italic for responses, eliminating the use of ℞ before each response . . . for to the average congregation the ℣ and ℞ would be unknown."[9] The Compline Service in *Authorized Services 1973* did not follow Updike's observation in this regard. While retaining the two conventions used to designate speakers in the rest of the book (titles, and alternation of roman and italics), it also introduced V (for versicle) and R (for response) in the suffrages before the Lord's

---

8. The 1928 Book of Common Prayer used "Minister" and "Answer" as designations. *The Liturgy of the Lord's Supper*, which had only the Eucharist, used "Priest" and "People." *The Book of Occasional Services* and *Authorized Services* used these two designations, but also added "Leader" and "People."
9. Daniel Berkeley Updike, "Some Notes on Liturgical Printing," *The Dolphin*, no. 2 (1935): 208–16, http://www.oremus.org/liturgy/printing/updike.html (accessed October 12, 2017).

Prayer. It differed from the remainder of the trial liturgy in another way as well. Unlike the version of nighttime prayers in *Services for Trial Use*, the instructions were not printed in red. As in *Services for Trial Use* the doxology was omitted from the end of the Lord's Prayer (as was also the case with Noonday Prayers)—a convention that ran counter to that in the appearances of the Lord's Prayer in most of the rest of the book.[10]

There was another important change in the three trial liturgies, one that Andrew McGowan has rightly noted elsewhere in this collection reflected the interest in the structure of the liturgy of Gregory Dix and other mid-twentieth-century Anglican liturgical scholars.[11] This new emphasis would be particularly evident in tables of contents. The 1928 table had listed all elements of the book in the same size type and with the same left margin. There were no subheads to indicate how parts of the book related to one another. *The Liturgy of the Lord's Supper* contained only materials needed for the Eucharist and did not include a table of contents, but *Services for Trial Use* divided material into nine categories. Four of these contained only single items: Preface, Holy Baptism

---

10. The Lord's Prayer had appeared without the closing doxology ("for thine is the kingdom, and the power," etc.) in the sixteenth-century editions of the Book of Common Prayer. The 1662 Book of Common Prayer, however, added the doxology in some places. The 1928 Book of Common Prayer adopted the practice of using the doxology, except for a few occasions with a penitential flavor (the priest's initial recitation of the Lord's Prayer at the start of the Eucharist, the Litany, the Churching of Women, the Visitation of the Sick, and the Burial of the Dead). The 1979 book further expanded use of the doxology; of texts carried over from the 1928 prayer book, only the Lord's Prayer in the Great Litany appeared without the doxology. The omission of the doxology from the new Noonday Prayers and Compline was an antiquarian choice that did not correspond to the use in the rest of the book and often created confusion among worshipers.
11. See McGowan's section titled "From 1928 to 1979: Tweaks" in chapter 3 of this volume.

with the Laying-On-of-Hands, the Calendar of the Church Year, and the Psalter. The remaining five categories—the Holy Eucharist; the Daily Office; the Pastoral Offices; the Ordination of Bishops, Priests, and Deacons; and the Proper of the Sundays and Other Holy Days—grouped appropriate material together. Morning and Evening Prayer, and the shorter services for noonday and the close of day were, for example, grouped together for the first time under a "Daily Office" heading. After some further experimentation in *Authorized Services 1973*, the *Services of Trial Use* pattern was essentially adopted in the 1979 prayer book, with one important difference. The editors of *Services for Trial Use* printed traditional language services—what would later be called Rite I—before the corresponding contemporary services but reversed that order in the listing of the collects in the Proper of the Sundays and Other Holy Day services. Officiants often found themselves reading the collect that did not correspond to the service that they were leading. The Standing Liturgical Commission responded to widespread complaints by separating the contemporary and traditional collects into separate sections. Once this change was made, it was no longer possible to list the lectionary and the proper liturgies for special days with the collects; as a result, the unified Proper of *Services for Trial Use* was broken up into four separate sections in the *Draft Proposed Book of Common Prayer*: Collects: Traditional; Collects: Contemporary; Proper Liturgies for Special Days; and Lectionary.

The services themselves were divided with various heads and subheads that had not appeared in the 1928 editions of the Book of Common Prayer. *The Liturgy of the Lord's Supper* included four major heads: the Ministry of the Word, the Offertory, the Consecration, and the Breaking of the Bread. It also included titles for most other elements in the service. *Services for Trial Use* include three major heads—the Proclamation of the Word of God, the Prayers, and the Celebration of the Holy Communion—and some titles that served as subheads, such as "the Breaking of the Bread." Morning and Evening Prayer, which was a combined office in *Services for Trial Use*, introduced titles for portions of the service (including English translations for the canticle titles) and numbered the canticles.

The trial liturgies received an uneven reception in the rank and file of the Episcopal Church. While some were excited by the changes introduced, others were not at all happy with the proposal. Critics of prayer book revision formed, for example, the Society for the Preservation of the Book of Common Prayer (later renamed the Prayer Book Society) in 1971 to campaign for the continued authorization of the 1928 Book of Common Prayer. The Standing Liturgical Commission and the General Conventions of 1976 and 1979 paid some heed to such critics and moved in a more cautious direction in *Draft Proposed Book of Common Prayer* and the Book of Common Prayer 1979.

Some of the most pointed criticism was directed at the format and style of the proposed books. The color of the cover of *Services for Trial Use* (olive green) seemed, for example, to attract particular censure. *Services for Trial Use* became almost universally known as the "Green Book," and wisecracks and jokes about it abounded ("If I could get hold of all those books and a Waring Blender, I could produce a heck of a dip."). When the Standing Liturgical Commission tried to head off such comments on the next round of revision by giving *Authorized Services 1973* a two-color cover with a chevron pattern, parishioners throughout the church responded by referring to it as the "Zebra Book."

A story circulated among clergy at the time that suggested another approach to revision. A parish rector of a well-heeled congregation in the Midwest, so the story ran, was concerned about the dissatisfaction with the "Green Book" that had been shown by parishioners in other nearby congregations. He ordered copies of the book for use in his parish, but before putting them in the pews sent them to a binder for rebinding with the familiar blue buckram covers that had been used on the 1928 editions of the prayer book. The result was that almost no one complained about the new text.

The story is probably fictional, but it does point to an important insight, one that the members of the Standing Liturgical Commission appeared ready to hear by the mid-1970s: the way in which a liturgical text is presented to a congregation makes a difference. Decisions about formatting, typestyle, arrangement of contents, and the like can add to or detract from a favorable impression about a text. Episcopalians may be more willing to accept significant change when it is packaged in a form that suggests continuity and stability. By 1976 the Standing Liturgical Commission was ready to curtail the degree of experimentation in graphic design.

## Bradbury Thompson and the Washburn College Bible

One response to negative reaction to prayer book revision was the seeking of advice from famed Yale designer Bradbury Thompson. Thompson provided expert advice on the graphic design of the *Proposed Book of Common Prayer* (1976) and the Book of Common Prayer 1979. At the time he was working on the *Washburn College Bible* (1979), a reprinting of the King James Version of the Bible, a master-project in which this leading figure in the field of graphic design offered his own vision of what had been the first major printing project in the Western World—Gutenberg's edition of the Bible. The project, undertaken for Thompson's alma mater, featured a coherent system of typeface, line justification, use of italics, and conventions for indicating quotation. Many of those same innovations would be incorporated in the 1979 edition of the Book of Common Prayer.

Thompson decided upon the Sabon typeface for the *Washburn College Bible*. Sabon was a new typeface created by European designer Jan Tschichold, but it was based on a sixteenth-century type created by Claude Garamond.[12] One of the characteristics of the type was that the roman, italics, and bold versions of Sabon occupied identical amounts of space, which Thompson reasoned was more pleasing to the eye and therefore easier to read.[13]

In addition, Thompson made the decision to abandon what the foreword to the *Washburn College Bible* explained was the tradition "since the time of Gutenberg" of setting "the text of the Bible in lines of type of equal length." Rather "the text of this Bible [was] set in lines of varying length, each accommodating a complete phrase, just as the words might be spoken." "The result," the foreword explained, "was a more natural type of configuration, aligned at the left and irregular at the right. This new system eliminates several awkward aspects of conventional typesetting. No words are hyphenated at the end of lines. Spacing between letters and words is uniformly consistent." Thompson also eliminated the use in text, titles, and headers of what he called the "less-readable all-capital characters used liberally in older Bibles." He made five exceptions: Lord, Lord God, Jehovah, I am that I am, and I am, "which appear in capital and small-capital letters."

For the main text Thompson limited the use of italics, which had been used in editions of the King James Bible to indicate words supplied for meaning in the English for which there was no equivalent in the original biblical language. (He retained the use of italics, however, for the page headings.) Thompson also limited the

---

12. Bradbury Thompson, *The Art of Graphic Design* (New Haven, CT: Yale University Press, 1988), 201. Tschichold had cooperated with Thompson on *Homage to the Book* (1967) and remained in contact with him. Tschichold was working at the time on a new *Sabon Antigua* typeface, and with Thompson's encouragement he created a phototypography version of Sabon type in 1972.

13. This is not the case with many other typefaces commonly used today such as Arial, Cambria, Garamond, and Times New Roman.

variation in type size, using one size "for every word of the Bible except for the main titles, which are set in an heroic size."[14]

Reformation Historian Roland H. Bainton of Yale Divinity School argued that Thompson's approach was a decided improvement. Bainton explained in the preface that he wrote for the *Washburn College Bible* that the arrangement of text was directed "not to the achievement of rigid regularity in length of line and column, but rather to the rounding out of sentences and phrases, so that the eye readily perceives and the voice readily conveys meaning."[15]

The foreword also commented on the arrangement of verse and chapter numbers in the *Washburn College Bible*:

> The numbers identifying the chapters and verses are placed in the left-hand margin rather than in the text matter. This departure from the traditional treatment expedites the search for particular passages, and further reduced the small intrusions that distract the reader. Also, by allowing the columns, as well as the lines of text type, to vary in length instead of prescribing an arbitrary bottom margin, it was possible to end each column with a complete verse and to avoid an interruption in reading.[16]

Thompson's edition of the King James Bible was a model for clarity and legibility.

While the critique offered in the front material of the *Washburn College Bible* was directed at earlier printings of the Bible, much of it also applied to the 1928 edition of the Book of Common Prayer. That book—and editions of the prayer book before it—had justified right margins and consistent text lengths. Some lines ended with

---

14. "Forward to the First Edition of the Modern Phrased Version," reprinted in Thompson, *Art of Graphic Design*, 211–12.
15. "Preface to the Washburn College Bible," reprinted in ibid., 209.
16. "Foreword," reprinted in ibid., 212.

hyphens. The verse numbers in the Psalter were printed with the text matter, rather than in a separate left-hand column.[17] In some cases Psalter verses ran over from one page to the next.

Some of the criticism would also apply with equal justice to *The Liturgy of the Lord's Supper* (1967), *Services for Trial Use* (1971), and *Authorized Services 1973*. *Services for Trial Use*, for example, generally had the justified right margins, the irregular spacing, and the hyphenation to which Thompson objected, with the exception already noted in the texts agreed upon by the International Consultation on Common Texts. All three books made use of capitals and small capitals. (*Authorized Services 1971* further increased the variety of typestyle by printing the book title in large lowercase letters.)

There were some elements, however, in which the Standing Liturgical Commission was already moving in the direction to which Thompson pointed. *Services for Trial Use* and *Authorized Services 1973*—the two trial liturgies that included the Psalter— listed verse numbers in a separate left-hand column and varied length so that no verses were split between pages.[18]

## The Book of Common Prayer 1979

Bradbury Thompson's input was incorporated for the first time in the *Draft Proposed Book of Common Prayer*, which was presented to the General Convention of 1976. The Sabon typeface was used throughout the book. All-capitals were avoided in texts, headers, and titles, with two of the four exceptions that Thompson himself

---

17. Prayer books through 1928 printed the full texts of Gospels and Epistles for Sundays and major Holy Days. Verses numbers were omitted for these lessons.

18. *Services for Trial Use* included only a partial Psalter, which was titled "The Psalter: Part I."

had allowed: the appearance in the Psalter of LORD and YAHWEH (the contemporary rendering from Hebrew of what the King James Version has called Jehovah). Text was arranged in phrase length, rather than right-justified lines. The length of the text on the page was not fixed but rather arranged in ways that corresponded to the specific material presented. If psalm or prayer ended near the bottom of a page, for example, the text concluded there. The verses numbers in the Psalter were also arranged in a separate left-hand column and no verse was split by a page break.

The heads, subheads, and titles of the portion of the service of the trial liturgies were continued. Curiously, however, the way in which the Rite I and Rite II Eucharistic services were divided did not correspond to the section titles in "An Order for Celebrating the Holy Eucharist," an outline of the Eucharist that allowed for local innovation and adaptation. The disagreement of the two sets of titles were a missed opportunity to make a point about common structure behind eucharistic celebrations.[19]

The anomalies in Noonday Prayer and Compline, and the division of the Proper of the Church year into sections continued.

The Book of Common Prayer preserved all the graphic conventions of the *Draft Proposed Book of Common Prayer*, except for the in the matter of the cover. The *Draft Proposed Book of Common Prayer* had a blue paper cover; the Book of Common Prayer 1979 returned to the buckram covers in blue and red that had been used with the 1928 edition. As in the *Draft Proposed Book of Common Prayer*, the rubrics no longer appeared in red in the pew editions as had been the case in the trial liturgies, though they would do so in altar missals and in the planned Standard Edition.[20]

---

19. Book of Common Prayer (1979), 402–3.
20. The Standard Edition of 1979 was never printed. See Society of Archbishop Justice, "The Standard Edition of the 1979 Book of Common Prayer,"

When the first copies of the 1979 book came off the press, Isabel Baumgartner wrote a review for the Episcopal News Service. Her comments indicated her conviction that following Thompson's advice had led to the desired effect. She commended the typeface, which she said, conveyed to her "gracefulness, strength, and integrity." She also wrote favorably about the "plain buckram-finish binding, the title on the spine in gold, [and] the front cover bearing a tall gold Latin-style cross whose slender arms broaden slightly toward their extremities." One short phrase summed up her overall reaction: "It looks like a prayer book."[21]

## Subsequent Developments in the Anglican Communion

The Episcopal Church was not the only member of the Anglican Communion to make changes in the format and style in the publication of revisions of the Book of Common Prayer. One way to categorize these efforts in the Anglican Communion is to divide them into two categories: (1) those books marked by continuing typographical experimentation, and (2) those books that seek something like the consistency of style suggested by Bradbury Thompson. Taken together, the English *Alternative Service Book 1980* and *Common Worship* (2000) are the best examples of the first category. They explore conventions beyond that of the trial liturgies of the Episcopal Church, and hint that the experimentation in style is not yet over. There are, to be sure, some features that had been approved for the American 1979 Book of Common Prayer, but even in those cases there were differences. The table of contents in

---

http://justus.anglican.org/resources/bcp/Standard1979.htm (accessed October 17, 2017).

21. Isabel Baumgartner, "Proposed Prayer Book a Massive Print Job," February 10, 1977, Episcopal News Service Archive, http://www.episcopalarchives.org/cgi-bin/ENS/ENSpress_release.pl?pr_number=77039 (accessed February 25, 2017).

*The Alternative Services* book was divided into sections, but the sections were not identical to the American divisions. *Common Worship*, moreover, moved back in the direction of simple listing of services, with only the Daily Office and the Eucharist grouped as sections with subsections. There were section titles in the Eucharist, though they also did not correspond to those in the American book.

The overall appearance of the English books is very different from the 1979 Book of Common Prayer. Bold and all-capitals were used more often in the English books than in either the 1979 Book of Common Prayer or the Canadian *Book of Alternative Services*. The English *Alternative Service Book* included a set of marginal numbers indicating parts of the service, an experiment dropped in *Common Worship*. The *Alternative Service Book* was printed in a serif typeface (Palatino) as was the case with the 1979 Book of Common Prayer, but the subsequent *Common Worship* appears in two different typefaces: Gill Sans for printed editions and Arial for electronic versions; both are sans serif forms.[22] The overall appearance of the English books lacked the consistency and uniformity of the American 1979 Book of Common Prayer.

The *Book of Alternative Services of the Anglican Church of Canada* (1985), *A Prayer Book for Australia* (1994), and the Church of Ireland's Book of Common Prayer (2004) are representative of the second category. They come close to representing a new normal, sharing a format similar but not identical to that of the American Book of Common Prayer (1979). The revisers of these books chose serif typefaces.[23] The books have tables of contents organized much like the American prayer book, use phrase-length lines, list verses

---

22. Paul Luna, "Texts and Technology, 1970–2000," *A Companion to the History of the Book*, ed. Simon Eliot and Jonathan Rose (Malden, MA: Wiley-Blackwell, 2009), 392.
23. Of these three, only the Irish Book of Common Prayer (2004) identifies the specific serif typeface on its publication page. The book is set in FF Scala.

in the Psalter in a separate left column, and vary text length on individual pages to avoid breaking up verses and prayers.

There are some differences, however. The pew editions of the books print rubrics in red; either include Latin (Ireland) or English (Canada and New Zealand) for Canticle titles, but not both as in the American prayer book; and in two of the three cases (Canada, and New Zealand) drop the Latin titles for the Psalms. All three group the collects, special services, and lectionary materials together, and refrain from the use of the abbreviations V (versicle) and R (response) of the Episcopal Church's Compline service. All three books use boldface to indicate congregational response. *A Prayer Book for Australia* also makes frequent use of all capitals and has greater variation in type size than in the 1979 Book of Common Prayer.

The *New Zealand Prayer Book* (1989) falls roughly into this second category but with two important innovations: the use of multiple languages (English, Maori, Fijian, and Tongan) and the addition of illustrations at the beginning of major sections. The Episcopal Church experimented with the use of multiple languages in *The Book of Occasional Services 2003*, which has some material in Spanish and French, and the Selected Liturgy series issued by the Convocation of American Churches in Europe.[24] The idea of printing illustrations is an old one that dates to the eighteenth century, if not earlier. At that point, printing and binding were separate steps, and illustrators provided drawings that could be bound with prayers books. To this point, however, the Episcopal Church has not followed the example of the *New Zealand Prayer Book, Evangelical*

---

24. The Selected Liturgy series (1999–2004) includes the public liturgies of the church from the Book of Common Prayer on facing pages in English and one other language. There are editions in Italian, Spanish, French, and German.

*Lutheran Worship* (2006), or the Presbyterian *Book of Common Worship* (2018) in including illustrations.

## Issues in Future Revision of the American Prayer Book

The 1979 editorial decisions have worn well. In general, the conventions of the 1979 Book of Common Prayer continue to shape more recent publications in the Enriching Our Worship series or the various editions of *Lesser Feasts and Fasts* and the *Book of Occasional Services*. There have been, however, some minor changes introduced by the Standing Commission on Liturgy and Music, such as the wider use of V and R to designate speakers in *Enriching Our Worship 1* and the reintroduction of the label *Minister* in *Enriching Our Worship 3*.[25] It might make sense to revisit the church's liturgical style sheet before publishing a revision of the Book of Common Prayer. Among the issues to consider are the following:

### Translation

How will translation be handled in the future? Will the Episcopal Church follow the lead of the Anglican Church in Aotearoa, New Zealand, and Polynesia and print editions containing multiple languages, or will there be parallel monolingual books? There are good reasons to take either path. Multilanguage volumes are useful for young immigrants or children of immigrants who are not entirely self-sufficient in their parents' language of origin; the inclusion of

---

25. See *Enriching Our Worship 1: Morning and Evening Prayer, The Great Litany, [and] The Holy Eucharist* (New York: Church Hymnal Corp., 1998), 42, for the use of V and R in the Daily Office. See *Enriching Our Worship 2: Ministry with the Sick or Dying [and] Burial of a Child* (New York: Church Hymnal Corp., 2000), 2, and *Enriching Our Worship 3: Burial Rites for Adults Together with a Rite for the Burial of a Child* (New York: Church Publishing, 2006), 43, for the use of *Minister*.

materials in their language can be both a helpful aid and a powerful sign of inclusion. On the other hand, multilingual publications quickly strain reasonable page and expense limits. Perhaps the initiative of the Convocation of the American Churches in Europe points a reasonable way forward—publication of a series of bilingual books that included liturgies selected for their frequent use in public worship.

## Typeface and Title

What typeface should be used? Two logical candidates are Sabon and Garamond. Sabon continues to be used in the Enriching Our Worship series, and is familiar to most Episcopal readers. Garamond is similar in appearance and is more widely available than Sabon, however.[26]

While American hymnals have dates of adoption as part of their titles, American editions of the Book of Common Prayer do not. Some other provinces of the Anglican Communion include a national designation in their titles: *The Scottish Book of Common Prayer*, the *New Zealand Prayer Book*, *A Prayer Book for Australia*, etc. With many different editions of the prayer book now easily available electronically, the possibilities for confusion are increasing. The General Convention should consider whether it is now time to add either a date, or a national designation, or both to the cover of the next Book of Common Prayer.

## Designation of Speakers

What convention is to be followed in designating speakers? With the exception of Compline, the Book of Common Prayer (1979)

---

26. Sabon is not, for example, included among the typefaces supplied in Microsoft Office 2016.

used two conventions: labels (officiant, priest, people, etc.) in small italic print or the alternation of roman and italic print. Compline in the Book of Common Prayer (1979) added the third designation of V and R. That designation has been repeated in a few other offices in the *Book of Occasional Services*—particularly those such as Stations of the Cross and Stations at a Christmas Creche that were based on Roman Catholic parallels—but it has not been picked up by other churches in the Anglican Communion. Our communion partners have offered their own convention by using roman and bold typeface to indicate the alternation of speakers. One recent liturgical work from Church Publishing—*Daily Prayer for All Seasons* (2014)—imitated that convention, but the book's circulation to this point has been limited. If we consider revision, it would make sense to ask what and how many conventions should be used in the future. Would the use of four conventions confuse visitors and newcomers? Would it make sense to limit future editions to one or two conventions?

One might also ask whether the designation of the bishop or priest who presides at worship as *celebrant* is the appropriate label. Some have pointed out that not all liturgical rites are celebrations, and that even when they are intended as such, celebration is the common undertaking of the whole congregation rather than the work of a single person. Should General Convention consider some other designations, such as *presider* or *president* for the one who leads worship?

## The Proper of the Church Year

Is it time to reunite the material related to the Proper of the Church Year in one place? The 1979 decision to divide that material was a pragmatic decision based on alleviating confusion about the order to the collects in *Services for Trial Use*. In the years since, other churches in the communion have figured out ways to keep changeable material related to the Church Year together in one place. Should the Episcopal Church follow suit?

## The Lord's Prayer

Is it time to consider once again the use of the doxology with the Lord's Prayer? The general trend in the Anglican liturgy since 1662 has been to add the doxology in more and more places. Is it time to reevaluate the few places in which a shortened form of the Lord's Prayer was introduced in 1979?

## Illustrations

Should the Episcopal Church follow the example of New Zealand Anglicans, the Evangelical Lutheran Church, and the Presbyterian Church (USA) and add selected illustrations?

Were the Standing Commission on Liturgy and Music to seek the advice of a graphic designer of the caliber of Bradbury Thompson in a future revision of the Book of Common Prayer, that designer would undoubtedly point to other ways in which the accessibility and appearance of the Book of Common Prayer might be enhanced.

# INDEX

Addai and Mari, 113–14, 117
Alexander, J. Neil, 96–97
*Alternative Service Book 1980* (Church of England), 60–61, 156n27, 179–80, 233–34
*An Australian Prayer Book* (1978), 60
Anselm, 107, 110
*Apostolic Constitutions*, 114, 205
*Apostolic Tradition*, xv, 8n9, 113, 129, 136, 141, 203–12
Atonement, 107–9, 111–12
Augustine of Hippo, 7, 95n20, 148, 191n33

Bainton, Roland H., 230
Balanced language, xiv, 39, 42, 45. *See also* Expansive language and Inclusive language
Baptism xii, xiv, 16–17, 26, 45, 47, 51–52, 71–86, 87–104, 127, 132n20, 159, 181, 184, 188, 190, 194–95, 197–98, 201, 207, 218, 223, 225
    Baptismal Covenant, 45, 83–84, 88–89, 92, 94–98, 100–101, 134
    Baptismal theology and ecclesiology, 17, 87, 94, 104, 105, 132n 20, 181, 184, 187–88, 190–91, 194–95, 197, 218

Barton, John, 210–11
Basil, St., *the Egyptian Anaphora of*, 114–15, 129n11, 130–31n16
Baumgartner, Isabel, 233
Baumstark, Anton, 10n10, 204
Bible
    as source for liturgical texts and lectionary, 60, 64, 100, 106, 143–44, 229
    Geneva Bible, 27n15
    Great Bible, 27, 28n16
    King James Version, 20, 22–24, 27n15, 228–30, 232
    Revised Standard, 23–27, 28n16
    Washburn College Bible, 228–30
Book of Common Prayer (English, 1549), 1–3, 15–17, 72, 76–79, 81, 115, 130, 131n17, 144–45, 148–49, 151–52, 164, 172–73, 176, 180, 183, 185
Book of Common Prayer (English, 1552), 15n17, 16n19, 72, 77–81, 130, 149, 152, 172–76, 180, 183, 204
Book of Common Prayer (English, 1662), 51, 55–56, 58n12, 60–61, 78–79, 81–82, 83, 131n17, 149–50, 152, 175–76, 180, 207n8, 225n10, 239

Book of Common Prayer
(American, 1928), xv, 12n12,
17, 20, 22n8, 27–30, 32–33, 43,
52–55, 58n12, 80–82, 90, 112,
145, 147, 149–50, 153–55, 165,
173–76, 207n8, 213, 215, 218,
222–28, 230–32
Book of Common Prayer, Proposed
(English, 1928), 58, 175–76,
179–80
Book of Common Prayer
(American, 1979), xii–xvi,
4, 6–8, 10, 12, 15n17, 16–17,
23–24, 29–31, 35–36, 38–39,
41n45, 43n50, 45–65, 67–70,
71–72, 82–86, 87–88, 91n10,
92–94, 96, 101, 104, 105,
106n2, 112, 115, 130–31, 139,
141, 152–59, 161, 164, 179–83,
186–87, 190, 194, 199–201, 207,
211, 218–19, 221–22, 225n10,
226–28, 231–39
Book of Common Prayer (Irish,
2004), 97n24, 117, 234
*Book of Common Worship*
(Presbyterian, 2018)
Botte, Bernard, 206
Bradshaw, Paul, 69, 209–10
Brent, Allen, 208–9
Buchanan, Colin, 117n23
Buddhism, 98n27, 108

*Celebrating Common Prayer*, 61, 64
*Common Worship*, 61–62, 67, 69,
95n21, 97, 99–100, 180, 183, 186,
207, 233–34
Confirmation, xiv, 22, 75–76,
78–79, 81–83, 85, 94, 101–2
Cranmer, Thomas 2n3, 3–4, 6–7,
9–10, 12, 14–16, 49n2, 50–51, 54,
56–58, 65, 69, 72, 76–81, 95, 115,
144–46, 148, 174–76, 183, 204

Daily Office 12, 27–28, 30, 49–70,
86, 104, 145, 147–57, 165, 167,
226, 234, 236n25. See also
Morning Prayer and Evening
Prayer.
Cathedral and Monastic forms
of the Daily Office, 51,
57–58, 65, 67, 69
*Daily Office SSF*, 60–61
*Daily Prayer for All Seasons*, xiin6,
50, 65–69, 238
Daw, Carl P. Jr., 220
Dix, Gregory 10, 53, 206, 225

Easton, Burton Scott, 206
English Language Liturgical
Consultation (ELLC), 39–40,
46, 158. See also International
Consultation on English Texts.
Enriching Our Worship series, xii,
39–40, 45–47, 50, 61–65, 67–69,
104, 115–16, 132, 135, 180–81,
200–201, 236–37
Eucharistic Prayers xiii–xv, 7n7, 10,
16, 25, 29n18, 30, 33, 43n50, 46,
54, 92, 99n28, 104, 105–19, 121–
41, 183–84, 204, 206–8, 210
East and West Syrian
Eucharistic Prayers, 72, 106,
113, 117–18, 210
Evening Prayer, xiv, 28, 50–58, 61,
64, 69–70, 154, 156, 217, 223,
226–27. See also Daily Office
Expansive language 40, 45, 62. See
also Balanced language and
Inclusive language.

Farley, Wendy, 110
Farwell, James W. xiv. 92–93,
105–19
Forester, Kevin Thew, 98–99
Fuller, Reginald H., 85

General Convention, xi–xiii, xv–xvi, 1, 21, 24, 28, 33–35, 40–41, 43, 45–48, 63, 83, 88n3, 93–94, 100, 102, 153, 158, 164, 168, 175, 213–14, 221–22, 227, 231, 237–38
Glover, Raymond F., 218, 220

Hippolytus, 8n9, 136n32, 204–9, 211–12
Hooker, Richard, 118
*Hymnal 1916, The*, 213, 220
*Hymnal 1940, The*, 41, 213, 215, 219
*Hymnal 1982, The*, 41, 48, 214–15, 216, 218–20

Incarnation, 107, 109, 111–15, 117–18, 126, 199–200
Inclusive language, 38–40, 62, 63n19, 64, 67, 135n27, 218. *See also* Balanced language and Expansive language.
International Anglican Liturgical Consultation, 106, 177, 225
International Commission on English in the Liturgy (ICEL), 26, 184n28
International Consultation on English Texts (ICET), 26–27, 33, 35, 40, 46, 224. *See also* English Language Liturgical Consultation.
*Intercessions for the Christian People*, 118

Jennings, Nathan G. xiv, 1–17
Johnson, Maxwell E., 129n9, 209
Joint Liturgical Group (Great Britain), 60n15, 156n27

Kähler, Martin, 109
Kavanagh, Aidan, 83n31, 84, 103
King James Version. *See* Bible.

Language of worship. *See* Balanced Language, Expansive language, and Inclusive language.
Lectionary, 3, 30n20, 47, 112, 143–68, 228, 235
  *Sanctorale*, sanctoral calendar, 66, 146, 148–49, 151, 153, 157, 159–60, 164, 166–67
  *Temporale*, temporal calendar, 151
Leo the Great, 138
Ligorio, Pirro, 204
*Lift Every Voice and Sing*, 40, 214
Liturgical Commission (Church of England), 61. For the Episcopal Church, *see* Standing Liturgical and Standing Commission on Liturgy and Music
"Liturgical Q," 205–06, 209–12
Luther, Martin, 3n5, 5, 76, 79, 82, 128n8, 130n15, 182, 184
Lutheran Churches, 3, 7–8, 106, 115, 118, 182, 207
  Evangelical Lutheran Church in America (ELCA), 97n24, 116, 184, 186, 235–36, 239
  Lutheran Church-Missouri Synod, 186
  North American Lutheran Church, 121n1
*Lux Mundi*, 111, 118

Malloy, Patrick, xiv–xv, 169–202
Mark, St., *Alexandrian Prayer of*, 114
McGowan, Andrew, xiv, 49–70, 225
McGowan, Anne, 130n13
Mertens, Herman-Emiel, 119
*Minjung* theologians (Korea), 110
Meyers, Ruth, 82, 101, 101–2n33
Morgan, Robert, 210–11

Morning Prayer, 12, 25n12, 51, 53–54, 112, 150, 152, 154, 158. *See also* Daily Office

Null, Ashley, 7n7

Ordination, xv, 22, 26, 86, 91, 205, 207–08, 210–12, 226

Paschal mystery, 93, 176, 186, 198
Pelagius, 95, 97n24, 191–93
Phillips, L. Edward, 209
Porter, Harry Boone, 212
*Prayer Book for Australia* (1992), 60, 185, 234–35, 237
Prayer Book Studies, 24–28, 32–33, 52, 63, 82–83, 101–2, 153–57, 160, 222
Price, Charles P., 30–31, 34–35, 220
Prichard, Robert W. xi–xvi, 10n10, 19–48, 221–39
Prosper of Aquitaine, 137, 188, 191–92
Psalms. *See* the Psalter.
Psalter, 5, 27, 27–28nn15–16, 33, 35, 50–51, 53–54, 57–58, 60, 62, 64–66, 69–70, 149–50, 154–57, 159, 163, 172, 175, 180, 223, 226, 231–32, 235

Ramshaw, Gail, 116–17
Raposa, Michael, 107
Revised Standard Version. *See* Bible
Rite I, 12, 16, 16n18, 19, 30–31, 35, 40–45, 47, 52–54, 115, 226, 232
Rite II, 10, 25n12, 31–32, 34–36, 39, 43, 46–47, 52–54, 56, 59, 62–65, 115, 207, 232
Roberts, William Bradley xv, 213–20

*Sanctorle*, sanctoral calendar. *See* calendar.
Schifrin, Amy C. xiv–xv, 121–41
Schmemann, Alexander, 125–26
Senn, Frank C., 130n15, 136n33
*Shape of the Liturgy, The*, 10, 53
Soteriology, 107–8, 110
Spinks, Bryan D., xv, 8n9, 70n25, 95–97, 113n14, 203–12
Standing Liturgical Commission, 21–24, 26, 29–34, 38–40, 52, 153, 221–22, 226–28, 231
Standing Commission on Liturgy and Music, xi, xiii, xvi, 1, 16, 40, 45, 94, 100, 153, 214, 218, 236, 239
Stewart-Sykes, Alistair, 209
Strout, Shawn O. xivn9, xv, 143–68
*Supplemental Liturgical Materials*, 39, 63, 63–64n20,
*Supplemental Liturgical Texts*, 39, 62–63

Tanner, Kathryn, 93
*Temporale*, temporal calendar. *See* calendar.
Thompson, Bradbury, 228–31, 233, 239
Turrell, James F. xiv, 71–104
Two-book approach (i.e. retaining a historic prayer book, while approving use of alternative books), 46–48, 61, 180, 185

Updike, Daniel Berkeley, 224

Vatican II, 6, 13, 26, 130

Wachner, Emily, 42
Weil, Louis, 84n34, 88n4
West Syrian Eucharistic Prayer. *See* Eucharistic Prayer
Wittgenstein, Ludwig, 36

www.ingramcontent.com/pod-product-compliance
Ingram Content Group UK Ltd.
Pitfield, Milton Keynes, MK11 3LW, UK
UKHW021840140426
5217IPUK00022B/1528